W0115497

NORTH CAROLINA

AND THE

TWO WORLD WARS

NORTH CAROLINA

AND THE

TWO WORLD WARS

Sarah McCulloh Lemmon

and

Nancy Smith Midgette

Office of Archives and History
North Carolina Department of Cultural Resources
2013

© 2013 by the North Carolina Office of Archives and History
All rights reserved
ISBN 978-0-86526-444-1

North Carolina Department of Cultural Resources
Susan W. Kluttz
Secretary

Office of Archives and History
Kevin Cherry
Deputy Secretary

Division of Historical Resources
David L. S. Brook
Director

Historical Publications Section
Donna E. Kelly
Administrator

North Carolina Historical Commission
Jerry C. Cashion (2013)
Chairman

Millie M. Barbee (2015)
Vice-Chairman

Mary Lynn Bryan (2017)   B. Perry Morrison Jr. (2017)
David C. Dennard (2013)   Freddie L. Parker (2013)
Paul D. Escott (2013)   Barbara Blythe Snowden (2013)
Valerie A. Johnson (2015)   Richard Starnes (2017)

Harry L. Watson (2017)

EMERITI: Kemp P. Burpeau, N. J. Crawford, H. G. Jones,
William S. Powell, Alan D. Watson, William S. Powell

Printed by Data Reproductions

Contents

Illustrations

Foreword

The North Carolina Office of Archives and History's Historical Publications Section has published numerous titles on the Tar Heel State's involvement in major military conflicts from the American Revolution through World War II. The two most popular titles in the military series—*North Carolina's Role in the First World War* (1966) and *North Carolina's Role in World War II* (1964)—have been out of print for several years. The late Dr. Sarah Lemmon of Meredith College used newspapers, documents, and photographs housed in the State Archives to research and write these two books. In response to customer recommendations that these two works be issued as a single volume, Historical Publications contracted with Dr. Nancy Midgette of Elon University to update and expand Dr. Lemmon's texts and to write a bridge chapter covering the interwar period between 1918 and 1941.

North Carolina and the Two World Wars provides readers with an introduction to and overview of the state's involvement in these two pivotal events in the twentieth century. It is not intended to be a comprehensive history of the subject. In addition to Dr. Midgette, several staff members contributed to the publication. Donna E. Kelly selected illustrations, wrote cutlines, obtained permissions, verified quoted material, and compiled the index. Susan M. Trimble designed and typeset the volume. Lisa D. Bailey proofread and edited all of the materials for accuracy.

The Outbreak of
World War I in Europe

I n the remote Balkan town of Sarajevo on June 28, 1914, a young Serbian nationalist assassinated Archduke Francis Ferdinand, heir to the throne of the Austrian Empire, and his wife. Most Americans thought little of this event. However, those with their fingers on the pulse of world tensions realized the potential. Powerful European nations greedily eyed the weak Balkan states to strengthen their regional control and gain vital access to warmwater ports. The Austro-Hungarian Empire had annexed Bosnia in 1908, an event that sparked widespread resistance to a similar fate in Serbia where nationalist organizations dreamed of a greater Serbian state. And so, as the Archduke and his wife Sophie drove through Sarajevo in an open car with minimal protection, they were easy targets for the plotters who saw the couple as a symbol of the domination they so hated.

The United States was not very concerned over this faraway event. Of much greater interest was trouble with Mexico that had developed because of a series of revolutions in that neighboring country. While the *Charlotte Daily Observer* (July 3, 1914) carried a lengthy account of the elaborate funeral of the Archduke and his wife, otherwise the front page reverted to headlines about Mexico. The United States had long felt a lack of involvement in European affairs, although as a result of the Spanish-American War the United States acquired a number of colonies and began to play a role on the world stage. Nevertheless, most Americans cared little for such foreign places as Serbia and the Balkans.

Following an investigation to determine Serbian involvement and an assurance of German support, the Austrian government on July 25 handed an ultimatum to Serbia with demands that no country in the world believed Serbia would or could accept. Austria seemed to be deliberately provoking war, hoping for a quick victory and the opportunity to annex Serbia. The *Charlotte Daily Observer* (July 26, 1914) took notice of this with the headline:

WAR CLOUD COVERS ALL EUROPE
AND HUGE FORCES ARE MOVING

The related article suggested that Austria had a right to be belligerent, indicating that Serbia had for many years tried to stir up rebellion within the Empire. "There is nothing brave about shooting a copperhead," commented the author, "but neither is there anything of which the shooter need be ashamed."

Events moved with frightening rapidity following Austria's ultimatum. Three days later Russia began preparation to mobilize the nation's entire army, calling up all the men who had served time in military training. One North Carolina editor feared Russia's intervention, saying that such involvement would be inviting "any amount of future trouble." Many people fervently hoped that this conflict would remain between Austria and Serbia, a localized war, if only other major European nations would remain on the sidelines. However, years earlier these same nations had allied themselves into the Triple Alliance and the Triple Entente, essentially turning Europe into an armed camp. With Russia's support for Serbia against Austria, the pledges of mutual support took on a life of their own. Germany, Austria's ally, declared war on Russia. On the morning of August 2, the *Charlotte Daily Observer*'s headline flared:

GERMANY DECLARES WAR ON RUSSIA;
TITANIC EUROPEAN CONFLICT HAS BEGUN

Under the terms of the alliance, France would come to the aid of Russia, so Germany wasted no time in declaring war on France, as well. From Germany's perspective, timing was of the utmost importance; Russia's poor railroads and highways and a lack of communication facilities meant slow mobilization. Germany therefore planned to fight and defeat France first while Russia was mobilizing, and then turn on Russia. Great Britain, not bound by an alliance to enter the war but only by an "entente," delayed a few days but ultimately declared war on Germany and Austria in support of France. Said the *Charlotte Daily Observer* (August 5, 1914):

"HERE IS YOUR ANSWER, GREAT BRITAIN: IT'S WAR FOR YOU, TOO," SAYS GERMANY

England Lifts War Gage as Burden of Honor for Beleaguered Allies

Kaiser Hurls Challenge into the Faces of Encircling Foes

Nations not in the war hastened to declare their neutrality, as did President Woodrow Wilson for the United States. On August 4 he announced that since "a state of war unhappily exists," no one in the United States "shall take part, directly or indirectly, in the said wars, but shall remain at peace with all of the said belligerents, and shall maintain a strict and impartial neutrality." The government would not, however, interfere "with the free expression of opinion and sympathy, or with the commercial manufacture or sale of arms or munitions of war." A North Carolina newspaper editor said, "The impending clash may shake the Nations, but thank God! Our own Government is safe!" America settled down almost to life as usual.

The first few days of the war produced some unusual events. A German steamer loaded with coffee put into Southport to avoid capture on the high seas, and found itself in company with another German vessel and two British ones waiting for orders. The *Fayetteville Observer* reported "sightings" of two "aeroplanes" near Wilmington, stated to be German, an obvious impossibility. American tourists were caught in Europe, sometimes without money and afraid to come home on a belligerent ship. Two schoolteachers from Salisbury were in Germany, and they had to walk three miles carrying their own luggage to the Swiss border in order to get home. They returned in the steerage of a ship, because all accommodations were crowded. Said one of the teachers, "I really enjoyed seeing fat, rich ladies covered with diamonds, climb the steerage ladders with ordinary citizens." Mrs. Lucy Halliburton of Charlotte, who was in Berlin, felt secure although she was warned not to speak English on the streets lest she be mistakenly identified as British. Later all Americans in Germany received little flags to distinguish them from the British; they were finally put on a special train and sent through the Netherlands to England and then on to the United States. The cruiser USS *North Carolina* was sent to Turkey carrying money for Americans stranded there by the war, but the Turkish

The USS *North Carolina* (Armored Cruiser #12), ca. 1916–1917. Image donated by Charles R. Haberlein Jr., 2008, and provided courtesy of the Naval History and Heritage Command, Washington Navy Yard, Washington, D.C.

government had already mined the Dardanelles, and the ship was not allowed to pass through.

North Carolina newspapers maintained a general tone of neutrality. They printed both sides of the war news, showed interesting pictures of the leaders of both sides, and kept careful watch on competing newspapers that might spread propaganda such as atrocity stories. Congressman Claude Kitchin of North Carolina pointed out that the war was a European power struggle, not an American quarrel. Judge Henry G. Connor asked for calmness: "While the American people are privileged to think as they please and form opinions about great issues, they should speak and write with moderation, always avoiding utterances calculated to stir up strife." Prayers were offered for the restoration of peace, as in this proclamation issued by North Carolina's Gov. Locke Craig on Thanksgiving Day, 1915:

Let us in humility and gratitude remember that we have been spared while the world is consumed by war. We should pray that to lands now stricken by desolation and death, the beneficence of Peace may be restored, and the power of Righteousness exalted in all the earth.

The first month of the war saw the Germans come close to achieving their timetable and strategy of defeating France first and then turning to face Russia. The German armies swept through the lowlands of Belgium, a noncombatant country, in a great arc pivoting on Paris; by the end of August Germany was on Paris's doorstep. Americans felt that the war would be over very shortly; most agreed that modern war was so deadly that it could not last long. However, the German soldiers were exhausted, and the army had outrun its logistical support, providing the French and the British a moment to hold the line at the First Battle of the Marne. The Germans fell back, establishing a defensive line approximately sixty miles east of Paris. Optimistic Americans then concluded that the war would indeed end soon, but in favor of the Allies. By winter, however, the troops settled down into a stalemated trench warfare that showed little hope of concluding for some time to come—"two years" according to armchair strategists—while the American newspapers again became absorbed in other problems and put news of the war on the front page only when an unusual event occurred.

Methods of fighting in the First World War differed radically from those of earlier ones, even the Civil War, which is often called the first modern war. In 1914, airplanes were used for the first time. Although invented in America, planes were taken up by European armies more quickly than in the United States. Primarily they were used to spot the enemy's defensive lines and artillery locations. Dirigibles, popular with the Germans, were used not only for observation but also for carrying bombs both over land and to attack naval vessels. These "new features in warfare," said American newspapers, "are already playing a part which adds fresh interests to the war news." While apparently not opposing the dropping of bombs on ships, the *Charlotte Daily Observer* (September 2, 1914) felt that to drop bombs on a city full of innocent civilians, as the Germans did on Paris during the First Battle of the Marne in 1914, was "a renaissance of ancient barbarity in new garb." The dramatic flights of the planes led to flights of language as well, one description picturing a plane shot down "like a wounded bird," while still another was said to have "volplaned

Shown here is an observation balloon flying over an unidentified camp in North Carolina, ca. 1918. Two men are seen in the airplane body attached underneath. This and all other images are provided courtesy of the N.C. Office of Archives and History, Raleigh, N.C. unless otherwise indicated.

earthward," allowing its pilot to escape successfully. Planes also attempted to shoot down dirigibles, and in at least one instance, to ram them.

The British first introduced the use of tanks on the battlefield in September 1916. Derived from the American farm tractor, the tank was what Col. E. D. Swinton, Royal Engineers, called, "a fighting automobile," manufactured in secret in Britain. Some thought tanks were to be used to carry water in desert fighting, but they provided excellent defense against machine guns as they could overrun a machine gun position with less danger to the attacking men than could the infantry. Col. Swinton described his first glimpse of a tank thus: ". . . the actual monster . . . loomed up through the mist . . . and amidst the laughter of our infantry heaved its bulk across the crater-pitted surface of No Man's Land toward the startled Huns." Not until late in the war, though, did tacticians find the best use for these tanks and employed them in great mass to break through enemy strongholds.

Poison gas was another new weapon of war, introduced by the Germans on the Ypres front at the Belgian-French border. Soon every soldier carried a gas mask and was instructed in its use. Some of the gases burned exposed flesh, however, even when not inhaled, and against these there was little protection. The use of gas was tricky because a sudden shift in the wind could blow it back upon the men who sent it. Nonetheless, it remained a fearful weapon throughout the conflict.

Submarines were also used for the first time in the First World War. Although a prototype of a submarine was tried in the American Civil War, these vessels were not fully developed until later. By 1914 most of the nations of the world had submarines in their navies, although their use was chiefly for coastal protection and guarding harbors from enemy fleets. The German navy developed the submarine into an offensive weapon in an effort to disrupt convoys ferrying war matériel from the United States to Britain.

With the advent of airplanes, tanks, and mechanized mobilization in support of the infantry, the cavalry became a relic of the past. Instead of a war of movement, a war of thrust and motion, dash and retreat, with pennons flying and bugles blowing the charge, this was a war of trenches slit into the face of the earth, facing each other in a double row from the boundary of Switzerland to the English Channel, the ground between the rows layered with barbed wire and marked with shell holes, a war in which men fought for days to advance ten yards, in which the battle for a farmhouse was as important as Napoleon's battles for entire cities. It was a strange and different war; there was none like it before, and there has been none like it since.

While most Americans fervently believed that the United States could remain aloof from this war, some young men volunteered to serve with the Allies. So many Americans volunteered to serve in the British army that the Germans falsely accused Britain of hiring American troops. Americans also volunteered to join the French foreign legion. Two North Carolinians from Asheville—Paul and Kiffin Yates Rockwell—were among those who went to France. Paul eventually joined the Information Section at French Army Grand Headquarters as an official war correspondent for the *Chicago Daily News*. Kiffin served in the trenches for a year; after receiving a severe wound in his thigh in the fighting in the Ypres sector in May 1915, he transferred to aviation.

The American Field Service, organized as an ambulance service by the American Colony of Paris, attracted many volunteers. These men drove ambulances, which was noncombatant work. The famous writer Ernest Hemingway drove an ambulance on the Italian front. Many North Carolinians sent money to J. P. Morgan and Company to pay for a hospital in Paris and for ambulances and staff to care for the wounded. A donation of $1.25 would pay a trained nurse for one day; $1.65 would keep a patient for one day; $37.50 would support a nurse for a month; $600 endowed a bed for a year; and $1,500 bought an ambulance and staffed it for six months. Owen Kenan, of Wilmington, enlisted in the American Ambulance Corps and served in France at the front. Edward G. Miles worked for the American Red Cross, driving a car on the front throughout the war. Two cars were blown to pieces under him. An Asheville woman gave an ambulance that was named the "Kiffin Rockwell," and it was driven by Dabney H. Maury Jr., also of Asheville. Madelon "Glory" Battle Hancock, daughter of Dr. Westray Battle of Asheville and wife of Mortimer Pawson Hancock, a British major, served as a nurse in Antwerp, Belgium, beginning in August 1914. Following the fall of Belgium she was transferred to Ypres and served at the front for the entire war, receiving twelve decorations. Other volunteers included Grover H. Cobb of Gastonia who joined the British army and served until May 1916; and June Potts of Columbus County, who enlisted in the Canadian army. A translated quotation from a French newspaper shows the appreciation by the French for these volunteers:

> Everywhere they are doing faithful, unremitting, merciful work. They are loved by us all. We bless their careless, selfless, chivalrous devotion. They have proven themselves to be worthy sons of that great and generous nation for which our ancestors shed their blood.

By far the most glamorous and well-known of all the volunteer units was the Lafayette Escadrille. This escadrille, or flying squadron, contained 38 American pilots, two of whom were from North Carolina—Kiffin Yates Rockwell and James Rogers McConnell of Carthage. An additional 180 men who flew with the French army, including James Henry Baugham of Washington and Arthur Bluethenthal of Wilmington, the son of a German immigrant, were dubbed the "Lafayette Flying Corps." The lives of Rockwell and of McConnell illustrate the work of the escadrille.

Kiffin Rockwell was born in Tennessee and spent much of his young life near his grandparents in South Carolina before his family moved to North Carolina when he was fourteen. In the fall of 1908, hopeful of a military career, he entered Virginia Military Institute. The following summer he received an appointment to the U.S. Naval Academy but never enrolled, thinking that he would never see any action. He attended Washington and Lee University for a time and then traveled the country until in 1914 he joined his brother Paul in Atlanta. On August 3, 1914, Kiffin wrote to the French Consul in New Orleans, offering his services to the French military. On August 7, without waiting for a reply, he and Paul were on board the *St. Paul* as it departed New York for Southampton, from where they would travel on to Paris. The evening before their departure, Kiffin wrote to his mother of their plans: "You know I have always been a great dreamer and I just couldn't keep myself from

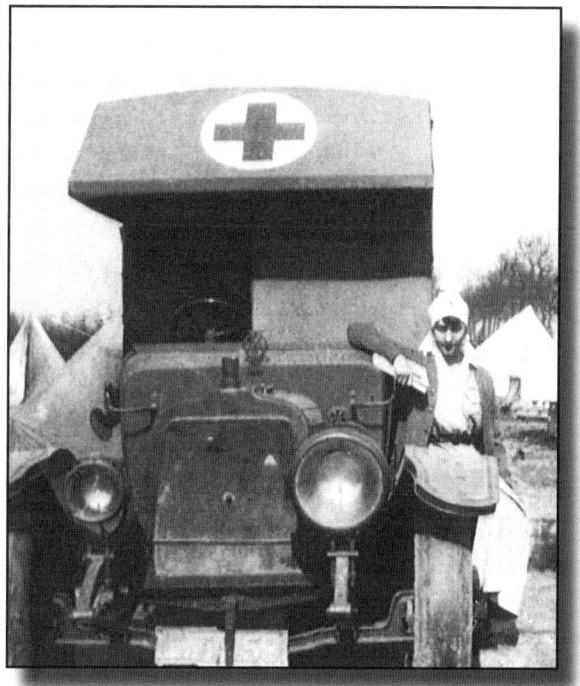

Madelon Hancock (1881–1930), who had family ties to Edgecombe County, served as a Red Cross nurse during World War I. Image provided courtesy of Anne C. Lewis of Tarboro, N.C.

Kiffin Rockwell and James McConnell were among several Americans who flew as part of the Lafayette Escadrille. Pictured from left to right are Victor Chapman (killed), Elliot Cowdin, Bert Hall, Lt. William Thaw, Captain Thénault, Lieutenant de Laage de Mux, Norman Prince (killed), Kiffin Rockwell (killed), and James McConnell. Image from James R. McConnell, *Flying for France, with the American Escadrille at Verdun* (Garden City, N.Y.: Doubleday, Page & Co., 1917), 18.

this trip, for I felt the call of opportunity." Kiffin was wounded twice while fighting in the trenches. In an effort to stay in the war he successfully transferred to the French aviation service. After a training period, in April 1916 he became one of the founding pilots in the Lafayette Escadrille. The fighter pilots flew alone, armed with a machine gun. Their tasks were to protect the French observation planes and balloons from German fighter planes and to attempt to shoot down German planes and balloons, which in turn were protected by German fighter planes. Hence there was little formation flying and few bombing raids. Instead, they engaged chiefly in "dogfights" with opposing planes about a mile high above the front lines. On May 18, 1916, on his first combat mission, Kiffin shot down a German plane, the first credited to the Lafayette Escadrille.

Much earlier, on November 26, 1915, he wrote to his mother of his dedication to the cause for which he fought: "I am giving the best that is in me in this war and will not stop at anything as long as it helps toward the final victory. This is a war of the world and means as much to the people of America as it does to anyone else. There is not one human being who is not being affected by the war. So no one has the right to forget about it or lose interest in it." Although he was officially credited with only four planes shot down, it is entirely possible that number was higher. Kiffin received multiple awards from the French government, including its highest honor, the Medaille Militaire. In September 1916, Kiffin's Nieuport was shot down over Alsace by a German observation plane, and his name became legendary. At his funeral, at the Luxeuil airfield, airplanes flew above and "showered down myriads of flowers." The French ambassador to the United States wrote to Mrs. Rockwell:

> Allow me . . . to express the sentiment of deep sympathy which was awakened in every French heart by your great loss. Your son was admired by all in France and his heroical death has left among us a lasting souvenir.

On April 27, 1918, American poet, Edgar Lee Masters, wrote the following in memory of Rockwell:

> Heights could not awe you,
>   Depths could not stay you,
> Anguished we saw you,
>   Saw Death waylay you
> Where the storm flings
>   Black clouds to thicken
> Round France's defender!
>   Archangel stricken
> From ramparts of splendor—
>   Shattered your wings!

Paul Rockwell, who survived the war, published *War Letters of Kiffin Yates Rockwell*, which contains many of his letters to his family and friends at home.

James McConnell of Carthage first went to France as an ambulance driver, receiving the Croix de Guerre for his work. But feeling that he was not doing enough, he joined the French flying corps and was in the Lafayette Escadrille. His first plane was a Nieuport biplane that traveled 110 miles per hour; it was armed with a machine gun on the roof that he had to fire with one hand while flying the plane with the other hand and with his feet. His group

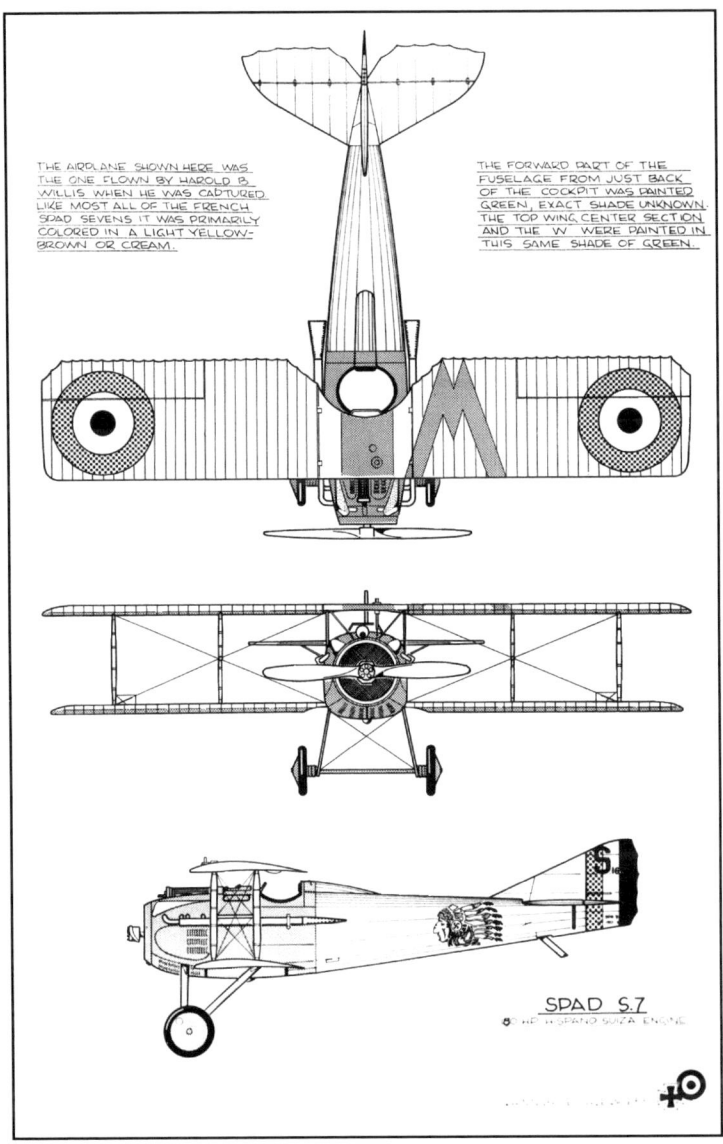

THE AIRPLANE SHOWN HERE WAS THE ONE FLOWN BY HAROLD B. WILLIS WHEN HE WAS CAPTURED. LIKE MOST ALL OF THE FRENCH SPAD SEVENS IT WAS PRIMARILY COLORED IN A LIGHT YELLOW-BROWN OR CREAM.

THE FORWARD PART OF THE FUSELAGE FROM JUST BACK OF THE COCKPIT WAS PAINTED GREEN, EXACT SHADE UNKNOWN. THE TOP WING, CENTER SECTION, AND THE "W" WERE PAINTED IN THIS SAME SHADE OF GREEN.

SPAD S.7

Drawing of a French SPAD S.7, by Ed Averkieff, similar to the one flown by James Henry Baugham. These aircraft were produced by Société Pour L'Aviation et ses Dérivés (SPAD).

consisted of six pilots and seventy ground attendants including mechanics and wireless operators. On a typical day he rose before daylight, had some coffee, and then motored to the airfield. The planes were trundled out, and as soon as there was light enough to see, the men prepared to take off. They wore fur-lined outfits, leather hoods, and goggles. After comparing notes for the day the men tested the motors, tried out the machine guns, decided at what altitude to rendezvous, and took off one by one. Each would circle the field at something like 4,500 feet waiting for the others to ascend. After two hours of duty, the planes returned. If needed, the men might fly an afternoon sortie as well as a morning one. McConnell said that a battle on the ground looked like a Gustav Doré picture of Dante's hell. After the battle of Verdun, McConnell received a new plane that could ascend to an altitude of 20,000 feet. His old 47-shot machine gun was replaced by a 500-round Vickers that was synchronized with the propeller. Like Kiffin Rockwell, McConnell was killed in action. Out of the hospital for only a week following an earlier crash, McConnell and a comrade were engaged in a dogfight with three German planes northwest of Paris on March 19, 1917. Edmond Genet managed to return his crippled aircraft to base, but McConnell did not. A month after his death the Southern Pines *Sandhill Citizen* (April 6, 1917) carried a lengthy article about his memorial service, held in the courthouse on April 1, 1917. Mr. Ralph W. Page, son of Walter Hines Page and editor of the *Pinehurst Outlook*, stated: "Oh the pity of it! With the enrichment, the enlarged experience, the broadened horizon, the expanded character of those tremendous years, what a wonderful career he might have had on his return, had he been spared."

Arthur Bluethenthal and James Baugham were also killed in combat. Bluethenthal was on an artillery observation mission on June 5, 1918, forty-seven miles northwest of Paris when his plane was shot down. Baugham, flying a SPAD pursuit plane, was wounded in a dogfight with three German planes on July 1, 1918. He managed to make a crash landing but died the following day. While many other Americans had joined these four in fighting alongside the French and British, that number would escalate exponentially once the United States entered the war.

War Comes to America

At the outbreak of the war most Americans felt that the United States should stay out of it, although Theodore Roosevelt and Gen. Leonard Wood, former Army Chief of Staff under President Taft, believed that it would soon become necessary to fight. President Woodrow Wilson and Secretary of State William Jennings Bryan were more pacifistic than Roosevelt and not only urged neutrality but also opposed additional expense in increasing the armed forces. By February 1916, however, the president decided to back legislation to strengthen the armed services. Angus McLean of Lumberton, a prominent politician who would be elected governor of North Carolina in 1924, stated that "considerable inquiry" on his part indicated that nine out of ten people went along with Wilson on national defense.

The National Defense Act of 1916, often referred to as the Hay Reorganization Bill (named for James Hay, representative from Virginia and chair of the House Committee on Military Affairs), was introduced first. Although the professional army officers sought a larger army and a smaller reserve, the final law, enacted on June 3, provided for a regular army of 175,000 in peace and a National Guard of over 400,000 men. It also established an Officers and Enlisted Reserve Corps, an expansion of the Medical Reserve Corps, and the modern ROTC (Reserve Officers' Training Corps) program. On August 16 a naval preparedness act passed, providing for 157 new ships during the ensuing three years. A final act established the United States Shipping Board and allocated $50 million to acquire and operate ships in order to enlarge the merchant marine. The entire program of preparedness would cost some $661,418,000.

On October 20, 1915, Congressman Claude Kitchin (majority leader in the House) wrote William Jennings Bryan that "the war goblins and jingoes had caught Wilson." Both Kitchin and the North Carolina Farmers' Union opposed the large naval expansion program, although Kitchin would have voted for a smaller one. Some disapproving people regarded Kitchin and William Jennings Bryan as "peace at any price" advocates. A second North

Claude Kitchin (1869–1923), from Halifax County, opposed naval expansion before the war and voted against declaring war on Germany. Later, however, he supported the war effort but opposed several war policies, including the sale of liberty bonds.

Carolina opponent of military expansion was Congressman Robert N. Page, felt so strongly that he chose not to run for re-nomination. In a speech announcing his decision in the Seventh District, he said:

> The loan of $500,000,000 to England by American capitalists, to say nothing of the profits of munitions manufacturers, has destroyed even the semblance of neutrality in the United States, and will probably lead us into war.

However, such views became increasingly unpopular, especially with the escalation of German submarine attacks.

The question of submarine attacks on surface shipping had haunted the American government since the beginning of the war. From time to time, as in the case of the *Lusitania* (a British passenger vessel on which 138 Americans perished when it was torpedoed on May 7, 1915), the United States government issued strong protests to Germany, who promised to be careful of the rights of neutral countries. However, protests and pledges ultimately

15

settled nothing, because a key component of German strategy was to disrupt the supply line between Britain and the United States. Subsequently, the submarine problem flared up and then subsided several times.

In January 1917, Wilson was hopeful that the warring countries would be ready to consider peace negotiations, since neither side could gain a strong advantage. The German government struck a rude blow to these hopes, however, on February 1 when it announced that henceforth it would initiate unrestricted submarine warfare, allowing only one American ship per week to go through unmolested to England, said ship having to follow a specified course and be marked plainly for identification. The *Charlotte Observer* (formerly the *Charlotte Daily Observer*) was surprised and stunned, fearing that hope for peace had been extinguished. However, the paper trusted Wilson to take all measures short of war, indicating that it would support him whatever course he should pursue. On February 4 diplomatic relations were broken, and the American ambassador to Germany was told to return home, while Count Johann-Heinrich von Bernstorff, the German ambassador in Washington, also packed up to leave. A headline proclaimed:

DIPLOMATIC RELATIONS WITH GERMANY
ARE BROKEN OFF: UNITED STATES IS ON
VERGE OF ENTERING WORLD WAR

The *Greensboro Daily News* (February 1, 1917) headed an editorial, "The Evil Day Has Come." The editor believed that Wilson had followed the wrong policy, placing the United States in a position of either entering the war or backing down humiliatingly. He thought the country should fight but was very clear that a different policy would not have resulted in such a dilemma. The *Robersonville Herald* urged a national referendum on war; those who voted for it should go to the front while the others stayed home.

Several days passed with no reports of submarine attacks; many people took heart and believed that Germany was merely bluffing. Wilson went before Congress on February 26 to ask for the authority to arm merchant ships. A resolution to this effect passed the House but was filibustered to death in the Senate. The *Fayetteville Observer* (March 14, 1917) labeled the twelve senators involved in the filibuster as "enemies of their country." The new Secretary of State Robert Lansing then informed the president that he had the authority to arm merchant ships without congressional action. Wilson proceeded to do so, and on March 12, the same day that the announcement was made, the American ship *Algonquin* was sunk. A week later three more American ships went down. As the *Charlotte Observer* (March 19, 1917) said:

VIRTUAL STATE OF WAR WITH GERMANY EXISTS

Said the paper, "The sooner war against the United States by Germany shall get under way, if it is to come at all, the sooner will the war be ended and peace declared." President Wilson called a special session of Congress to meet on April 2:

CONGRESS EXPECTED TO DECLARE WAR ON GERMANY; PRESIDENT ADVANCES DATE OF SPECIAL SESSION TO CONVENE

Some North Carolinians fostered a lingering hope that Germany would realize that it could not win and therefore would not let matters come to war. Several North Carolina newspapers believed that soldiers would never have to go to Europe; if war came, only the American navy would be involved plus goods and money to aid France and England. The *Durham Morning Herald* stated that, "It would be nearly a physical impossibility for the United States to render a great deal of assistance to the enemies of Germany in that way." It would be much better just to send $1 billion. The *Greensboro Daily News* believed that "the masses of the people of this section have little desire to take a hand in Europe's slaughter and confusion," but peace was no longer possible. On March 23 the editor of the *News*, W. A. Hildebrand, wrote:

> Some of us have done our small best to keep the peace, always fearing that this best would be of little avail. Very soon the world, looking on, may find it a ca[u]se of America, with but a single thought—the will to win.

He hoped the congressmen would search their hearts when they arrived for the special session. A Confederate veteran from Asheville expressed his willingness to fight to preserve his home, but he did not want to be sold for "a mess of pottage even to England." On the other hand, the *Fayetteville Observer* and the *Charlotte Observer* were strongly in favor of fighting to preserve the national honor. They felt Germany had forced war upon the United States. As the Greensboro newspaper *Everything* said, "We must accept the challenge—war is not ours to choose, but has been thrust upon us." The *Durham Morning Herald* declared that war was already here for all practical purposes.

On the evening of April 2, 1917, President Wilson faced the assembled House and Senate and many distinguished visitors in the chamber of the House. After pointing out that while property could be paid for, the loss of lives could not, he asked the Congress to declare that Germany's recent actions were in fact a state of war against the government and people of the United States. He followed with a declaration of America's war aim: "The world must be made safe for democracy." After admitting that it was a fearful thing to lead a great nation into war, Wilson concluded:

> But the right is more precious than peace, and we shall fight for the things which we have always carried nearest our hearts—for democracy, for the right of those who submit to authority to have a voice in their own Governments, for the rights and liberties of small nations, for a universal dominion of right by such a concert of free peoples as shall bring peace and safety to all nations and make the world itself at last free. To such a task we can dedicate our lives and our fortunes, everything that we are and everything that we have, with the pride of those who know that the day has come when America is privileged to spend her blood and her might for the principles that gave her birth and happiness and the peace which she has treasured. God helping her, she can do no other.

The *Greensboro Daily News* (April 4, 1917) said that the president's war message was:

> not indignation at a betrayal on the part of Germany nor a railing accusation against the Teutonic government; it is rather a reluctant admission that the United States cannot live at peace with the type of sovereignty represented by the imperial German government.

The article continued, "He has been bold enough to base the fight on the rights of mankind."

The Senate, on April 4, passed the war resolution with six dissenting votes; the North Carolina senators voted for it. In the House, however, more opposition surfaced. After lengthy debate, on the evening of April 5 a roll call vote began. When Claude Kitchin's name was called, he went up to stand at the right of the clerk's desk to explain the reason he was going to vote against war. He wore a blue business suit, a high white vest, and a black string tie. A hush fell over the entire assembly as he prepared to read his five typewritten pages. He said, in part:

> The depth of my sorrow, the intensity of my distress in contemplating the measureless step proposed, God only knows. . . . [M]y conscience and judgment, after mature thought and fervent prayer for rightful guidance, have marked out clearly the path of my duty, and I have made up my mind to walk it, if I go barefooted and alone. [Applause.] I have come to the undoubting conclusion that I should vote against this resolution. [Applause.]

He said that he would, however, take off his coat and struggle "with all of his soul and might in defense" of his country because he knew the resolution would pass. Kitchin told a friend later that he wanted his children to know that their father never voted against his conscientious convictions. The House sincerely respected his views, but the war resolution passed by a vote of 373 to 50.

Some North Carolinians were ashamed of Kitchin and felt that he should resign, or at least should step down as the majority leader in the House. They called him selfish, a coward, a member of the "petticoat brigade." Others said that millions were with him in spirit. One man wrote a letter in which he said, "You are what I call a MAN," and he was proud of him. Once war was declared, however, public sentiment clearly supported the war effort. As an editorial in the *Charlotte Observer* (April 7, 1917) phrased it:

> The President of the United States has formally proclaimed that a state of war exists between this country and Germany. Coincidentally he has made call[s] upon all American citizens to give support to all measures of the Government. The final word has been spoken. The war is under way. The people must be for one country or the other. There is no neutrality—no middle ground. The time for argument, for debate, for dissention, is passed and it is for all America to prove loyal to the Flag.

Later, 2nd Lt. J. W. Smoot of the 374th Infantry and a 1917 graduate of Trinity College (later Duke University) wrote while in France:

> . . . we'll pay most willingly and proudly our debt to Lafayette and Rochambeau for their substantial and moral help they gave us in 1776. Our hearts

are right, our mission is glorious and we are equal to the task, and soon Old Glory will be flying over Germany.

A woman wrote to Gov. Thomas Walter Bickett saying, "We must stand by the FLAG. The world is on fire and we must all fight and after it is out then argue over the cause." In a May 21, 1917, proclamation, "Call for Volunteers," Governor Bickett himself said, "This Republic has unsheathed its sword in defense of humanity and to prove that republics have a right to live. America has planted the emblem of liberty and democracy in the pathway of the tyrant and the autocrat. And she now calls upon her sons to keep it there." He continued, "This is no ordinary war. It is a war of ideals." Judge H. G. Connor wrote to North Carolina Chief Justice Walter Clark:

I am finding fresh inspiration in my old age in seeing the monarchies and autocracies of Europe crumble and fall at the command of a long suffering people. Before this war, brought on by autocracy, ends, I hope that not one of them will remain. They have failed and should give way to the last hope of mankind—genuine democracy.

The *Greensboro Daily News*, although it had opposed war, nevertheless felt that it might be a blessing in disguise to the soldiers. The editor said:

. . . many a man who, heretofore, has not been able to control himself, will hereafter become master of himself, his habits and his circumstances. Many a man now regarded by himself, and his friends, as a failure; with nothing to hope for in the future, will come back from the war, with head erect, eye steady, grip firm and an air of confidence in himself, never seen before. He will see the unsuccessful boy transformed into a seasoned, disciplined, efficient man.

On May 16, 1917, at its annual convention, the Episcopal Diocese of North Carolina endorsed the declaration of war. A resolution introduced by Joseph Hyde Pratt was adopted unanimously. In part it read:

we believe that in entering this present war we do so with no selfish purpose or desire and with no feeling of hatred towards those people with whom we are now at war; . . . we believe that it is now our righteous duty to participate in this world war and do all in our power to resist the wrong and

Thomas Walter Bickett (1869–1921), of Anson County, led North Carolina in her war efforts by making patriotic speeches and proclamations just three months into his term as governor. Image from the Library of Congress, Prints and Photographs Division.

> maintain the rights of other nations and peoples as well as our own; . . . we . . . will strive in every way possible by our efforts, prayers and influence to bring to a successful finish this world-wide war, to the end that there shall be established a permanent and righteous peace; and to prepare ourselves to lay hold of the wonderful opportunities which will then be offered to extend the Kingdom of God on this earth.

Three speeches by Governor Bickett reflect a variety of reasons why most Americans and North Carolinians thought they were fighting the war. In a February 18, 1918, letter to the president of the North Carolina

Federation of Woman's Clubs, the governor indicated these factors: "the sanctity of the person of woman, which sanctity is unknown to the Hun. . . . that motherhood may enter into its just rewards and may not be forever impaled on Militarism's iron cross . . . and that the ideals of woman may live and brighten and bless the earth." In delivering the Founders' Day address at the University of North Carolina in Chapel Hill, he declared that common gratitude to France was one of the chief reasons. Peace and prosperity came next. Also, the people hope to "mold and color the civilization of the whole world." The question was, "Who and what shall rule the earth? . . . if the Allies shall triumph war will come no more upon the earth." He urged the students to work and think; to be able to say, "Here am I, send me." In the name of the university, he appealed to them "to run and not be weary, to walk and not faint." The final review of reasons for entering the war was contained in Bickett's Thanksgiving Day proclamation for 1917, delivered on November 18:

> In the providence of God the world is today engaged in blood-red debate to determine whether government shall henceforth be guided by the love of justice or by lust for pelf and power.
>
> Not in rashness nor in anger, but thoughtfully, in the fear of God, and out of respect for its own conscience, this Nation has consecrated its unlimited resources and its unconquerable spirit to the maintenance of governments that will guarantee fair treatment to every man and every nation.
>
> It is cause for universal thanksgiving that in the most awful and most [a]ugust hour of human history the conscience of our people triumphed over the counsel of selfishness and fear.
>
> This is the blessing of the year.

A poem in *The Independent* magazine (December 15, 1917) expressed the spirit of America thus:

THE MARCHING MEN
by Harry Kemp

The brown lads, the brave lads go marching down the street;
It sets one's head a-whirling,—the motion of their feet!
Their legs go swinging, swinging, in row on rhythmic row,
As down the street, down the street the marching soldiers go.
They are stepping, stepping, stepping as if they hummed a song
That soon must burst in thunder a mighty million strong. . . .
The Kaiser, O, the Kaiser, if he had seen this hour
When first he dreamed a vanquished world lay sprawled
    beneath his power,
Had taken thought, had taken thought, and then had paused
    again
Before he roused the valor of all these marching men!

Upon the United States' declaration of war, all German ships in American ports were seized and all credits and deposits of money frozen. The crews on the ships, approximately 3,000 men and a few wives, were to be interned for the duration of the war. The Immigration Commissioner came to the mountains of western North Carolina in search of a suitable yet remote location. There was some opposition, because of possible harm to the summer tourist trade; but most thought it necessary to be patriotic and accept the camp. Kanuga was first selected as an appropriate site, but the objections of some summer residents of Hendersonville blocked this choice. Waynesville citizens then asked for the camp to be located at White Sulphur Springs. A third offer came from the manager of the Mountain Park Hotel at Hot Springs, which had experienced a decline in business; since buildings were already there and the site included a large tract of land, the federal government accepted this offer and leased it for the duration of the war. For over a year the German internees remained there.

An immediate task was to create an army; the question was, should soldiers volunteer or should they be drafted? England's experience with volunteers suggested not a dearth of men but that too often the wrong men volunteered, or the right men at the wrong time. A steady flow was necessary, neither

From 1917 through 1918, the grounds of the Mountain Park Hotel in Hot Springs, N.C., housed German civilians who found themselves on American soil at the outbreak of the war in 1914. In 1917, after the United States entered the war, these men were designated "enemy aliens" and transported from New York Harbor to Hot Springs for internment. Photograph was taken by Adolph Thierbach, one of the detainees. Image provided courtesy of the Madison County Public Library, Marshall, N.C.

too fast to be trained nor too slow to leave camps and installations unoccupied. Nor should men with skills critically needed to manufacture explosives, for instance, or airplanes, be accepted to fight on the front line. Special difficulties arose in North Carolina with physicians. Some towns with young physicians were completely denuded when they all volunteered; in other places, almost none volunteered. Within six weeks of entering the war, Congress passed a national conscription act. Governor Bickett telegraphed the president in support of drafting men aged twenty-one to thirty years old. On May 18, 1917, the bill became law; in addition to the draft, the president was authorized to accept volunteer expeditions if he wished. June 5 was set as the day for all men in the designated age bracket to register and receive numbers; these numbers would later be drawn at random, and all men bearing drawn numbers, wherever they lived, would have to report for duty.

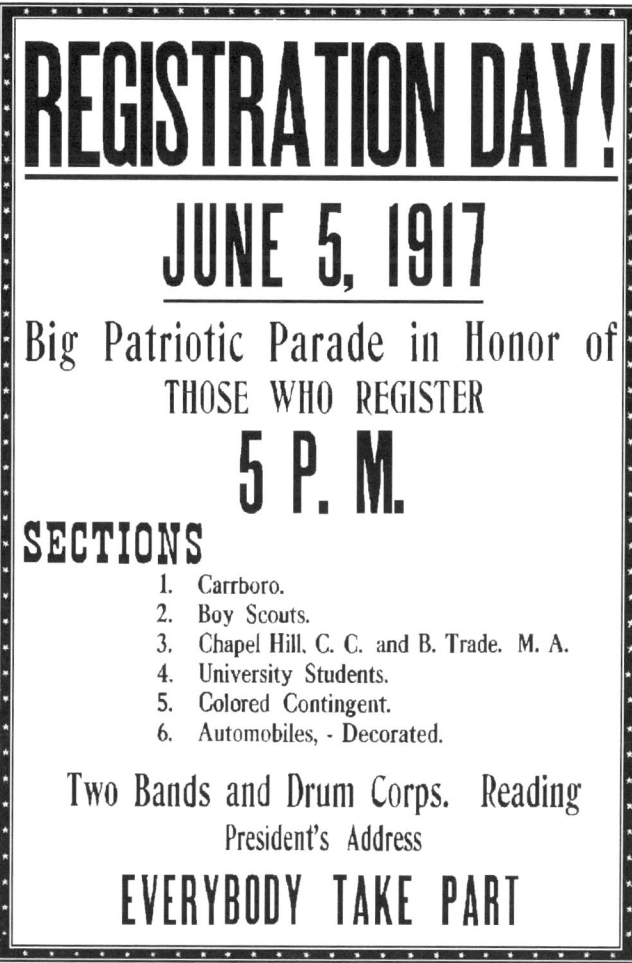

REGISTRATION DAY!

JUNE 5, 1917

Big Patriotic Parade in Honor of
THOSE WHO REGISTER

5 P. M.

SECTIONS

1. Carrboro.
2. Boy Scouts.
3. Chapel Hill, C. C. and B. Trade. M. A.
4. University Students.
5. Colored Contingent.
6. Automobiles, - Decorated.

Two Bands and Drum Corps. Reading
President's Address

EVERYBODY TAKE PART

A poster from Orange County dated June 5, 1917, announced events regarding registration day activities.

Across the United States, registration day became one of consecration for all American people. Registrants were honored with arm bands, dinners, and parades. A poster for registration day in Chapel Hill on June 5, 1917, announced a parade at 5:00 P.M., to be followed by the reading of President Wilson's address on the subject. While there was some concern about the potential for disorder in protests against registration, as had occurred during the Civil War, the day went smoothly everywhere. Throughout North Carolina more men registered than the census indicated were in that age group; instead of 100 percent registration, the figure was 106 percent. Some towns ran out of forms and had to extend registration to the next day. The selective service boards in each community were local men, who then classified the registrants into categories, with Class I being subject to military duty. On July 20 Secretary of War Newton D. Baker drew the first number from a large bowl. A man from Hamlet who was in Washington on business was a spectator at part of the drawing; he was seated within a few feet of the big table on which rested the bowl with 10,500 capsules in it. The total number registered in the nation was 9.5 million; in North Carolina, 480,491 men registered: 337,986 were white, and 142,505 were black. The *Charlotte Observer* declared that "The Army which came into existence in America during the single day of June 5 is an Army born to conquer."

Other wartime legislation followed apace. Senator Lee S. Overman of Salisbury introduced and led to passage the Overman Act on May 20, 1918, granting extraordinary powers to the president during wartime to coordinate various government agencies. Some criticism suggested that this bill gave Wilson dictatorial powers. A cartoon in the New York *Tribune* (March 21, 1918) showed Uncle Sam working feverishly to coordinate various resources to support the war effort. However, *The Independent* magazine (May 4, 1918) had proclaimed that this act would give Wilson the power to say, "Here, clean up your business; cut out the dead wood; hitch up your teams; pull together!" Upon Overman's death in 1930, Senator Claude A. Swanson of Virginia said in a memorial address to Congress:

> . . . as acting chairman of the Judiciary Committee he championed the measures recommended by President Wilson for the effective prosecution of the conflict. He became the exponent of a well-defined and aggressive policy—that of giving the Commander in Chief unlimited power and resources. This policy demonstrated superior wisdom. It inspired confidence, shortened the conflict, and economized both blood and treasure.

Claude Kitchin, chairman of the Ways and Means Committee, piloted through the House the war revenue bill, which made the income tax the chief source of revenue during the war. Some northern congressmen protested, declaring that Kitchin was unfairly taxing their region and protecting

This cartoon titled, "It Wouldn't Take Long If We'd All Form a Bucket Brigade" from the March 21, 1918, issue of the New York *Tribune*, shows Uncle Sam trying to mix buckets full of resources like ship construction, food conservation, and the Red Cross, in order to put out the fires of war. Image from the online project, "Chronicling America: Historic American Newspapers" http://chroniclingamerica.loc.gov/lccn.

the South since incomes and corporations were larger in the North. Kitchin also supported all other necessary war legislation in the House despite the fact that he had voted against the war. A Republican said to him:

> . . . you have fully equaled the standard of leadership set by your predecessors on either side of the House. In the matter of tolerance and patience, you have set a higher standard than I have observed during the fourteen years of my service in Congress.

This was indeed high praise from a member of the opposite party.

The war gave impetus to legislation forbidding the manufacture and sale of alcoholic beverages, better known as Prohibition. Opponents to the prevalence of alcohol near army camps claimed that soldiers would be corrupted by drink. Others opposed the European practice of having wine and other drinks served at all times, and still others insisted that wheat should not be used for whiskey when it was needed for bread for the army. A leaflet from the Committee on War Prohibition was entitled, "Save 11,000,000 Loaves of Bread a Day" which became the committee's slogan.

North Carolina was a stronghold of Prohibitionist sentiment. In 1908 the legislature had passed the first state law calling for a popular referendum on the subject; prohibition won by a vote of 113,612 to 69,416. The *Washington Progress* (May 28, 1908) declared: "North Carolina first at Bethel, farthest at Appomattox [*sic*] and the first State in the Union to banish the liquor traffic by popular vote, a glorious history. . . . Each man should record his vote in the family Bible." On the other hand, the Greensboro *Daily Industrial News* (May 27, 1908), which favored saloons, said, "the Old North State is now scheduled to become the 'toddy less Sahara' for which the prohibition forces have long labored." North Carolina Congressman Edwin Y. Webb carried his views into Congress and became co-sponsor of the Webb-Kenyon Act of 1913 making it illegal to ship liquor from a "wet" state into a "dry" state. When the Eighteenth Amendment to the Constitution was submitted to the states for ratification on December 18, 1917, North Carolina became the twenty-eighth state to ratify on January 16, 1919. The legislature tightened state laws to conform to the national law, so that the *World's Work*, edited by Walter Hines Page, wrote of North Carolina in November 1920:

A Helping Hand

Cartoon by Billy Borne from the *Asheville Citizen* (June 15, 1918).

> There is no prohibition issue in North Carolina. The affair is settled. If a vote were taken on the question to-day the dry majority would be far greater than it was when the wets and drys lined up against each other for their state-wide fight in 1908.

The war also gave impetus to the woman suffrage movement, although North Carolina was not as supportive of this movement as of Prohibition. The woman suffrage movement really began in the state in the summer of 1913, and by 1914 clubs had been organized in fifteen cities. Mrs. Archibald Henderson of Chapel Hill served as the state president, and a number of men including Judge Walter Clark favored women's demand for the ballot. In 1915, headquarters were set up at the Yarborough House (Hotel) in Raleigh, and supporters launched a drive to petition the legislature to amend the state constitution. Although bills were introduced, action on them was tabled.

Following this defeat, supporters changed their strategy to seek the ballot for women only in municipal and presidential elections. Once again, however, in 1917 the legislature refused to grant women suffrage even on such a limited basis. Legislators' speeches indicated that among other objections they did not want black women to have the vote. Then came the war, and women devoted most of their energies to volunteer work in the war effort. Their leaders believed that such work indicated they were worthy of the ballot. They could not convince the men, however, for when the Woman Suffrage Amendment was voted on in Congress, only representatives Zebulon Weaver and Hannibal Godwin from North Carolina voted for it. The Farmers' Union, the labor unions, and the Republican State Convention of 1918 all went on record favoring the Nineteenth Amendment. However, sentiment in the state remained strongly divided, even among women. While many women supported the amendment, others joined the Southern Women's Rejection League, claiming that allowing black women to vote would threaten white supremacy. A special session of the North Carolina legislature was convened in the summer of 1920 to consider this amendment and other business. At that time only one more state was needed to ratify the Nineteenth Amendment. The House rejected a resolution to ratify; Tennessee ratified the next day, on August 18, and women throughout the United States voted in November 1920 for the first time. In a meaningless gesture the North Carolina General Assembly finally ratified the amendment in 1971.

Several North Carolinians held positions of great importance during the war. As previously mentioned, Thomas W. Bickett served as governor of North Carolina during the war years, from 1917 to 1921. He was born of Irish and English descent in Monroe in 1869. After graduating from Wake Forest College, he studied law at the University of North Carolina and was admitted to the bar in 1893. In 1916 he was nominated as the Democratic candidate for governor in the first statewide primary ever held in North Carolina and was elected over his Republican opponent in November. Bickett was an excellent orator whose many patriotic addresses helped to lead the state and inspire citizens during the war. He personally took a hand in solving the deserter problem in two western counties; he made valuable suggestions to the director of the Selective Service Act; and he was frequently asked by New York newspapers to express his opinion on current events as they occurred, and he always did so graciously with good common sense. He also accumulated a good record in promoting social legislation for the betterment of the state, even though the war absorbed most of his energies. After his term expired, he practiced law in Raleigh until his death in December 1921.

Angus W. McLean of Lumberton, mentioned earlier, was named by President Wilson as one of four directors of the War Finance Corporation, an extremely powerful war agency in Washington that extended credit to war industries, bought and sold United States bonds when necessary to keep their price stable, and had the power to issue $3 billion worth of bonds. Born on a small farm in Robeson County, McLean came from a long line of Scotch and Scotch-Irish forebears. He received a law degree from the University of North Carolina in 1892. That year he joined a law firm in Lumberton and became actively engaged in business interests, including founding the city's first bank and organizing the Lumberton Cotton Mills and the Virginia and Carolina Railroad (serving for a time as its president). He was also an active member of the Democratic Party and a strong supporter of Woodrow Wilson's campaigns for president. In 1920, in addition to his duties with the War Finance Corporation, McLean became assistant secretary of the treasury. President Wilson wrote to McLean: "You have performed this war duty with signal ability and devotion, and you are deserving of a large share of credit for the successful operations of the Corporation." In 1924 Angus McLean was elected governor of North Carolina.

Chief Justice Walter Clark of the North Carolina Supreme Court was appointed by President Wilson to serve as an umpire to sit with the National War Labor Board when it could not reach agreement on problems involving such factors as working conditions and wages in disputes affecting the war effort. Clark, a native of Halifax County, served briefly in the Confederate army. Upon completion of his law degree at the University of North Carolina, he practiced law in Raleigh and wrote widely on both history and law. In 1889 he became a member of the North Carolina Supreme Court, and in 1902 he became chief justice. He performed his wartime service in addition to his regular duties during 1918 and 1919.

Josephus Daniels, editor of the *News and Observer* in Raleigh, was appointed secretary of the navy by President Wilson to follow in the footsteps of four other capable North Carolinians who had been secretaries of

Angus W. McLean (1870–1935) (*left*), of Robeson County, was appointed to the War Finance Corporation, which gave financial support to industries and banks essential to the war effort. He had founded Lumberton's first bank as well as three textile mills, giving him the necessary experience to fill that post. Walter Clark (1846–1924) (*right*), from Halifax County, served as an arbiter for the National War Labor Board, an agency established to ensure reliable labor and efficient productivity during the war. Clark was also a strong supporter of woman suffrage.

the navy in the preceding century. As a young man growing up in Wilson, Daniels acquired a job at a printing house, which fired his lifelong passion for the newspaper business. After studying law at the University of North Carolina, he moved to Raleigh in 1885 where he owned and edited a series of small newspapers. They lost money, however, and so from 1892 to 1895 he held a position in the U.S. Department of the Interior. In 1894 he purchased the *News and Observer* and merged it with two of his small newspapers.

Daniels was a strong and knowledgeable secretary of the navy. He made patriotic speeches throughout the United States and fought steadily for larger appropriations to build a stronger navy. His "big navy" policy was in line with the policies advocated earlier by Admiral Alfred Thayer Mahan and Theodore Roosevelt, and by his own assistant secretary of the navy, Franklin Delano Roosevelt. Anticipating that war might come to America, he moved

Josephus Daniels (1862–1948) (*right*), from Wilson County, earned prominence operating newspapers, primarily the Raleigh *News and Observer*, which he used as a political mouthpiece for the Democratic Party. Daniels supported Woodrow Wilson who appointed him secretary of the navy, serving from 1913 through 1921 when Edwin Denby (*left*) succeeded him. Daniels was the last member of the cabinet to vote for war in 1917. Image from the Library of Congress, Prints and Photographs Division.

toward preparedness by ordering a survey of all merchant ships that might be available in war. When the order came from President Wilson to arm the merchant vessels, Daniels was able to carry out the order on the same day, and to place naval crews aboard all the ships. He directed the building of 355 submarine chasers; naval industries were put on a war-operating basis with vessels ready, munitions stored, and supply ships held ready to sail. When war was declared on April 6, the fleet was mobilized within the hour. Only twenty-eight days later a flotilla of destroyers reported in England for duty, which completely astounded the British. By the end of the war, over 300 vessels and 75,000 men under the command of Admiral William S. Sims were serving in Europe.

The navy patrolled the route to Murmansk, Russia, the Adriatic Sea, the Azores, and the vicinity of Vladivostok in East Asia. It provided and protected the transportation of two million soldiers and all their necessary supplies to Europe. The American navy suggested the North Sea mine barrage that reduced the loss of shipping to submarine attacks. American naval guns were even carried overland to defend the city of Paris. Daniels offered the United States Marines to the army upon the declaration of war; although the generals hesitated because such a move was unorthodox, Secretary Baker accepted. Thus the marines fought in the front line in France at Château-Thierry and Belleau Wood, far from the waves of the ocean. Daniels also accepted women in the navy as yeomen (F), and in the marines as marinettes. These women worked in offices, but drilled just like the men and had every privilege and duty that the men did except for fighting. A company of yeomen (F) served as President Wilson's guard of honor upon his return from the Versailles peace conference. These were the only women eligible to join the American Legion.

North Carolinian Walter Hines Page, mentioned earlier, was appointed ambassador to England by President Wilson in 1913 and served until becoming ill near the end of the war when he was forced to resign. Page was born in Cary and attended Randolph-Macon Men's College in Virginia before enrolling in The Johns Hopkins University for graduate study in Greek. In 1882 he returned to Raleigh and soon thereafter founded a newspaper, the *State Chronicle*. Finding southern life very stagnant in this period following Reconstruction, he sold his paper to Josephus Daniels and went to New York City where he edited the *Forum* and later the *Atlantic Monthly*. In 1899

Walter Hines Page (1855–1918), from Moore County, founded the *State Chronicle* in Raleigh and edited various other newspapers, magazines, and journals, including the *Atlantic Monthly* and *World's Work*. Page was a strong supporter of the Allies and often encouraged the Wilson administration to intercede prior to the United States' entry into the conflict. He was appointed ambassador to England. Image from the Library of Congress, Prints and Photographs Division.

he founded the magazine, *World's Work*, and became a member of the publishing firm of Doubleday, Page and Company.

Page was an excellent speaker, genial, and magnetic. When the war broke out, he consistently argued that the British were fighting for democracy and eventually was a strong voice in garnering U.S. support for the Allies. Page was a great personal friend of the British foreign secretary, Sir Edward Grey, and they often conferred informally and worked together. Some of Page's critics, including members of President Wilson's inner circle, inferred that he was entirely too pro-British, given that his duties in London included not only helping war-stranded Americans get home and the sponsorship of relief funds and organizations, but also presenting the American notes of protest when the British seized American ships and searched the mails. Moreover, with the departure of the German ambassador at the outbreak of the war, the American Embassy also oversaw German interests in London. Page's work-load was enormous; that, combined with the frequent acrimonious cor-respondence with the government in Washington, took a toll on his health.

When the United States broke diplomatic relations with Germany, Page excitedly informed the Foreign Office that his duties no longer included overseeing German interests. He closed the note with a flourishing signa-ture. Page helped plan an April 20 special service in St. Paul's Cathedral in London to celebrate America's entry into the war. In attendance were mem-bers of the royal family, most members of the cabinet, and the archbishop of Canterbury. One person in attendance noted that Page was "so full of enthusiasm and satisfaction that he looked almost 6" taller!"

The subsequent year, however, continued to take its toll on Page's health. In the summer of 1918 his diagnosis included hardening of the arter-ies, high blood pressure, and emphysema (he was a heavy smoker). He soon complained of vision problems, the result of retinal hemorrhages. Unable to work full days, and sometimes ill for weeks at a time, he clearly could not continue as ambassador. He left London on October 2, 1918, and became so ill on the transatlantic passage that an ambulance awaited the docking of the ship and immediately took him to St. Luke's Hospital in New York. He recovered sufficiently to return to North Carolina and to see the end of the war; he died on December 21 and was buried in Aberdeen (Moore County) in Bethesda Churchyard. In 1923 the British government dedicated a plaque to Page in Westminster Abbey, on which he is described as "The friend of Britain in her sorest need."

North Carolina Girds for War

Shortly after the United States entered World War I, Congress created the National Council of Defense to coordinate war preparedness throughout the nation. This Council (six members of President Wilson's cabinet) and its seven-member Advisory Commission (nationally known businessmen) were to create "relations which will render possible in time of need the immediate concentration and utilization of the resources of the Nation." The National Council directed each state to create a state Council, which North Carolina did on May 31, 1917, with Daniel Harvey Hill Jr., the immediate past president of the State College of Agriculture and Engineering (now North Carolina State University), as its chairman. State councils were assigned the work of directing, marshaling, organizing, and producing the food, clothing, money, supplies, and other needs of a nation at war. The purpose of this council was to "mold public thought and sentiment; and to get into the minds of the people the truth." It was also to practice conservation through such devices as the "carry-home-your-own-parcels" campaign; to detect deserters and help draft boards; to stimulate food production; to develop

Daniel Harvey Hill Jr. (1859–1924), resident of Raleigh, chaired the North Carolina Council of Defense, modeled after the National Council of Defense. Through his leadership various state committees were established for important aspects of the war effort, ranging from historical preservation to woman's work. Image from Samuel A. Ashe, Stephen B. Weeks, and Charles L. Van Noppen, eds. *Biographical History of North Carolina: From Colonial Times to the Present*, 8 vols. (Greensboro, N.C.: Charles L. Van Noppen, 1905–1917), 7:145 (folio).

a rural motor express; to use county road crews to thresh and cut hay; to set up bureaus to register vacant rooms, especially in cities near war camps or with war industries; to provide legal aid to servicemen; to report to the Alien Property Custodian anything belonging to citizens or corporations of the enemy powers; to carry on social welfare work among the industrial plant workers; to control vice, especially near army camps; and to keep civilian morale high.

The federal government did not provide funding for state councils. In its first annual report dated May 30, 1918, the North Carolina Council of Defense reported that it had not received any state funding either, and had relied on the generosity of private citizens to provide labor, materials in kind, and the $3,591.23 that it had spent since its inception. The Council was not pleased with this lack of state funding, noting that eight states had each received over a million dollars from their respective state legislatures, and other states had received lesser amounts. Nonetheless, this report indicates that the Council accepted its responsibilities with great seriousness of purpose and engaged in a wide range of activities that included informing the citizens about the war and encouraging their support, remaining alert to signs of disloyalty, marshaling the state's resources for the war effort, supporting Liberty Loan campaigns, and assisting the Red Cross and other organizations as they met the needs of both citizens and soldiers. North Carolina women, black and white, found new opportunities for leadership by working with county Council of Defense initiatives.

Keeping citizen morale high as the realities of war struck home was an enormous challenge. Those on the home front needed not only news of the war's progress but also encouragement to continue their work, whether it was directly or indirectly related to the war effort. Throughout the war, newspapers and patriotic speakers, many of them famous, spread their words of cheer and encouragement. The state Council of Defense sponsored many "four-minute speakers," most frequently in movie and vaudeville show houses, so that vital information could reach people "too busy to read." Commissioner of Public Safety D. Hiden Ramsey delivered one such speech in the Galax Theater in Asheville, as reported in the *Asheville Citizen* (October 10, 1917). He encouraged citizens to purchase war bonds, proclaiming that it was every American's duty to see that the government's call for funding did not go unheeded. "Uncle Sam is asking us to save that we might support the men in

Let's Fill It Up.

This cartoon drawn by Billy Borne and titled, "Let's Fill It Up," appeared in the *Asheville Citizen* (October 5, 1917).

France," said Mr. Ramsey. "We are not lending our money to a stranger; we are lending it to ourselves, and the supreme question of the hour is what can we give?"

While many parts of the country saw hysterical anti-German outbursts, Governor Bickett reassured the citizens of North Carolina that those of German descent had done much to build up the state. The *Charlotte Observer* praised the "excellent comportment" of the many Catawba County citizens of German extraction. In another effort to shore up morale, in his proclamation "A Call to Prayer," June 17, 1918, the governor requested every church to ring its bells for two minutes at 7:00 P.M. each evening until victory came, to remind the people to pray "to the God of battles, to give to our forces on sea and land wisdom and foresight, courage and fortitude, and make them more than conquerors of the powers of evil arrayed against them." The state Council of Defense listed ways in which "purposeful loyalty" would manifest itself:

1. In cheerful obedience to law.
2. In prompt conformity to Governmental requests.
3. In the forebearance of criticism.
4. In bold dealing with anti-American sentiment.
5. In giving our best thought to our country.
6. In honest sacrifice, if sacrifice is needed.

In honor of Flag Day (June 14, 1918), schools, factories, and fraternities were encouraged to display the American flag:

> For the first time in the history of America the Flag is being carried in European countries by legions of fighting Americans.
> For the first time men of all nationalities who have adopted America as their country are banded together under the Flag, in foreign lands.

Music was also used to keep up morale. A newly appointed state music director asked each county to name a five-man committee to encourage a "Liberty Chorus" in every town. Nationally popular songs such as "Over There" were always on the program bill, but so too were some homegrown compositions with first lines such as, "Just like Washington crossed the Delaware, General Pershing will cross the Rhine" and "America I love you (and I hear you calling me)."

At the outbreak of the war some North Carolinians feared that spies and saboteurs might try to stir up race riots and encourage African Americans not to register or serve in the armed forces. Some incidents occurred in St. Louis and in Houston, but none in North Carolina. Around Thanksgiving the *Charlotte Observer*, in describing the annual football game between Livingstone College and Biddle Institute, remarked on the patriotic singing by the spectators, especially a song with the refrain, "We'll never let the flag hit the ground." Said the *Observer*, "Seems like it is about time for all that silly talk about the probable disloyalty of the negro to be given a back seat—or better still, toted out and given burial." In an address titled, "How War Came to America and What It Means to Us," delivered in Raleigh on August 14, 1917, James H. Pou, a prominent Raleigh lawyer and former North Carolina congressman, sounded as if he wanted to look beyond the segregation laws of the era when he said:

There will be a fuller understanding and a deeper sympathy between the races here at home. Misfortune has prevented that heretofore. Black men fought bravely in the Civil War, but against us. Politics estranged us. Now we will fight together.

In spite of all efforts to keep civilian morale and loyalty at a high pitch, reports of sabotage, sedition, and spying surfaced from time to time. Fortunately, in North Carolina most of these reports turned out to be spurious. In December 1917, the chairman of the Nash County Council of Defense received a letter reporting "foreigners supposed to be Germans" in the vicinity, but could never locate any. A Raleigh man reported a German working for the American Tobacco Company who kept a notebook with data on troop trains passing through, and the number and time of drafted men leaving for camp. A security check revealed that the man was completely loyal. James Sprunt, a prominent Wilmington businessman, reported a "German spy" in Columbus County who approached an elderly African American to say that the Germans would not molest blacks after they won the war, but no such person was found. A group of conscientious objectors known as Russellites from the International Bible Students Association in Brooklyn passed out literature in Wilson encouraging people not to register for the draft. More serious was the case of two men impersonating federal officers who urged the 750 employees of the Atlantic Coast Line Railroad at Wilmington to strike and tie up the system. Two hundred men went on strike, but James Sprunt and others influenced the remainder to stay at work. Sprunt also alerted the Standard Oil Company in Wilmington that their storage tanks near the Seaboard Airline Railway were poorly protected at night and could easily be set on fire. Then there was an amusing letter to Governor Bickett from a man in Wilson: "Have I as a private citizen the legal right to shoot a man who utters slanders and seditious threats about the President and the government?" Despite these reports, in the Eastern District Federal Court, in a year's time, only seven cases of sedition actually came to trial. Of these one defendant was found not guilty and one was convicted, two cases were dismissed, and three were still pending at the end of the war.

In addition to maintaining high morale, another important matter in wartime was keeping the public in good health. Two problems in particular plagued North Carolina: typhoid fever and the Spanish influenza epidemic.

THE WORLD CANNOT LIVE HALF SLAVE, HALF FREE

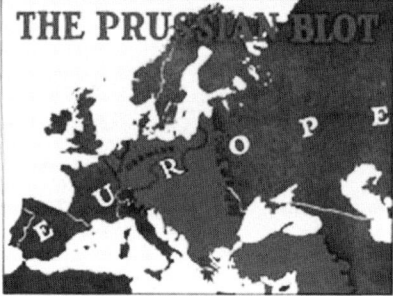

THE PRUSSIAN BLOT

100,000,000 PEOPLE ALREADY ENSLAVED BY GERMANY

President Wilson Says of the Germans:

"Their plan was to throw a broad belt of German military power and political control across the very center of Europe and beyond the Mediterranean Sea into the heart of Asia. They have actually carried the greater part of that amazing plan into execution."

THE KAISER PROCLAIMS:

"Woe and death unto those who oppose my will. Death to the infidel who denies my mission. Let all the enemies of the German nation perish. God demands their destruction."

WHILE GERMANY DREAMS OF DOMINATING THE WORLD BY FORCE
THERE CAN BE NO PEACE

State Councils of Defense issued posters that were used as anti-German propaganda. This one claims to echo a quote by Kaiser Wilhelm II. The title is an adaptation of a quote from Abraham Lincoln's "House Divided" speech.

North Carolina's death rate from typhoid fever was next to the highest in the nation. Between 1914 and 1917, 2,911 people died of this disease, 31.9 percent of those who contracted it. The chief causes were the use of open-backed privies and unscreened homes. In 1917 public health officials launched an attempt to wipe out typhoid fever with an educational campaign explaining the causes and encouraging parents to take their children for inoculation. Officials asked clergy to promote the campaign, and posters appeared in conspicuous locations. Meetings across the state informed people of the seriousness of the disease. It was suggested that a woman be chosen in each county to assist the health officer and to visit homes where she could talk "tactfully and kindly" with the woman of the house and get her cooperation. This was the start of a campaign that resulted in a great reduction in the number of cases of typhoid.

The Spanish influenza epidemic also hit North Carolina hard. In the fall and winter of 1918–1919, 13,644 persons died from the "flu," including Edward Kidder Graham, then in his sixth year as president of the University of North Carolina. A letter from Raleigh in October stated that 55 people had died, but the situation was improving. A letter from Wilmington said:

> We have indeed fallen upon evil days for added to the strain of war, comes its consort pestilence, striking down the loved ones at home and those abroad. Dr. Wood tells me this morning that this influenza pneumonia, is as deadly as the yellow fever. We are losing personal friends every day—the last victim being young Victor Grainger greatly beloved.

The Grove Park Inn in Asheville lost thirty of its employees at one time. The State Board of Health ordered the closing of all schools, churches, movies, fairs, circuses, and other public gatherings as soon as the first case appeared in a community. Other public gatherings, such as funerals, became more private in an effort to control the spread of the disease. The tobacco warehouses, a major industry in the state, were closed until October 28, and other businesses suffered in proportion.

To meet the epidemic, schools and other public facilities were converted to hospitals to enable doctors and nurses to attend to all the patients. The story of Clarkton is illustrative. Two young friends were taken ill the same day, died the same day, and were taken to the cemetery in the same hearse. Then in the home of one, his mother, two sisters, and three brothers became violently ill. A friend of theirs named Clarence Clark "came up with his hospital proposition . . . which has saved many lives." This hospital was in a schoolhouse. His father wrote to a friend:

> And it did make me proud to see Clarence as he came to hospital with his patients (men, women, and children) and take them in his strong arms and put them in their beds, then go for others. . . . Of all treated there has not been a death.

In High Point, Fred N. Tate and Clara T. Cox did noble work for the ill. They raised $2,000 in donations for a diet kitchen, medicine, clothing, and nursing care. Women made soup in their homes while others carried it to the hospitals and the homes of the ill, "mitigating the horrors of this fearful scourge." Twelve white nurses, 28 black nurses, and 6 male nurses cared for 224 families in one way or another. In Wilmington, a Miss Wood devised a block system for daily reports and was highly praised by Sprunt, who said she "has perhaps done more than any other person except Dr. Stiles, to overcome the plague here. . . . Dr. Stiles has left the whole management of the City in her hands."

Thousands of men, women, and children helped with the various volunteer organizations in the state, including the Red Cross. Before the war Red Cross local units were largely nominal. By the end of the war, 250,000 members comprised 140 chapters, 360 branches, and 250 auxiliaries and had raised $2 million in individual and corporate donations. Most of the active members were from the more affluent sections of the population, and their contributions of time and money persuaded others to participate. A report published in 1918 by the State Normal and Industrial College tabulated county by county the number of Red Cross chapters, the work accomplished, and the amount raised in Liberty Loan drives. While this report does not distinguish between black and white members, no doubt black chapters and auxiliaries existed. By this time, women in North Carolina had grown accustomed to joining the forces of their various separate organizations to work toward the same causes.

Three Red Cross drives directly solicited funds, but chapters utilized a variety of means to augment this source. A tobacco warehouse in Wilson donated half of its commissions on October 12, 1917, to the Red Cross. The Scotland Neck chapter sewed 169 convalescent robes, 271 underpants, 122 pajama suits, and 174 hospital shirts; it knitted 173 sweaters, 148 pairs

Posters were used to promote patriotism through Red Cross membership drives and fund raising. Wladyslaw T. Benda (1873–1948), a Polish-American artist, designed posters for Poland and America during World War I. Image (*left*) provided courtesy of the Library of Congress, Prints and Photographs Division. This World War I-era poster (ca. 1919) (*right*) was designed by Howard Chandler Christy (1873–1952).

of socks, 144 washcloths, and 232 property bags. It collected 1,440 pounds of clothing to be sent to refugees and also made surgical dressings. It conducted a first-aid class and gave help to the families of twelve soldiers. The canteen at the Raleigh railroad station served refreshments to some 250,000 soldiers as they passed through on troop trains and arranged for the soldiers to take cool showers when their trains stopped long enough. Wives of these soldiers wrote many thank-you notes to the Raleigh women who had been kind to their husbands. At the railroad station in Monroe, every soldier who passed through received a cold drink, a slice of melon, some fruit, or something to smoke. A poem of appreciation from one soldier reads:

I'm the fellow that helped to squeeze the lemons,
I'm the fellow that fell in love with you,
And after I've put the germ in the germans
I'm coming to claim a little kiss or two.

Women from the Red Cross canteen served refreshments to soldiers as they passed through Raleigh.

Emma Ingold Bost of Hickory wrote this poem about the Red Cross:

> Everybody knits but father and he winds yarn all day,
> Forming the big balls swiftly that knit so slow away;
> Mother casts on stitches, for she can do it right;
> Then everybody knits at our house, morning, noon and night.

The total North Carolina war output by the Red Cross was: 1,930,675 surgical dressings; 102,014 hospital garments; 44,646 refugee garments; 99,674 knitted garments; and 155,471 miscellaneous items. Several years later in an address titled, "North Carolina in the World War," delivered to the North Carolina Bar Association in Blowing Rock on July 5, 1923, Chief Justice Walter Clark praised the women of the state in saying:

> As to the women of North Carolina, who joined the Canteen, the Red Cross and other allied organizations, who cheered our soldiers at home and abroad, and as to the women of North Carolina, who ministered to the sick, the wounded and the dying, there can be no praise too high. Many sacrificed their health and others their lives. I cannot mention all and I am unwilling to mention only a few of these heroic women.

The second most active volunteer work in North Carolina was carried on by a national group called the War Camp Community Service (WCCS), which had centers in Raleigh, Fayetteville, Charlotte, Wilmington, and Southport. The purposes of this organization were to entertain soldiers and "surround them with the influence of home while in . . . training camps." In Raleigh, Red Circle Social Clubs in the churches provided recreation for the men. Fayetteville had a scarcity of recreation halls so the WCCS organized entertainment troupes that went out to Camp Bragg. The city of Charlotte, with 40,000 men in nearby Camp Greene, provided eight downtown lounges. In addition five churches served cold drinks on Sundays, six churches opened reading and writing rooms, and $4,000 was raised for a Christmas tree with gifts. The "Get Together and Sing Together" programs at two churches, followed by supper, proved to be very popular among the soldiers. The old Presbyterian Hospital served as an inexpensive hotel for soldiers' families, and a theater was started. The Wilmington WCCS secured reduced rates for the soldiers at nearby beaches and on at least one occasion sponsored an oyster roast at Masonboro Sound. Asheville was especially concerned with its hospitals and soldiers' families who came there, although that city's volunteer work was not a part of the WCCS. In Durham another independent agency did outstanding work with black troops. All this work required money, and North Carolina donated $1,422,485 to help pay for it.

The war exerted a significant impact on education. As the Council of Defense noted:

> . . . the welfare of our public schools is menaced by the shortage of teachers, who have been drawn into other fields by a difference in salaries. Surely we are not to let our children fall into the hands of incompetent novices and blunderers. We need to throw the whole weight of our shoulders into [a] campaign for saving our schools from disaster. The fact that 41,000 illiterates were found in the physically fit men of the first draft, shows plainly the need of strengthening our schools rather than allow any decline.

Short of raising salaries, however, which the state did not do, it was not possible to keep the teachers from leaving for better-paid war work or, in the case of men, for joining the armed forces.

On the positive side, schoolchildren, in addition to their parents, aided in collecting scrap, in buying war savings stamps, and in planting gardens and canning. College students contributed significantly in a variety of ways.

This patriotic ca. 1918 poster, designed by Haskell Coffin, featured Joan of Arc as an appeal for women to buy war savings stamps.

At Peace Institute in Raleigh, during the summer of 1918 the students carried on gardening, farming, dairying, canning, a wheat-saving campaign, and Red Cross work. Flora Macdonald College students at Red Springs picked 11,636 pounds of cotton. Students of the Agricultural and Technical College in Greensboro cut and shucked corn in the fall of 1918, dug sweet potatoes, mowed and raked the 25-acre campus, and gathered nuts for use in manufacturing gas masks. (The nuts were crushed, burned, and used as filters similar to charcoal filters.) They maintained a diet kitchen during the flu epidemic and gave $10,312.10 to war fund drives. College students registered in May 1918, for summer work under the United States Public Service Reserve, following a slogan of "Work or Fight."

Most of the men's colleges joined the Students' Army Training Corps. The activity on the campus of the University of North Carolina in Chapel Hill mirrored that across the state. Many students were almost pacifists in 1915 and 1916, but by January 1917 activity quickened considerably. By April a small group of military preparedness advocates had blossomed to include 500 students and faculty. On May 8, 125 students left campus for Camp Oglethorpe, Georgia, for officer training. The university offered a comprehensive curriculum of military training when it reopened in September. The space behind South Building was lighted at night for drills. In the fall of 1917, the university canceled football for the duration of the war. When eleven professors volunteered for military service, President Frank Porter Graham said in that year's University Day address, "The bitterness of having them taken is swiftly lost in the larger happiness of giving them and in the gallant fashion of their going." By December hysterical war propaganda was sweeping the campus. Poetry in the college magazine was ghoulish, to say the least, against the Germans. Religious lectures correlated "Religion and Patriotism." Bonfires and pep rallies had a new cry: "Beat Germany" replaced the old cry of "Beat Trinity [Duke]." In the fall of 1918, 750 students participated with 150,000 others across the nation in having eleven hours of training and three hours of recitation per week in addition to their regular college classes. Military French was added to the curriculum. Army headquarters moved into the Sigma Chi fraternity house; Memorial Hall became the armory and Swain Hall the mess hall. Trenches were dug near the Raleigh road, and the local girls played Red Cross in serving coffee and doughnuts to the "fighting" students. The movie house in Chapel Hill closed from lack of patronage. In all, 2,240 alumni and students went into service; 15 were killed in action; 3 received citations.

Two requisites for war were food for the fighting men and fuel for transporting them to France and for operating military manufacturing plants. Raising more food with fewer farm workers would be a challenge; and in particular North Carolinians could no longer rely on foods from other sections of the country because of transportation shortages. One poster proclaimed:

FARMERS
Plant it now
If you have not already done so
Right now is the time to plant your
VICTORY ACRE
Sell the crop and buy war savings stamps
ACT AT ONCE

Mrs. Lindsay Patterson of Winston-Salem became state chairman for the School Garden Army. All boys and girls were asked to join a Corn, Pig, or Poultry Club, the goal being 100,000 student members. The Mining and Metallurgical Society of America wrote all its members asking them to urge farming and food divisions at all mines and smelters where members worked. Governor Bickett and clergymen throughout the state threw themselves into the "feed yourself" campaign, advocating for victory gardens in town and country. As a result, food production in 1918 was four times that of 1917; 56,000 gardens were planted, Wilmington alone having 3,000. Governor Bickett, from time to time, appealed to the women to can, dry, and preserve all the food they could. In a July 14, 1917, address titled, "That Nothing Be Lost," he said:

> Let me close this appeal by giving you the salutation that I hope will greet you every morning for sixty days, "Good morning! Are you going to dry today? If not, what are you going to can?"

Conservation of food was critical. A sign in one restaurant said, "Use less sugar and stir like h - - -." Garbage was valuable as it could be fed to hogs, made into fertilizer and soap, and used in explosives. The public was asked to substitute plentiful foods for foods either scarce or needed overseas, such as potatoes instead of wheat. A poem by Ellen H. M. Brooks of Oxford put it this way:

We'll get the best of Kaiser Bill,
If all of us will eat our fill
Of mealy, plump potatoes;
So let us hasten to the store,
And buy a peck or two, or more,
Of Victory Potatoes.

Corn meal and rice were also used as substitutes for wheat. A recipe for Patriotic Biscuits was:

Patriotic Biscuits

1 pint white flour
1 pint finely ground corn meal
1 scant teaspoon soda
1 teaspoon baking powder
Lard the size of an egg
Salt

Directions: Mix all with buttermilk and bake as other biscuits.

Food conservation efforts included observing meatless days, wheatless days, and porkless days. Poultry, game, and fish were to take the place of beef. Restaurants were expected to serve meals that conformed to conservation suggestions, such as no white bread or meat, a minimum of sugar, and very little fat. The U.S. Food Administration launched the following pledge that 20 million people, mostly women, signed:

> I am glad to join you in the service of food conservation in our United States and I hereby accept membership in the United States Food Administration, pledging myself to carry out the directions and advice of the Food Administrator in the conduct of my household, in so far as my circumstances permit.

Signers received stickers for their home windows and buttons to wear; local newspapers carried their names. The farmers' pledge was:

> I hereby certify that the wheat this day delivered by me to (name of miller) was grown by me on my farm. I pledge myself to use such flour only in my own household or establishment and not to resell any of it without permission.

Top: This image shows the Asheville Community Cannery in the summer of 1917. *Bottom*: Posters urging food conservation were distributed by the United States Food Administration.

○

garbage *is* valuable
Don't waste it

UNITED STATES FOOD ADMINISTRATION

EXPLOSIVES
FERTILIZERS
SOAPS —
vital War
necessities
are being
made from
Kitchen
Refuse

Clean Garbage is also excellent food for hogs. Keep it free from broken Crockery-Glass -Tin Cans-Sweepings and other household Rubbish.

Use every ounce of food fat for human consumption, then —

make *the* Garbage Pail do its part

In many cases the war proved to be a boon to North Carolina farmers. John Paul Lucas, Executive Secretary of North Carolina's Food Administration, announced that by the autumn of 1917 the state's corn production had increased from 55 million bushels to 70 million bushels for a net increase of $22,500,000. Irish and sweet potatoes, sorghum, cowpeas, soybeans, and hay occupied significantly more acreage than the year before, and he estimated the increase in the value of the hog crop to be approximately $20,000,000. The great demand for military clothing and other fabric items meant that cotton farmers were able to sell all they could grow and textile mills whirred with activity. Tobacco farmers and cigarette manufacturers also saw a significant increase in demand for their products. Smoking was becoming increasingly socially acceptable, and tobacco companies developed clever advertising campaigns to make their specific brands more appealing.

The pressure of demand on other scarce items caused prices to rise. The military need for leather meant that shoes grew scarce; while the price of shoes was not governed by law, retailers signed a pledge not to charge more than a predetermined value and placed a sign in the store window to that effect. The scarcity of metal meant that furniture manufacturers had to secure a permit to purchase enough metal to go into the springs in rocking chairs. Construction already under way could continue, and farm buildings could be erected; other construction had to be by permission from the Council of Defense. The Council turned down the request of a man who asked for enough lumber to build a summer cottage at Lake Junaluska, and a great outcry arose against the congressman who secured construction materials for a new post office in his district.

North Carolina had no particular worries about food, but the state experienced a shortage of fuel, especially coal. A. W. McAlister of Greensboro and later R. M. Norfleet of Winston-Salem served as fuel administrators, directly under the national administrator. In October 1917, a survey of the coal needs of the state determined that the supply was inadequate, and a severe shortage developed as winter came on. The railroads that were carrying men and matériel to the Atlantic ports for shipment overseas required massive amounts of coal. At times railroad administrators confiscated carloads of coal being shipped to another customer. The situation as described in the Asheville newspaper on December 29, 1917, indicates the severity of the situation.

To prevent any actual suffering for lack of fuel the fuel administration yesterday borrowed twenty tons of coal from the Grove Park Inn, and this was distributed in small lots to consumers who came after it armed with the proper order from R. H. Luther, the man in charge of dispensing the coal. . . . To meet the most urgent demands today the fuel administration has arranged for the purchase of a car load of coal from the Southern Railway company, now at the depot, and will today haul this to the city coal yard on Market street. Until the dealers receive some of the many cars they have ordered this one car is all that is available.

That month the fuel administrator sent the following telegram to Washington:

Fuel situation in North Carolina most serious and becoming more serious every day. We request that order as to giving preference in shipment of coal applicable to Georgia and Alabama be extended so as to include North Carolina. Believe this will help to avoid calamitous situation. Please advise.

As a result, 255 carloads of coal soon arrived in the state, and the crisis was temporarily averted. By February 1, 1918, however, coal was running out again; this time the national administrator sent 140 carloads. In November 1917 the United States Fuel Administration decreed that electric signs could not be turned on before 7:45 P.M. or left on after 11:00 P.M.; one month later the "lightless night order" mandated that no electric lights would be allowed on Thursdays and Sundays. This order was suspended in April 1918, but the fuel administrator warned that it might be reinstituted if electricity consumption rose too high. Schoolchildren tied instruction tags on every coal shovel explaining how to save coal, and wood grew in home usage. In a proclamation on February 20, 1918, the governor urged the cutting of wood to conserve coal. With a facility for paraphrasing and for catchy expressions, he said:

Cut wood, cut wood, and cut more wood. . . . In time of sunshine prepare for blizzards. Eternal vigilance is the price of warmth. . . . [T]he man who chops a tree in this cause serves his country no less than he who digs a trench.

Gasoline conservation was every bit as important; the fuel administrator requested that gas not be used for pleasure riding on Sundays. One North Carolina local fuel administrator reported:

We have gone after the conservation of gas here so vigorously that most of the people here look upon one who violates the requests of the Fuel Administration as being as much of a slacker as one who evades military service. I see no other way of considering it.

One man with a sense of humor wrote this:

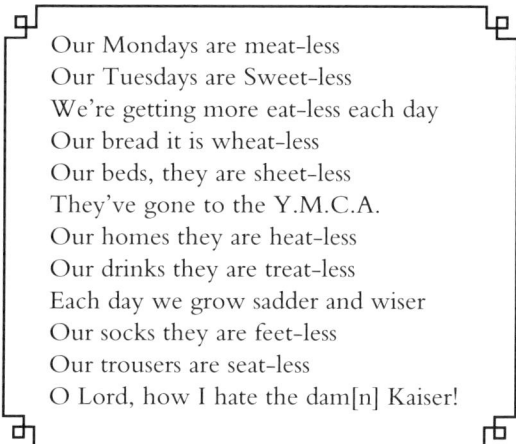

Our Mondays are meat-less
Our Tuesdays are Sweet-less
We're getting more eat-less each day
Our bread it is wheat-less
Our beds, they are sheet-less
They've gone to the Y.M.C.A.
Our homes they are heat-less
Our drinks they are treat-less
Each day we grow sadder and wiser
Our socks they are feet-less
Our trousers are seat-less
O Lord, how I hate the dam[n] Kaiser!

Given the huge military need for products that Americans had become so accustomed to consuming, it is remarkable that so much conservation could be carried out solely by appeals and voluntary action. Public opinion served as a powerful factor; no one wanted to be known as a slacker, and a majority of the public eagerly sought the recognition of window stickers, buttons, and newspaper notices of their conservation efforts. Moreover, the war effort afforded women an opportunity to expand their lives beyond the home, and thousands took advantage of the opportunity to head up local and state chapters of various relief organizations and to become leaders in the movement for conservation of resources.

Although North Carolina was not a great manufacturing state, 198 war industries were tabulated. High on the list of importance was shipbuilding. Three such industries operated in Wilmington. The schooner *Isabel C. Harriss* was christened in Wilmington June 25, 1918, at the Wilmington Wooden Shipbuilding Company, and four more ships were under construction. Several barges were transformed into coastal schooners. The Wilmington Iron

Works constructed two seagoing vessels, the *Hauppauge* and the *Commack*. The Carolina Shipbuilding Corporation began in November 1917 in Charleston with a contract for sixteen ships of 7,500 tons each, but the high construction costs in Charleston led the shipyard to move to Wilmington. No ships were completed, however, before the end of the war. Another shipyard operated at Morehead City where Daniel H. Hill Jr., the director of the state Council of Defense, tried to encourage a second one. Elizabeth City also had a shipyard.

The state geologist, Joseph Hyde Pratt of Chapel Hill, aided in the search for rare minerals in North Carolina such as platinum, manganese, iron, pyrite, tin, chrome, tungsten, molybdenum, antimony, and fluorite. An aluminum plant at Badin processed 90 tons a day. The Raleigh Iron Works made shells for the army and navy, while a munitions plant opened in Sanford in April 1916. Other products included spruce wood for airplanes from the Black Mountain region, an airplane propeller plant at High Point, a wagon wheel plant at Hickory, a sulphuric acid plant at Wadesboro, and a leather plant at Asheville. The shortage of French briar roots for smoking pipes led to the substitution of mountain laurel roots from North Carolina. B. R. Jolly of Raleigh offered a new range finder to the army, but officials determined that it was not enough of an improvement to warrant the expense of changing over the manufacturing plants. Every textile plant in the state had some war contracts, whether for blankets, socks, tents, duck, or any of the many cotton goods needed by the army. Between 1914 and 1919 North Carolina rose from second place nationally in value of tobacco products to first place.

The labor shortage grew increasingly critical as more men joined the armed services. A Public Service Reserve registered men with special skills who agreed to go wherever needed. Particularly needed were aviation mechanics, canners, blacksmiths, masons, nurses, saddlers, shipworkers, tailors, telegraph operators, wheelwrights, and machine woodworkers. High wages lured men away from North Carolina at times. Governor Bickett attacked the professional labor agents who tried to hire workers away from their jobs, and he urged mayors and sheriffs to arrest these agents. Camp Bragg needed 15,000 workers; Camp Polk needed 3,000; Biltmore needed 2,000; and Wilmington needed 1,000 in October 1918. Local councils of defense secured lists of men who had an income and were not employed, men who worked less than forty hours a week, and men who were not working at all, with the intention of calling them before the council and telling them their labor was needed.

This image shows the manufacture of shells for the United States Army and Navy, by the Raleigh Iron Works. Shells had also been made there for North Carolina during the Civil War.

The cities of Greensboro, Asheville, and New Bern passed ordinances against vagrancy. In a proclamation on May 14, 1918, Governor Bickett said, "At this time idleness is a crime that savors strongly of treason, for the men at the front cannot fight unless the men at home work." Farm work and cotton picking suffered from lack of hands, so that schoolchildren were asked to sign up for such work. A lady in Elizabeth City wrote to the governor describing her hardships in trying to run the farm and harvest the crop with her son in France and asked if he could "do something to help farmers out."

Another very important wartime activity was raising money to finance the war. Since taxes could not pay for it all, the federal government borrowed money through the sale of bonds and savings stamps. These bonds and savings stamps were good investments because the government paid interest on them to the purchaser. However, persuading people that they should buy war bonds rather than new hats, luxuries, or other products sometimes proved challenging.

The Spruce Squadrons

When the United States entered the war, it was soon discovered that the nation did not have the capacity to build a sufficient number of warplanes. While the airplane had been invented in North Carolina, by 1917 the European countries spent many years developing it for warfare and using it in

Top and Background: Camp of the 7th Provisional Squadron, Spokane, Wash. *Bottom*: Members of the 38th Spruce Squadron, U.S. Army, Raymond Wash., ca. 1918. Nelson Carr "Carl" O'Quinn from Harnett County served as a cook in this squadron. *Opposite*: Unidentified lumberjacks near Spokane, Wash.

combat. They needed to produce enough planes to occupy the skies over the front lines in France. The United States was supplying the Allies with spruce timber, which was vital to wing construction. However, output was small, and the lumber industry suffered from labor problems.

To help resolve some of these issues, the army took over the production of airplane spruce, most of which took place in the Pacific Northwest. Army personnel built a wood-processing plant and built roads and railroads to access and cut the timber. Lumber workers were organized into the "Loyal Legion of Loggers and Lumbermen" in order to provide good wages and working conditions, and to prevent labor strife. Production soared to unheard-of levels.

The Spruce Squadrons were officially part of the Signal Corps because this organization was charged with overseeing all army aviation. The term "squadron" was normally reserved for a flying group, but in this case, it was also the moniker for construction and logging units. Many men would have preferred to take part in combat overseas, but their expertise in cutting timber was needed elsewhere. Approximately 50,000 soldiers, overseeing around 100,000 lumber workers, were stationed in Oregon and Washington in 1918. One-fifth of these soldiers built roads and railroads that extended deep into the forests to provide access to the spruce trees that had never been logged commercially. Other soldiers worked at small lumber camps throughout the coastal areas. Because of their experience in both logging and the sawmill industry, many Tar Heels made their way to this region, some settling in the Darrington area. They brought traditional ways, food, and music that are still evident today. An annual Bluegrass Music Festival is held there in mid-July.

A Victory Loan Drive, featuring a load of helmets, with the sign "TO HELMET DER KISER [*sic*] BUY VICTORY LOAN BONDS," in front of the Raleigh post office on Fayetteville Street.

The government sponsored four "Liberty Loan Drives" and one "Victory Loan Drive," employing a variety of tactics. Prominent men wrote fifty personal letters each; salaried men were asked to accept war stamps for part pay; farmers were asked to give the proceeds of certain pieces of ground; movie stars such as Charlie Chaplin made public appearances and asked people to buy bonds. One elderly lady joyously invested her entire lifetime savings in a $100 bond, buying it with a thousand dimes unearthed from an old jug buried beneath the floor of her little cottage. A woman over sixty years old who had an invalid husband and worked in a factory a mile from her home, and who had been helped by the board of public welfare, when solicited said she would be glad to give the boys five dollars if she could pay a quarter a week. In Union

County, black citizens raised $1,000 for the United War Work fund. At a rally in Tarboro, one man bought $1,300 worth of war bonds, and another bought $50 in war savings stamps. Others sent telegrams to Adjutant General B. S. Royster of North Carolina volunteering their services and affirming loyalty and patriotism.

A school song went like this, to the tune of "I've Got Six-Pence":

> I love a thrift stamp
> A jolly little thrift stamp
> I love a thrift stamp
> As I love my life
> I earned a quarter for it
> I spent a quarter for it
> I put the thrift stamp where it was safe.

Special days became holidays to promote sales. April 26, 1918, was such a day, as was Sunday, October 6 (Heroes' Day), and October 12, when all stores and factories in North Carolina closed until 4:00 P.M. while schoolchildren sold bonds on the streets. During the flu epidemic workers sprayed their noses and throats and went from door to door. In an appeal to the public titled, "A Dash for the Home Plate," on October 14, 1918, the governor said of this drive, "It is the last inning of the war. Our boys have found the enemy, hit him hard and the bases are all full. A six-billion-dollar hit will bring them all over the home plate and win the war. A strike-out now would be a world tragedy." A newspaper advertisement read:

> NO QUARTER For The Hun
> EVERY QUARTER For Uncle Sam
> BUY THRIFT STAMPS

In an address on April 9, 1918, Governor Bickett said, as a reason for buying bonds, "They will yield more solid comfort for the inner man than 'possum and potatoes, and more juicy sweetness than the apples for which our first ancestors threw Paradise away."

The Asheville Times noted on May 8, 1919, the following figures represent- ing North Carolina's financial contribution to the war effort: $110,208,950 purchased in liberty bonds; $37,000,000 purchased in war savings stamps; $100,574,417 paid in federal taxes; $1,750,000 contributed to the Red Cross; $323,870 contributed to the YMCA; $1,422,485 contributed to the United War Work Campaign; and $154,000 contributed to the Jewish War Relief fund. In addition, North Carolinians donated thousands of hours in volunteer service to support the war effort. Although mindful of those men and women who had volunteered to serve in the war, North Carolina citizens always considered their support of family, friends, and neighbors to be part of the national effort.

Preparation for Combat

More than 86,000 men and women from North Carolina served in the armed forces during World War I, including the army, the navy, the marines, and the Coast Guard. The largest number served in the 30th Division of the army, nicknamed the "Old Hickory" Division, and the 81st Division, known as the "Wildcats." The 321st Infantry Regiment of the "Wildcat" Division contained more Tar Heels than the other regiments. The Wildcats were the first to wear an insignia patch, which Gen. John Joseph Pershing, although at first disapproving, finally ordered every division to emulate. The 316th Field Artillery of the Wildcats was from North Carolina. North Carolinians were scattered in other divisions, as well. The 42nd or "Rainbow" Division had a North Carolina engineer train, the 117th Engineers. The 3rd and 4th Divisions, the latter known as the "Ivy" Division, were organized at Camp Greene near Charlotte, but they were not notably North Carolinian. Forty-nine black men from North Carolina attended Officer Training School at Fort Des Moines, Iowa. Most black soldiers from North and South Carolina served in the 371st Infantry Regiment and trained at Camp Jackson before going overseas. In addition, two hospital

The Carolina Wildcat insignia is a shoulder patch worn by units of the 81st Infantry Division during World War I. It shows a black wildcat on a black bordered olive drab disk. Although the division included troops from Florida, Puerto Rico, and New York City, the insignia recognized the fact that most of the troops in the 81st were from the Carolinas. They actually trained at Camp Jackson, S.C., near Wildcat Creek. Image provided courtesy of the North Carolina Museum of History.

units went overseas, one under Dr. Addison Brenizer of Charlotte and the other under Dr. John W. Long of Greensboro; and 195 nurses from North Carolina saw medical service.

The largest grouping of men in the army is called an army corps, which in turn is subdivided into divisions, each division being given a number for convenience. A division is broken down into three brigades, under the command of a brigadier general; and in turn a brigade is subdivided into regiments, under the command of a colonel. Divisions also contain artillery units, machine gun units, engineers, and ambulance and hospital personnel. A headquarters company handles the paperwork: roster lists, payrolls, messages, letters, and supply orders. The supply company is responsible for providing adequate food and ammunition. Thus, an army requires many different types of service personnel with a variety of skills in addition to soldiers trained for combat.

When the North Carolina National Guard returned from assignment on the Mexican border in March 1917, the soldiers were immediately put back into federal service and transformed into the 119th and 120th Infantry, 60th Brigade, 30th Division, which trained at Camp Sevier, South Carolina. While the United States had not yet entered the war, this move indicates that the army was preparing for that day, which came on April 4, 1917. In August of the same year, additional guardsmen were called up to make the 105th and the 117th Engineers as well as the 113th and 117th Machine Gun Battalions. A cavalry squadron commanded by Maj. Warren A. Fair of Lincolnton was called into service on May 26, 1917; the coast artillery was divided into six companies and stationed at Cape Fear. The naval militia, like the first national guardsmen, was called to the colors even before war was declared, and North Carolina members reported to Norfolk for orders.

Volunteers were called for immediately following the declaration of war in order to fill out the National Guard units to war strength and to secure naval and marine personnel. A volunteer had the advantages of choosing his outfit and thus staying with his friends, and probably earlier promotion. Naval recruiting stations opened in Asheville, Charlotte, Fayetteville, Goldsboro, Raleigh, Wilmington, and Winston-Salem to meet a quota of four hundred men in less than a month. In an appeal made on April 19, 1917, Governor Bickett urged, "I cannot conceive it to be possible that the State that has had five Secretaries of the Navy will fail to do its plain duty in this

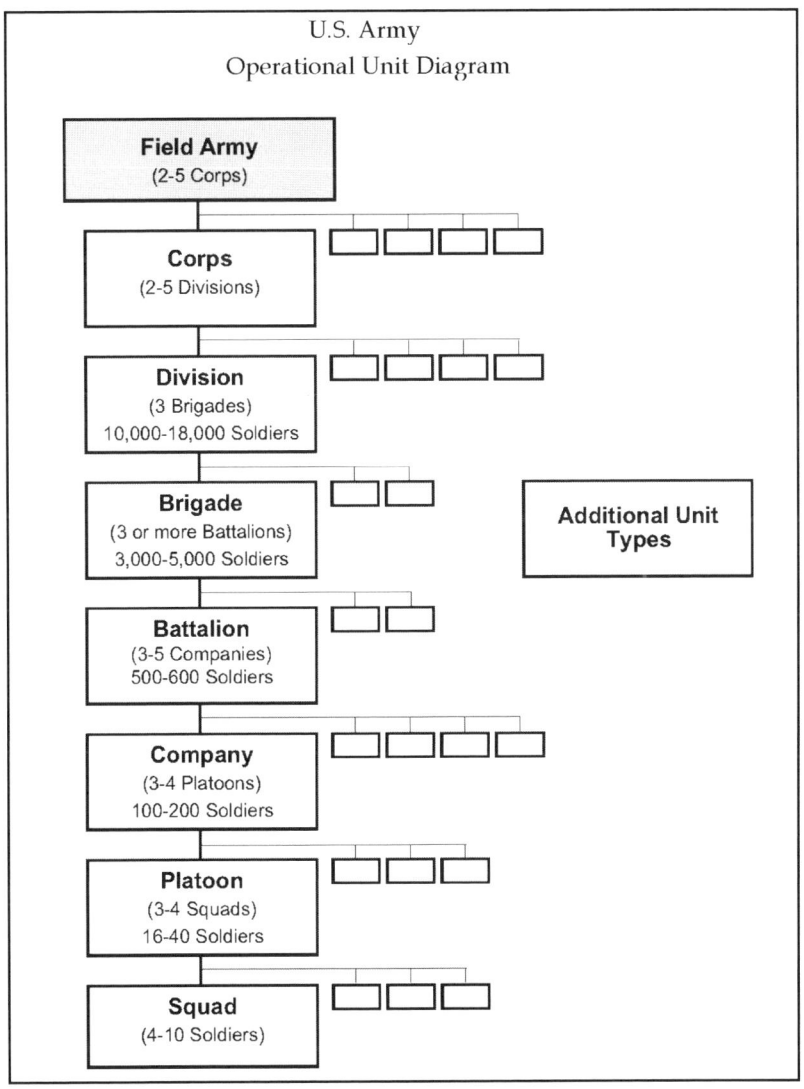

U.S. Army
Operational Unit Diagram

Field Army
(2-5 Corps)

Corps
(2-5 Divisions)

Division
(3 Brigades)
10,000-18,000 Soldiers

Brigade
(3 or more Battalions)
3,000-5,000 Soldiers

Additional Unit Types

Battalion
(3-5 Companies)
500-600 Soldiers

Company
(3-4 Platoons)
100-200 Soldiers

Platoon
(3-4 Squads)
16-40 Soldiers

Squad
(4-10 Soldiers)

This diagram provides information on how army operational units are organized today, which would have been similar during World War I. Image adapted from www.army.mil.

crisis of the Nation's life." Marine enlistment stations appeared in Charlotte, Durham, Raleigh, and Winston-Salem. One poster announced enticingly:

Here Is Your Chance To See
FRANCE
AND THE RHINE
ENLIST IN THE UNITED STATES ARMY TO-DAY

Another poster said:

THE NAVY
NEEDS YOU!
DON'T READ
AMERICAN HISTORY
MAKE IT!

The great bulk of soldiers came from the draft, however, instead of National Guard units or volunteers. On June 5, 1917, all men between the ages of twenty-one and thirty-one registered; on June 5, 1918, those who had reached the age of twenty-one during that year registered; and on September 12, 1918, those between eighteen and forty-five who had not already registered did so. North Carolina was proud of its 106 percent registration; a member of President Wilson's cabinet thought some registrants must have lied about their ages. Sixty-five percent of those who registered passed the physical fitness test, a record exceeded only by a few other states.

One of the problems connected with the draft was that of calling up doctors. The government predicted that at least 17,000 physicians would be needed, which meant that all M.D.'s below the age of forty-five would be called, leaving the older and the retired physicians to handle the patients at home. The hardship on the civilian population was a necessary one, as the North Carolina Council of Defense appealed: "Think of 5,000 wounded men lying on the battlefield all night moaning for help, and no man to give them succor."

Treat 'Em Rough!—Join the Tanks. This poster, ca. 1917 poster was created as a recruiting poster for the U.S. Tank Corps and features an attacking cat leaping over a tank, the trademark of the Tank Corps. Drawing by August William Hutaf, National Printing & Engraving Co., Chicago, New York, St. Louis.

Conscientious objectors presented another challenge. During the course of the war, over 64,000 men nationwide requested noncombatant service based on their moral opposition to fighting. Local draft boards recognized approximately 57,000 such claims as legitimate, based primarily on a man's stated religious faith. Ultimately the army drafted 20,873 of these men, 4,000 of whom maintained their position for the duration of the war. The army had little experience with such individuals, and so treatment of them varied greatly. Those who accepted noncombat duties in camp usually fared well;

however, those who refused even noncombat duties often found themselves in prison. Not until November 1920 were the last such men released.

In 1918 another controversy arose over the exemption of college students. The provost marshal general of the United States, Gen. E. H. Crowder, wanted to exempt college students from the draft, to which Governor Bickett and others strongly objected. The governor made the counterproposal that students be drafted; if the army then saw fit to send them to college, well and good. Chief Justice Walter Clark also opposed exemption. He wrote to the *News and Observer:*

> But the boy between the plow handles, who may be the chief laborer on the farm or the support of a widowed mother, is doing fully as much for his country out of the army as the boy whose father is able to send him to college. A discrimination along these lines will cause the deepest dissatisfaction. . . . We have no privileged class in this country and should have none. . . . There is already some dissatisfaction expressed that so many young lawyers who should be at the front have shunted themselves off into safe berths, out of cannon range.

He also wrote to the University of North Carolina president, Edward Kidder Graham, in Chapel Hill:

> Having been a witness to the class discrimination which caused such serious disorganization in the Confederate Army, I do not think that the somewhat similar exemption in favor of the educated youths over their comrades will be prudent. . . . We need to make bombs and bomb throwers and not "bomb-proofs."

President Graham, however, supported the policy of exemption. The students joined the Students' Army Training Corps and thus formed a pool that could generate officer candidate material, if desired by the army, or privates, as the commanders might see fit. Graham pointed out that by the spring of 1919, no fewer than 90,000 officers would be needed; he felt the provost marshal general's plan to be sound. These plans were put into effect, although the end of the war in November 1918 fortunately prevented the need for additional soldiers.

Draft boards also had to cope with "slackers," men who failed to register or who did not appear when called up. Such behavior was a federal offense and in the Eastern District Federal Court for the year July 1, 1917, to

July 1, 1918, 390 cases resulted in 52 convictions. Some of the cases were probably because of ignorance rather than disaffection. In Chatham County unscrupulous agents solicited funds from men called for military service in order to employ counsel to test the constitutionality of the Selective Service Act. The Chatham County sheriff said they were "using language that is calculated to arouse the ignorant against the Government." In an August 4, 1917, letter, Governor Bickett told the sheriff and solicitor of Chatham County to notify the United States district attorney if anyone should:

> by word or deed, give aid and comfort to the enemy by seeking to palsy the Nation's arm as it is raised to strike. Immediate and drastic action will be taken upon every report, and men who thus desert their country in its hour of peril will be made to feel the strong arm of the law.

No massive resistance developed in Chatham following the publication of this message. To reiterate the sentiment, the following notice was used:

> If you are a shirker or a
> slacker or if your sentiments
> are opposed to the selective
> draft, and your habits are to
> air your opinions, then YOUR
> place is on the OUTSIDE.

A more difficult problem was that of men already sworn into the army who deserted. North Carolina reported approximately 4,000 deserters. The local council of defense and the women's committee did all they could to report such cases to the adjutant general. In some cases men who left their units did so with absolutely no intention of returning. In other cases the desertions resembled those of the Civil War, when soldiers received woebegone news from a family member and returned home to attend to the situation, always intending to return to their unit but not having notified anyone of their absence in advance. In a February 8, 1918, address to clergymen, Governor Bickett urged them to preach that families should write cheerful letters to their loved ones in service. He had just visited Camps Jackson and Sevier and reassured the ministers that the men were:

better fed, better clothed, and lead more wholesome lives than ninety-five per cent of the men of the same age at home. They are a husky, handsome lot, with muscles as hard as nails, and with hearts aglow with a high purpose to serve and to save the world in this supreme crisis.

By writing positive letters, parents would not risk sending their sons to prison or getting them shot for desertion because of a tale of woe from home.

A grave problem developed in Ashe County in June 1918 when forty deserters chose to hide in the hills for the duration of the war. An armed civilian posse attempted to bring them in, but the renegades held them off; one member of the posse was killed in the exchange of gunfire. Upon being notified of the situation, Governor Bickett immediately went to Jefferson (the county seat), where he addressed a large crowd at the courthouse. He said, in part:

Men of the mountains: I come to you today to save and not to destroy. I come to save the fair name of a county in which the whole State takes . . . peculiar pride. I come to save you . . . your birthright of honor and chivalry; I come to save wayward and willful boys from the sad and certain consequences of ignorance and sin.

I have tried honestly to get at the real cause of this unlovely situation. . . . Certainly, it is not because they are afraid to fight. . . . It is not because they are unwilling to do or to give their share. . . . I am forced to the conclusion that these mountain boys are giving trouble because they have not been told the truth about this war and because they have been told a lot of lies about it.

As was his way, Governor Bickett then recounted for his audience the history of the U.S. involvement in the war in the most patriotic of terms. That day one of the deserters surrendered to the governor, who then provided the AWOL soldier with a letter to take to his commanding officer at Camp Jackson in South Carolina attesting to the young man's loyalty and asking for leniency. Following the governor's return to Raleigh, sixteen more of the deserters reported and asked to be sent to camp and reinstated. Four more promised to come in the following Saturday. Most of them said they had stayed overtime at home and were then afraid to return; but the governor's visit encouraged them to report. In Mitchell County there were thirteen deserters at one time. When one came in, he was used as a liaison to reach the others, who were persuaded to come in also. The draft board chairman accompanied them to their camps and asked for leniency. Some of the units had gone overseas while the deserters were away, so they were assigned to new units that were ready to sail for France.

With the National Guard in federal service, the state was left without military protection in case of riots, rebellions, or sabotage. The state called up 5,000 men from the thirty to forty-five age group, at least twenty-five men from each county, and organized them into a reserve militia. Because of a shortage of rifles, some cities purchased their own in order to arm their militiamen; the men bought their own uniforms. Fortunately, the only time the militia was called out was in Winston-Salem when a mob threatened to lynch a man held prisoner in the city hall. When a firehose failed to disperse the crowd, the militia fired two volleys over their heads and held them at bay. Companies arrived from Charlotte, Greensboro, and Raleigh to relieve the Winston-Salem guards; by noon of the next day all was quiet, with only four men injured. Had any large outbreak occurred, however, the soldiers stationed at Camp Greene in Charlotte could have been called on for duty.

The War Department built thirty-two cantonments or camps in which to train the new army, primarily in the South. Camp Greene, just west of Charlotte, was the largest such facility in North Carolina. The first troops arrived in September 1917, with construction still in progress. By February 22, 1918, when Camp Greene reached its maximum population of 41,000 soldiers, roads and sanitation facilities still were not completed, and the *New York Times* (February 23, 1918) reported that the War Department was considering abandoning the camp for all but aviation training. Shortly after this report the 3rd Division departed for Europe, and the 4th Division did likewise in May. While the facility was never pristine, neither was it repurposed until the end of the war, when it closed.

The North Carolina National Guard trained at Camp Sevier near Greenville, South Carolina; North Carolina draftees went first to Camp Jackson in South Carolina for their basic training. These camps contained wooden buildings because lumber was available and tents were not. They were simple, only semi-permanent, with water, sewers, roads, and supply terminals. In September 1918, an artillery camp opened at Camp Bragg near Fayetteville. Named for Gen. Braxton Bragg, it consisted of 118,000 acres where the artillery could have a school and a firing range. After the armistice,

At Camp Polk a tank is pictured in the foreground with its crew outside the State Fairgrounds Exhibit Hall in 1918.

Fayetteville waited breathlessly to see if the camp would be closed. When the War Department announced that it would be retained, the Chamber of Commerce gave a banquet to celebrate.

Around the same time Camp Bragg opened, Camp Polk near Raleigh was authorized. Some training was carried out at the state fairgrounds while the camp was being erected slightly farther west, at a railroad station named Method. Tanks were stored under the grandstand at the fairgrounds. Some carried two cannons, others only one. A drill field was graded flat and was used also for airplane landings. Before the permanent camp was finished, the war ended, and construction stopped almost as fast as it had begun.

While these large camps proved to be a boon to the local economies of Charlotte, Fayetteville, and Raleigh, they also created new problems. One significant issue was housing for construction workers who often came great distances for the work. In addition, some soldiers' families came to be with them until they went overseas. For instance, Fayetteville needed 750 more rooms to rent and 200 apartments. There were only two hotels, one of which was very small.

Training at Camp Sevier was probably typical of the other infantry training cantonments. The infantry was the most important fighting unit of the war. In European armies the individual man was one of a mass, but in the American army he was part of an eight-man squad that could act independently if need be. This system, a part of American frontier and individualistic heritage, proved extremely valuable on the front in France. More than once pre-dawn attacks, sometimes in heavy fog, would have floundered had squad leaders, trained in directional and map-reading skills, not been briefed in advance of direction and target.

Gen. George W. McIver, a native of Moore County and an 1882 graduate of West Point, praised the quality of the southern draftees sent to Camp Jackson. He said they inherited the "hardihood and the military virtues of their pioneer ancestors." He continued, "I doubt very much if any mobilization point in the country received a body of drafted men who excelled them in the fundamental qualities which go to make up good fighting men." They brought "the fine battlefield traditions of the valiant Army which fought for the Southern Confederacy."

When the National Guard arrived at Camp Sevier, it was still under construction. Arthur Lloyd Fletcher of the 113th Field Artillery, 30th Division, described it as "grub stumps, pile brush, rake trash all day long and the bugle called you again early the following morning to start it all over again." Each man had a cot with a straw mattress and four blankets. He brought his own pillow, if he had one. He was issued a kit bag for his underwear, two shirts, four pairs of socks, his uniform, and two pairs of shoes. There were showers in the bathhouse. As one fellow said, "General Headquarters officially ran the Army, but the unofficial source of all orders, rumors, dates of movement overseas, and much unofficial army intelligence was the company latrine." Soldiers nicknamed their officers "Sears-Roebuck Lieutenants" because they had been rapidly trained or "mail-ordered." French and British officers came over to serve as instructors. John Otey Walker of the 120th Infantry, 3rd North Carolina, 30th Division, wrote to his family: "One army characteristic, which we were taught to do then, has left such an impression on me that I am still doing it and that is, shave every morning. Those English officers were sure strict about that."

Pre-war training methods were useless because trench warfare outmoded the older military tactics. Winning the war would require crushing offensive power, not mobility. Line-smashing and modified open-rank warfare for going "over the top" were emphasized. Training courses included rifle and bayonet, machine gun, automatic rifle, hand grenade, gas defense, sniping, reconnaissance, camouflage, radio and telephone, patrolling, and cooking. At first the men had to train with wooden sticks for guns, but soon their weapons arrived. The early recruits had no electric lights either, so they went to bed in the dark until electric wires had been strung. To Ben Muse, a native of Durham who served as a lance-corporal in the 11th King's Royal Rifles, bayonet practice was "nauseating, though I tried not to show it." A typical letter follows, showing life at the camp:

> We are working hard and I just can't write as often as I want too. Out at five and work until six o'clock. No lights to write by and we are putting in full time.
>
> I have to report to Brigade Headquarters every day for two hours work with the bayonet. Was sent over by the Major of our Batallion, and I am to learn it so I may be able to teach the company.
>
> By the way, I don't remember whether I wrote you that I had been promoted to Sergeant. More work all the time but am doing my part. Was vaccinated once week before last, and twice this, all are taking but have lost no time yet. My arms are sore, as we get stuck in both, and at the same time.

Another man wrote, "We could never understand how 'passing in review' would help us chase the German Army back across the Rhine where it belonged. But Colonel Halstead said to parade and we did just that." Some of the promising men were sent to San Antonio for additional training as instructors. One such man wrote home that he was drilling with 36-inch steps, 135 steps to the minute. "That's almost a run." He also patrolled, crawling on hands and knees. There were new exercises, too. He had "developed muscles that I didn't know was in my body." There were hikes with packs and map study. When these men later led their squads into battle, they put these skills to good use.

Entertainment for the soldiers' morale fell into two categories: that which was conducted at the camp, such as the YMCA, the Liberty Theater,

Seven organizations, including the YMCA, the YWCA, the Salvation Army, and the American Library Association raised funds to support American troops and keep up their morale during leisure time. "The fighting man's play time is recognized as no less important than his work time," so the United War Work Campaign was organized in September of 1918 as a coordinated effort. Posters like this one published by the U.S. Food Administration served as pictorial publicity and helped motivate the home front effort.

the Red Cross Building, the Knights of Columbus Building, the library, and the Hostess House; and that which was officially or unofficially carried on in the nearby towns. In camp the soldiers organized minstrel shows, and they played baseball and other games. In Greenville, South Carolina, the Imperial Hotel had Saturday night dances, and extra trains ran from the camp to town. Motion picture theaters were filled. Parents and friends could send soldiers "Smileage Books," which had coupons of admission to theaters. Soldiers received weekend passes once every six weeks at first, becoming less and less frequent as the pace quickened. Mass singing was conducted at the camps by trained musicians who led in the national anthem, "Tipperary," "Over There," "There's a Long Long Trail A-winding," "Pack Up Your Troubles in Your Old Kit Bag," and "Brighten the Corner Where You Are." One favorite soldier song was:

> Good-bye, Maw! Good-bye, Paw!
> Good-bye, mule, with yer old hee-haw!
> I may not know what this war's about,
> But you bet, by gosh, I'll soon find out;
> And O my sweetheart, don't you fear,
> I'll bring you a King for a souvenir;
> I'll bring you a Turk and a Kaiser, too,
> An' that's about all one feller can do!

Another one went like this:

> Old Uncle Sammy, he needs the infantree,
> He needs artilleree, he needs the cavalree.
> When he gets them, we'll all go to Germany.
> God help Kaiser Bill!

Not only was soldier morale a concern, but the health of these men was also a grave concern, especially during the unusually severe winter of 1917–1918. The flimsy wooden buildings that provided shelter did little to help. Spinal meningitis broke out, proving 80 percent fatal until doctors learned new treatments. Mumps and measles were brought into camps by recruits; quarantining the new men until the incubation periods had passed solved that problem. Local doctors were asked to report to public health officials any diseases with which a soldier on furlough might have come in contact, so that he could be quarantined when he returned to camp. A vitally important health problem was that of venereal disease. In the regular army in 1917, 88 out of 1,000 men were ill "as the result of immorality," while among the draftees, 388 out of 1,000 were ill. As a pamphlet put it:

> The Problem?
>   The lonely boy.
> Where?
>   Outside the camp.
> When?
>   On furlough.
> What does he crave?
>   Diversion; Companionship; A touch of home!
> Why?
>   Stale from drilling; homesick. Because he's a human being.
> When strikes the danger hour?
>   When he stands on a street corner, LONELY, waiting for something to happen.
> The Penalty:
>   Impaired fighting efficiency; disease; discontent.
> The Solution:
>   Organized hospitality.

Communities were warned that if they did not co-operate in controlling vice, the camps would be moved to other locations. Given the cost of relocating camps, this threat was no doubt an idle one. However, towns benefited economically from nearby camps and so made strong efforts to cooperate. Secretary of War Baker appointed Raymond B. Fosdick, a long-time acquaintance of President Wilson, to lead the Commission on Training Camp Activities. This organization, housed within the War Department, was charged with working with local governmental and social agencies to provide a wide variety of recreational opportunities that would hopefully offset the lure of prostitutes and saloons. On May 24, 1917, in an open letter to all the governors, Secretary Baker said: "The greater proportion of this [fighting] force probably will be made up of young men who have not yet become accustomed to contact with either the saloon or the prostitute, and who will be at that plastic and generous period of life when their service to their country should be surrounded by safeguards against temptations to which they are not accustomed."

The War Camp Community Service clubs, mentioned previously, were part of Fosdick's answer to the problem, as were camp singing sessions and visiting professional entertainers such as Sir Harry Lauder, renowned Scottish singer. North Carolina cities did their best to clean up undesirable situations such as the "blind tigers" or illegal saloons that were operating at one time or another. In every way possible, the men of the United States were being turned with amazing rapidity into one of the world's finest fighting forces, ready for combat. That came next.

The American Expeditionary Forces (AEF) in France

The United States was woefully unprepared for war when Wilson asked Congress for such a declaration in April 1917. At this time the American army ranked seventeenth in the world in terms of size, numbering 135,000 troops. Congress immediately authorized increases to 287,000 men in the regular army and 450,000 in the National Guard, and recruiting stations went to work. Volunteers, however, did not keep up with even the initial authorization, let alone the demands from Gen. John Pershing, who had arrived in France in June. That month Congress approved the first of three selective service bills that would be passed during the course of the war, and immediately nearly ten million men entered the pool for potential military service. General Pershing insisted that America should have an army of one million men in Europe within twelve months, with a final goal of three million men.

The first American soldiers departed for Europe in late June 1917. For nearly a year they fought embedded in either the British or French armies. General Pershing continuously and loudly argued for a separate American command with himself in charge, but until the spring of 1918 the number of American soldiers available could not support this request. Not until March 1918 did the number of U.S. troops in Europe reach 250,000. By July that number was one million, and by November it was two million. Of this number, over 200,000 were African American. They fought with the British and French, since the American army refused to use them in combat. Black soldiers encountered considerably less racism than they had in the United States, and enjoyed significant social freedom while on leave. Their experiences translated into a new level of social activism on their return to the United States.

Although the majority of Americans who served in World War I did so as part of the army along the western front, the navy, Coast Guard, and marines also played significant roles. Guarding the shores of the United States from enemy submarines was one such duty. Since the Diamond Shoals Lightship,

This is the Diamond Shoals Lightship No. 71 (*LV-71*) a few months before being sunk by a German U-boat in World War I. On August 6, 1918, the *LV-71* reported by radio the presence of a German submarine that had sunk a passing freighter. The message was intercepted by the submarine *U-104*, and after giving the young master, Walter Barnett, and his crew an opportunity to abandon ship in the lifeboats, the *LV-71* was sunk by surface gunfire. Image provided courtesy of the U.S. Coast Guard and reproduced by permission.

off Cape Hatteras, was sunk by a submarine, this fear was not an idle one. Marines also served in the war, although not in what would become their traditional role of securing beachheads. Two marine units served with the 2nd Division and fought along the western front in 1918. Their commander was Marine General John A. Lejeune, for whom Camp Lejeune was named.

The United States Navy's roles included ferrying men and supplies to Europe, returning the wounded and the remains of those killed to the United States, and warring against enemy submarines. The navy was in no way equipped to transport millions of American soldiers to Europe, but managed the process by confiscating German ships that had languished in American ports since the start of the war, seizing some neutral passenger liners, and utilizing British vessels. American destroyers were crucial in escorting the troop convoys across the Atlantic. Josephus Daniels, secretary of the navy, noted in his memoirs that the U.S. Navy escorted 82.75 percent of troop transports, the remainder being escorted by the British and French navies. Frank X. Britt of Enfield kept a diary of his trips across the Atlantic escorting troop ships.

In a heavy fog on one trip, two ships were lost and collided with each other, forcing them to return to the United States. He experienced two submarine warnings but no attacks. The troop ships arrived at Brest, France, but did not unload until they went on to Bordeaux. On the return trip his ship carried 3,500 sacks of mail and 70 convalescent soldiers. On another trip, Britt was in the harbor at St.-Nazaire, France, when a submarine boldly came into the harbor and attacked. One ship was hit. As he described the incident:

> . . . the oil tanks were blown up and the oil on the waters was blazing up about six feet high, if they [the men] stayed on board they were doomed to be cremated alive—now just imagine how I felt watching these poor fellows burn to death while screaming for help.

Britt's ship missed its convoy going back that time, which was fortunate for him because six of the eight ships in the convoy were sunk by submarines.

A sailor named Donald from Cumberland County described his trip across on the *Princess Matoika*, a confiscated German ship, sailing from Norfolk with 4,000 black troops.

> We went in convoy with 11 other troop ships and were convoyed by 14 destroyers, a cruiser and 2 seaplanes. Two days out all but the cruiser & 2 destroyers turned back. . . . Every day or so some ship would sight an object in the water & then every ship in the convoy but ours would open fire on it. It invariably turned out to be a can or barrel but we took no chances.

At Brest he had two days' rest, and then the ship returned. "We brought about 100 terribly wounded soldiers. Some with both arms & legs gone. One with only one lung. Some blinded by gas & two crazy. . . . Oh, but I am thankful I am in the navy!"

Two navy commanders from North Carolina had harrowing experiences. David Worth Bagley, born in Raleigh and a graduate of the U.S. Naval Academy, was in command of the *Jacob Jones* when, on December 6, 1917, while on antisubmarine patrol near the French coast, the ship was hit by a torpedo that punctured the fuel tank. The ship sank in only 8 minutes. Sixty-four crew perished; Bagley and 37 others survived, thanks to the humanitarian concern of the submarine commander who radioed their location. Bagley received the Distinguished Service Medal and went on to a long and productive naval career, retiring in April 1947 with the rank of Vice Admiral.

David Worth Bagley (1883–1960), was the brother of Worth Bagley, the only U.S. Navy officer killed in action during the Spanish-American War. His grandfather was Jonathan Worth, governor of North Carolina. After commanding the *Jacob Jones*, he served as Chief of Staff of Naval Forces in Europe. Image provided courtesy of the Naval History and Heritage Command.

Percy W. Foote, of Wilkes County, also lost a ship to a German submarine. On May 31, 1918, the USS *President Lincoln* (a German interned ship) was about 600 miles from Brest, France, after delivering American soldiers, and was returning to the U.S. with its crew and some sick and wounded soldiers when it was struck by a total of three torpedoes, one of which immediately killed seven men. Foote ordered that the ship be abandoned. The lifeboats and rafts were lashed together, and that night all survivors were rescued by two destroyers, the *Warrington* and the *Smith*. Foote later served as aide to Secretary of the Navy Josephus Daniels. He was awarded the Distinguished Service Medal and on his retirement was promoted to Rear Admiral.

The vast majority of North Carolinians who served in the war, though, did so as soldiers in the U.S. Army. When the 30th Division left Camp Sevier in May 1918 to head for France, the soldiers sailed from various ports in twenty-five ships, and landed in Liverpool, England. One group sailed from Boston on the British tramp steamer *Bohemian*, "slipping out quietly to prevent leakage of information. No manifestation of farewell could be permitted," wrote Lt. Charles W. Perry. The cooks on these tramp steamers were Australian, and the Americans were not accustomed to their kind of food. The ships were overcrowded and by the time they reached Halifax, Nova Scotia, where they waited for their convoy to assemble, the grumbling reached dangerous proportions. Lieutenant Perry wrote:

On account of growing unrest of troops, caused by extreme hunger, it was found necessary to substitute our own cooks and methods of rationing for the British. An immediate change for the better was the result and the usual cheerful spirit of the troops became manifest.

A member of Company A, 115th Machine Gun Battalion, 30th Division, described a submarine attack on May 18, 1918, at 3:30 A.M.

First there was the electric alarm in every compartment of the ship, then there was the siren whistle of the ship. This was the signal for everyone on deck. . . . Submarine destroyers were on the job, darting here and there around the ship. On board everything was deathly quiet. Thus we awaited the order to lower boats, but the order never came.

The 30th Division was assigned to the British army and fought with them for the duration of the war. Upon arrival in England the American soldiers were issued British rifles since the supply of American weapons was not adequate until late in the war. Initial training gradually accustomed the American soldiers to the techniques and the sound of fighting. James Otey Walker wrote about the British:

We often disagreed, but they accepted us and treated us as one of their own. They gave us their splendid Australian Artillery, they fed us, they equipped us, they clothed us, they protected us in the air, and we profited by their four years of experience in warfare. We feel honored in having been selected to serve with them.

In a January 21, 1918, letter Lt. James W. Cheshire (1st Infantry Division, 2nd Brigade) of Raleigh thought the British were:

a whole sight nicer than our own fellows & were far & away ahead of our crowd in everything pertaining to good manners, taste & the like. I am sorry to say that frequently some of our fellows made me feel quite uncomfortable with their blatant assaninity and rudeness.

The 30th Division experienced a zeppelin raid while in England. Col. E. D. Swinton wrote:

. . . a faint humming noise made itself heard afar off on high. The sound approached, grew louder, and gradually changed to a high-pitched purring, which seemed to fill the whole sky as a Zeppelin droned up overhead and circled . . . like a night owl quartering a field of corn above a colony of paralysed field-mice.

This time the zeppelin did not drop any bombs.

Crossing to France, the men received additional training "somewhere in France" under Scottish troops known as the Black Watch and Gordon Highlanders. They also had three French interpreters, the "Duke," the "Count," and M. Jacques Rouilly who was killed in action. They were not thrown immediately into battle; at first they observed, then they relieved troops in a quiet sector. Only after this seasoning did they go into the thick of the fight. From May 27 to June 15 the men had no baths; when the time came for one, they marched four miles to the bathhouse and four miles back. Another day they marched seven miles to receive their gas masks. On June 5, a fairly typical day, the 120th Infantry had one hour of close order drill, one hour of response to bombing, one hour of route march, special classes in musketry and Lewis machine guns, and gas lectures to the sergeants. On other days they practiced map reading and litter bearing, had buglers and signalers classes, and practiced advancing through woods. Haystacks in a field were designated as machine gun nests, and the men practiced crawling, running and falling, using mud balls for hand grenades, and concluding with a bayonet charge. The engineers studied French camouflage and prepared shops at Dijon where they made hangar covers and snipers' suits. They camouflaged machine gun positions and those of the field artillery, if the latter were not protected by woods. During the training period King George V of England visited the troops, and they were also entertained by Scottish bagpipe bands. Church services were held each Sunday, and one baseball game was played. Periodically the sanitary officer conducted inspection for lice and vermin. Following this final training, 2nd Lt. James W. Smoot remarked appropriately:

> . . . when they can shave, take a bath, and have drinking water left all from one canteen of water they can say they are soldiers. And when they can ride cattle cars for two or three days and live on canned goods and bread; get off and hike 20 miles in the rain with a pack that weighs 75 to 90 pounds—then they can call themselves soldiers.

On May 9, 1918, a battalion of the 3rd Regiment N.C. National Guard, later the 120th Infantry, U.S. Army, assembled on Capitol Square on their way to France. Despite the rain that day, many gathered to send them off. They were on the front line near Ypres three and a half months later.

In July, having met the above qualifications, the division was moved up nearer the front, and small groups of men visited the front lines. On July 17th the 2nd Battalion moved up to the front line on the Ypres sector with the others being gradually worked in. Their initial assignment was to rebuild the trenches, originally constructed in 1914, a task for which the American soldiers had little taste. They had come to fight. However, their British counterparts quickly instructed them on life in the trenches: "Don't shoot; if we don't shoot, they don't shoot."

Nonetheless, they soon got their first taste of the fighting. Most of the 30th Division, including the 119th and 120th infantries, originally North Carolina National Guard units, were sent to the front line near Ypres on August 30. The British commanders had intelligence suggesting that the Germans were withdrawing from their forward lines and were determined to occupy that territory. On the morning of August 31, the soldiers stormed out of their trenches only to encounter stiff and unexpected resistance after going less than two hundred yards. The Germans had not withdrawn. By late in the day on September 1, the American forces had established a new line and captured a few German positions. They withstood a German counterattack on September 2, then received word that on September 3 they would be replaced by British troops. This shift was not an insult to the American forces, but rather a common tactic used throughout the war in an attempt to ensure fresh troops at the front. Between July 17 and September 4, the 30th Division lost a total of 777 soldiers. Most of those casualties were North Carolinians; the 119th Infantry had 296 casualties, and the 120th suffered 269.

The American military was completely segregated until the end of World War II, and so during World War I black North Carolinians served in segregated units. Blacks from throughout the nation volunteered for service, hoping that the nation would, as a result, begin to open doors that had long been closed to African Americans. Black North Carolinians were no different. John Ward of Goldsboro had eighteen sons, nine of whom served in the 9th and 10th regiments of the First United States Cavalry. Mrs. Sarah Mason of Kinston gave seven sons to the army, all of whom returned safely. Forty-nine black North Carolinians attended Officer Training School at Fort Des Moines, Iowa.

The 371st Infantry Regiment was composed of drafted African Americans from North Carolina and South Carolina; the unit trained at Camp Jackson in South Carolina before going overseas. Assigned to the French army, the men served alongside white Europeans as well as French colonial soldiers with many skin colors. They trained for several weeks with French instructors and interpreters before heading to the trenches northwest of Verdun as part of the 157th French Division. They experienced significant action in this sector before being moved in September to support an offensive in the Champagne region. The 371st, in the forefront of the action, suffered significantly more casualties than the remainder of the division. A total of 146 individuals received citations for their valor: 22 received the American Distinguished Service Cross, 1 received the French Legion of Honor, and 123 received the French Croix de Guerre. Col. P. L. Miles, commanding officer of the 371st, offered high praise for the regiment, commenting "I never heard of similar performance by any regiment of any nation." The 371st remained in action for the duration of the war.

Lt. Thomas J. Bullock of Wilmington, who was born in Henderson, served as a volunteer in the Spanish-American War, enlisted in the regular army, and served in the Philippines. After he was mustered out, he enrolled in Lincoln University, and graduated in 1911. When the 15th Regiment of the New York National Guard was organized he enlisted; at Fort Des Moines he entered Officer Training School and received his commission. He was killed in action September 2, 1918.

James William Alston, born in Wake County, provides a particularly insightful glimpse into the life of a black soldier in Europe. Prior to the war he served as a janitor and messenger for the North Carolina Museum of History, and wrote several letters from the battlefield to H. H. Brimley, director of the museum. Alston enlisted in the army, attended Officer Training School in Des Moines, and was commissioned first lieutenant in the 372nd Infantry. His initial letter to Brimley, on June 21, 1918, recounted a color-blind experience: "A British barrage when viewed from the British trenches is the most wonderful sight imaginable, but a German barrage experienced in the British trenches is something far worse than horrible." On September 3 he wrote to Brimley: "I have been commanding my company since July 30th and it is some job believe me. I took command while in the front line and have been in the front line all the month of August except <u>8 days</u>. I hope to get a new Captain soon and if it is a white Capt. let him be from the south is my prayer." Alston reported some conflicts among officers, observing that most problems seemed to involve officers from the North. In his letter of September 3 he wrote that he was proud of the performance of black soldiers:

> I am glad to know that <u>my</u> people are doing their bit to win the war, they sure make good soldiers and seem to take delight in sticking Fritz with a bayonet or clubbing him with but[t] end of a rifle, but their main weapon is the hand grenade.

On November 1 Alston wrote from a field hospital: "My wound is all healed and with the exception of a very little stiffness I am as good as ever. There is so much talk of peace I want to get back and have another try at Fritz before the finish." Armistice came before Alston returned to the front.

When the men were not on the front lines, the YMCA, the YWCA, and other groups attempted to make life better for them. Canteens and huts offered stationery, chocolate, a little reading material, someone to play the piano and lead singing, a movie projector, ice, and similar amenities. Familiar American "ragtime" sounded out over the French countryside. Vespers at one hospital hut ended with "the famous Brek-ek-ek-ex Yale cheer, which must have astonished the Germans if they heard it in their trenches over the hills not far away." Football teams and baseball games sprang up. The YWCA provided social workers, a club in Paris for army nurses, and helped French women form canteens for female war-industry workers. It also supported Hostess Houses at large camps. Small French towns and villages where the troops might be resting had their own forms of entertainment. At Camp Coëtquidan, Arthur Lloyd Fletcher wrote: "The men fell for vin rouge, vin blanc, cognac and other concoctions, mixing them indiscriminately. This proved disastrous to their stomachs and to their records and the infirmary and guardhouse did a rushing business." Another soldier (Frank X. Britt) wrote, "I have a good time with the girls over here and they think a lot of the American soldiers but I think more of the Enfield girls than all the rest." A Trinity College alumnus wrote home of Christmas Day in France:

Christmas Day expected to be bright & sunny as we had hoped. However, we have a holiday; we are going to have chicken, pumpkin pie and cake for dinner; and I see no reason to complain. I am going to have a very pleasant Christmas this year in France, the happiest and only one I'll ever spend in France I hope.

If the men had a long enough leave to get to London, they went to the Eagle Hut, operated by the YMCA. May F. Jones of Asheville and her sister Elizabeth worked there. Other workers included Mrs. Walter Hines Page (the wife of the American ambassador), Lady Astor and her sister, and the sister-in-law of the Earl of Leicester. May Jones wrote: ". . . they wore aprons & overalls & did a hard days work as a common laborer—& felt richly paid in being allowed to serve." There were nine staff members, one "Hut Mother," and 800 volunteers, providing sightseeing, meals, theater parties, and French lessons for the troops. As Elizabeth Jones said, "It was great fun at times; very pathetic & heartrending at other times, —& a very great joy & privalege [*sic*] at all times." May Jones wrote: "We have heard all their love affairs, told their fortunes & mended & sewed on buttons for them." Elizabeth described an air raid in London:

The exterior of the YMCA Eagle Hut in London is provided courtesy of the Woodrow Wilson Presidential Library Archives. It was obtained via photostream on flickr.

> Well!—an air-raid is not just my idea of heaven, but we are not frightened and not downhearted, although they dropped leaflets saying they were coming again. . . . We went into the cellar & declared the Truth out loud. . . . [I]t sounded as if each bomb was coming right through our roof. The noise is awful—it took me all day to get over it.

But the grim business of the war was carried out in the trenches. These long lines gashed the French landscape from the mountains to the sea; the men in them looked across no-man's-land at each other and from time to time in massed attacks attempted to drive the other out. Life in the trenches was miserable, for they were chiefly mud slits. A news reporter wrote:

> Parts of the trenches are less muddy, but others are rushing rivulets, with the water ankle deep. . . . Anybody who goes through the trenches will be caked with mud to the knees, spattered with mud to the hips, and rubbed with mud to the elbows and sides from scraping the narrow walls.

The 115th Machine Gun Battalion lived in "small bevies and holes along the railway and canal bank like so many musk rats." The dugouts were dark and candles were few, but the men found that a tin of bacon grease could be burned with a twisted rag for a wick; sometimes they sneaked a little gun oil to burn. Edward Miles wrote to his father in Asheville:

> We can build fireplaces in any corner of any of them, and collect sticks & branches along the road, those that have been cut down by pieces of shell, and then, like the rats who live with us, we shall be snug & warm underground.

Willard Newton, of the 105th Engineers, wrote in his diary on July 11, 1918:

> During the night my partner and I had rolled our equipment in a bundle and sit on it the remainder of the night to keep out of the water. In spite of the mud and water we roll packs and 9 a.m. finds us on the move, with rain coming down. . . . Most of us had wet and muddy blankets with which to make a bed for the night.

Besides rats, there was the problem of lice. On September 17, 1918, Newton reported, "At first we had only one kind; but now we have the gray-back, the red, the black, and almost every color imaginable." These could not be gotten rid of until the men went back to a rest area, where they would bathe and be issued new clothing.

The principal food was "Bully Beef," which the men disliked, cheese, coffee, and bread, plus a mixture from the rolling kitchen that they called "slumgully." The slumgully was made of meat, rice, tomatoes, potatoes, water, macaroni, cheese, and anything else that had been left over from the previous meal; at least it was filling. While on the march they ate hardtack and the "Bully Beef," also known as "willie"—as Newton put it, an "imitation of beef" made by Swift and sent to the soldiers as "souvenirs"—plus a slice of bread, together with pork and beans.

All along the western front troops were constantly shifted from one location to another, sometimes slowly and sometimes in a rush. At one point the British used old London city buses to carry men to the front. The French "taxicab army" that saved Paris at the First Battle of the Marne is famous. American troops sometimes rode in Ford trucks that had railroad wheels attached and traveled on a light railway line. Camions driven by laborers from Indo-China transported the marines to Belleau Wood. A sophomore from Guilford College wrote of the incongruities of that morning. They were on their way to battle, but "The trees along the road were in bloom and some of us had blooms stuck in our helmets." The most typical vehicle, however, was the "Forty and Eight," a small boxcar built for either forty standing men or eight horses. When the 321st Infantry Regiment boarded its first French cars, they were counted off in groups of forty and packed into the little boxcars, "which bore unmistakable signs, which were equally distinguished by sight and smell, of a recent cargo of cows." One soldier discovered that the best way to ride was to sit in the side door and dangle one's feet. In between rides, there were miles and hours and days of marching. When shifting from one position in the line to another, the men saw the awful destruction of the years of war. On September 22, 1918, Newton wrote in his diary:

> From Amiens to Bernes all we could see was destroyed villages and barren fields with trenches running through them, with shell holes everywhere. The whole country between these two places lies in ruins. Here and there crosses, rifles drove into the ground, and other similar tombstones, mark the resting places of friend and foe alike, who have fallen in the recent fighting.

German prisoners working on the roads begged the Americans for cigarettes, and the steady roar of big guns provided a background for it all.

A gas attack was one of the most feared hazards at the front. The protective mask consisted of a clip to go over the nostrils and a mouth tube to hold between the teeth. It terminated in a can filled with chemicals at the bottom of the mask. A mask would provide protection for 72 hours. Within two miles of any front, the troops were supposed to keep them ready for instant use. An attack was described by J. R. Graham in *Tar-Heel War Record*:

> Just as we entered the woods near Brocourt we received a welcome that sounded like a hundred thousand Fords—Gr, Gr, Gr, Gr, Gr, then a crack and a boom, boom, then someone said GAS. Scared? No, we were paralyzed—didn't know whether to put on our gas masks or turn and run. Finally our masks were on and then somebody gave: "Permission is given to remove face pieces." We would not mind the gas alarm so much if it wouldn't come around meal times.

The infantryman's supreme moment, the one for which he had spent months in training, came when the command was given to go over the top. This meant to come out of the trenches, cross no-man's-land, and jump down

A soldier wearing a WWI uniform and gas mask.

in the enemy trenches to drive the Germans out—if the attack were success-ful, that is. During the night before, the engineers laid white tapes across the ground from which every man was to start; watches were synchronized up and down the length of the front for perhaps four or five miles; before dawn the big guns would lay down a barrage; and at the proper moment, whistles blew, and the men went over. No-man's-land was eerie and weird. Hamilton Holt, editor of *The Independent* magazine, wrote on July 27, 1918, after spending three months in the field:

> Spread out in front of us was No Man's Land, as still as death, while the thin thread of earth on the opposite slope indicated where the German front trenches seamed the earth. Several villages half in ruins dotted the vista and except for them and the pocked earth and the splintered forest one would have thought all was peace and plenty.

Col. Sidney W. Minor, commander of the 120th Infantry, addressed his men the night before an attack over the top:

We have worked and labored together for the past sixteen months and to-morrow comes our supreme trial. Remember, the eyes of the world are upon us and our native state expects us to do our duty.

Col. Frank Halstead addressed the 321st Infantry Regiment:

I never say goodbye. When you get an order carry it out, but first understand it. You have to use your head. In the present fighting I understand it will be on a mountain, and we have the Germans on a down hill push. Goodnight, and I again wish you a pleasant trip.

Ben Muse described going over the top on September 20, 1918:

Weighted down with rifle, bombs, entrenching tools, ammunition and still other impediments, climbing over shell craters was hard work. I had considered myself a moderately tough physical specimen, but I didn't see how I could keep going much longer. Heroes must be pretty strong, I reflected, along with their other qualities. I wondered how heroes managed to keep on going if they were as tired and out-of-breath as I was.

The field artillery operated from behind the front lines, usually sheltering in woods where enemy planes could not spot their placement. Their duty was to lay down barrages in front of advancing infantry to keep down the enemy. The 113th Field Artillery under Col. Albert Cox was equipped with 24 French 75-millimeter guns. Although supposed to serve with the 30th Division, they were sent elsewhere, and the Royal Australian Artillery fought with the 30th. The artillery was one of the few outfits still using horses; they pulled the caissons that bore the big guns. Each artillery battalion had an ammunition train to keep it supplied. Edgar Warren McCullers of Clayton was in the ammunition train for the 105th Field Artillery. On October 4, 1918, in the days of the final big drive by the Allies and Americans, McCullers wrote: "The trucks have kept running day and night, we working by relief. We have been handling ammunition as fast as possible." When the ammunition wagoners had nothing else to do, they helped the engineers keep the roads in shape for the artillery to pass over. McCullers wrote, again in October 1918, "I haul 5 loads of rock from St. Remy to Dommartin road winding on hillside mountain on one side, precipice on other, anti aircraft gun nest, get in after dark, rainy night—tired."

Old German Cannon Returned with Interest

Duties at the front consisted of patrolling to ascertain any enemy movement and to recover the bodies of the dead. Occasionally a patrol would capture a stray enemy soldier; on August 31 a group of 14 Germans was captured in a dugout. A private bored with guard duty aroused everyone one night with his own personal hand "gunnade" barrage. One soldier wrote his family, "I have been up to the front lines trench and I like it right well it is not so bad all I do not like are those big shells which come over singing home, sweet, home." A man in the 82nd Division described a day at the front:

> After our morning meal, it was always too late to be called breakfast, we would slip out in front of our line. Shielded by trees and rocks and the crest of the ridge, we would carefully make our way forward a few feet at a time. We wanted so badly to get the hands on the town clock which we could see lying at the foot of a pile of debris. What wonderful souvenirs they would have made!

But every time they approached the clock hands, someone started shooting at them, and they never succeeded in getting them.

Soldiers from Asheville, however, successfully brought home a German cannon captured on the last day of the war about 15 kilometers south of Verdun. Wagon Sergeant Theodore B. Sumner of Company I, 371st Infantry Regiment, hitched a team of mules to the cannon and dragged it with the rest of the regiment's equipment to their debarkation point at Brest. Realizing that bringing home captured enemy equipment was against orders, several men in the company took the cannon apart and packed it into three crates labeled U.S. Government Property. These crates made it with the soldiers all the way to Camp Jackson, where they were mustered out. Many months later the cannon arrived in Asheville and was placed on display in front of the Zebulon B. Vance monument.

Photograph of the WWI "Old German Cannon" on Pack Square at the foot of the Vance Monument, prior to 1942. It was taken by Ewart M. Ball Jr. and is provided courtesy of the D. H. Ramsey Library Special Collections, UNC Asheville.

In 1942, with the United States again at war, the War Department decreed that all old field pieces would be turned in for scrap metal. In August the cannon was dismantled and taken to a collection depot. However the protests of Sumner and others were so vociferous that by August 26 the cannon was back in its accustomed place. On October 30, 1942, though, it vanished forever. Two men claimed that they had returned it to the scrap heap to make up for Buncombe County's deficiency in the scrap metal collection drive. Rumors immediately began to circulate that, once again, it had been rescued and was sequestered away. The *Asheville Citizen*, in a much later story about the incident (May 27, 1956), concluded that "More likely, the metal from the old German cannon was returned with interest and a vengeance to its native soil in the air raids on the Fatherland."

Members of the 165th Engineers of the 30th Division repairing a road near Bellicourt after the smash of the Hindenburg Line, September 29, 1918.

One can well understand that McCullers was tired. Machine gun battalions were attached more directly to the infantry and moved forward or backward with them, aiding in their advances and covering their retreats. The principle drilled into the machine gunners was:

Machine-Gunners stand fast!
Machine-Gunners fight to the last!

The duties of the engineers included providing water supplies, operating both light and standard gauge railroads, keeping roads in repair, building bridges—sometimes just in time to have them blown up again—and providing electricity. As the Germans were driven back in 1918, they destroyed roads and bridges, and these had to be rebuilt quickly for the pursuing Americans and Allies. Engineers built pillboxes for machine guns, laid barbed wire entanglements in no-man's-land, laid the white tape to guide the infantry going over the top, and cleared mud out of trenches. They cut enemy barbed wire during the night to clear the way for tanks and infantry the next morning.

For example, the 117th Engineers, from North Carolina and South Carolina, served in the 42nd "Rainbow" Division, taking care of the roads and constructing new positions. The 105th Engineers were attached to the 30th Division, which in September was moved from the Ypres area to just in front of the Hindenberg Line near Bellicourt. Willard Newton served with the 105th Engineers, and on his first day at the front he reported that the men in the 117th were so tired that the cook gave them mashed potatoes, beef steak, and hot "real" coffee to bolster their spirits. Col. Joseph Hyde Pratt of the 105th Engineers, the State Geologist of North Carolina who before the war had been instrumental in locating war-needed minerals throughout the state, wrote in his diary on September 28, 1918:

> Last night a preliminary survey was made and tonight we actually lay the white tape which will guide the infantry and insure their leaving on a straight front. I hope to have word by midnight that the work is accomplished, and without casualties. In the meantime I am waiting amidst the booming of guns, the crash of shell and the *meaner* noise of bursting bombs, dropped by aeroplanes. . . . I should receive word by 1:00 a.m. that the tape is laid. Then it is just a wait until zero hour when the battle begins.

At 9:30 A.M. on September 29, Bellicourt fell to the Allies, led by the 120th Infantry Regiment from North Carolina.

The tank corps protected soldiers who were trying to wipe out machine gun nests and break through enemy trenches. The men inside the tanks, however, had low visibility, and their machines were not as maneuverable as they later became. According to James Otey Walker, before the 120th Infantry went into battle they were cautioned to "look out for tanks so as to avoid being run over. Infantry will assist tanks by rushing strong points." During the attack on the Hindenburg Line on September 29, the 115th Machine Gun Battalion, which included Capt. Robert Gregg Cherry of Gastonia, later to be governor of North Carolina, was passed over by tanks. One man wrote:

> One tank driver made a short turn and ran squarely over Corporal Gibson's gun at which the gunner was firing, and came dangerously near crushing the entire team. In a few minutes a second tank started across the identical spot and a big shell struck directly upon top of the tank killing the officer in charge and wounding several of the men.

The major duty of the air force was to be the eyes of the army. Both from balloons and planes, observers located the targets for the field artillery, corrected their firing range, and watched for enemy movements. The larger part of the observation was from balloons, first used in the American Civil War, which were protected by a cover of higher-flying planes, in turn protected by the highest-flying and farthest-ranging planes, such as those flown by the Lafayette Escadrille. The artillery officer on the ground, by telephone, told the balloon, "Battery ready." The answer was, "Ready to observe." The artillery officer then said, "On the way." The observer watched where the shells hit, reported how many yards over or under, right or left, the explosion was from the intended target; and the artillery officer then corrected his range. Some planes made air attacks on factories and cities, and a few dirigibles or zeppelins raided England. Mass bombing raids were unknown, however.

Lt. James A. Higgs of Raleigh served in the balloon corps. He arrived in France for training in November 1917; on January 13 he made his first ascension. "I was surprised by the fact that there was really no sensation to it. The thing that impresses you most is the wonderful view you get of the country, and how it all lays out before you just like a map." The balloons were inflated with hydrogen, each inflation costing $1,000, and attached to the ground with a steel cable. When enemy planes approached to shoot down the balloon, the cable was quickly wound down, if time allowed. If not, a strip of white cloth called the "jump panel" was unrolled on the ground, and the two men in the balloon observation basket jumped to safety, opening their parachutes and floating down. Often balloons caught fire from machine gun bullets fired by attacking planes. Higgs always rose before daylight; reveille was at 3:00 A.M. The men went up just at dawn, and stayed up until noon, then changed observers. On August 30, 1918, Higgs had a busy day. The balloon was hauled down to 900 feet altitude twice because of the approach of enemy planes. On the fourth approach of the planes, he was attacked; the telephoned order from the ground said, "Jump." Higgs forgot his French and told his French companion to "jump," but the man just stared. Finally Higgs remembered to say "sautez"; then their parachute ropes tangled, but finally they both got out. "Believe me," he wrote, "that first drop before your parachute opens is no job that I would relish every morning before breakfast." The balloon was saved, and Higgs was back up in the air again fifteen minutes later.

North Carolinians participated in flight training at Hampton, Virginia; Hempstead, Long Island; and Miami, Florida. A soldier at Hampton wrote of his first plane flight:

> I could sit and look over the sides of the cockpit very easily from my seat, I had the safety strap across me, every machine is provided with one for each seat, and I knew I couldn't fall out even if we looped the loop. . . . Well the downward and the slide slant [while landing] at the same time while you are descending at about 60 or more miles a hr is not quite the same sensation as riding along a nice country road in a Ford at 20 miles an hour.

The observation planes carried a man trained in map reading and aerial observation in addition to the pilot; the fighter planes carried only the pilot and flew much higher. Pilots who were too heavy to fly fighter planes were relegated to the lower-flying observation or bombing planes. Planes seldom flew at night, but when they did searchlights immediately tried to pin them so that the antiaircraft could fire. Arthur Lloyd Fletcher described the first night flight he ever observed. The sound of the German plane gave it away, and the searchlights began to sweep the sky. Finally they spotted him, and Allied planes gave chase. "The wily Boche side-slips, plunges, dips, does a back-flip and drops out of the light, making a clean get-away."

Backing up all these men was the essential medical corps. Base Hospital No. 65, organized by Col. Fred Hanes and Col. J. Wesley Long and staffed by many North Carolinians, was an important medical facility established in western Europe. Located near Brest, France, a port city in a sheltered position on the extreme western edge of the Breton peninsula, this hospital treated thousands of soldiers. Charles Gibson, a native of Rockingham County who trained with a medical unit at Fort McPherson, Georgia, arrived at Base Hospital No. 65 in August 1918. At first he treated disembarked soldiers with influenza, but soon wounded soldiers from the front arrived. Those with less serious wounds were treated and returned to their units; those more seriously wounded were cared for until a transport ship arrived in port to take them to the United States.

The 317th Ambulance Company, organized in Raleigh before war was declared, was assigned to the 81st Division, which it followed to France and served at the front. Medics such as Charles H. Warren of Lenoir saw

Army nurses are shown at Base Hospital No. 65, which operated from September 1918 through July 1919. The nucleus of the professional staff (20 medical officers, 100 nurses, and 200 enlisted men) was formed from North Carolina physicians. This image was taken outside the Kerhuon hospital, which served as an embarkation hospital to receive patients from the American Expeditionary Forces.

many grim and grisly sights. He spoke of "one pal driven stark mad by the bursting shells." He wrote in his diary, "Not yellow—but in thinking of this madness I think how long! Oh! Lord! How long!!" Female nurses served in evacuation hospitals only eight or ten miles behind the front lines, where bombs and shells were not unknown. More severely wounded men were taken to London or other British hospitals when they could be moved; convalescents eventually found their way back to America on returning troop ships. Azalea Hospital was opened at Asheville during August 1918 for tubercular soldiers and sailors; multiple additional veterans' hospitals opened in other places.

A few Americans were taken prisoner by the Germans. Two such North Carolinians were Ben Muse, identified above, and Edgar M. Hallyburton. In his memoirs Muse recorded that he felt that "to fight against Germany was to fight for peace and freedom," and that if he did not come home, it was a "worthy cause" in which to give one's life. Instead, he was captured in November 1917, and marched to a German prison camp along with British captives. As they passed on foot through captured French towns, the people slipped loaves of bread to them. Rations were so slim that the men became "shabby, hungry, begging wanderers about the camp." After several months in camp, Muse was sent to work on a farm in Mecklenburg, although he knew nothing about farming. He had five meals a day and a bed, however, and he learned how to farm before it was over. In the summer of 1918 he tried to escape. Covering his prisoner's stripes with black cloth and a stolen coat, he made his way successfully through several towns, heading for the Netherlands. He was caught because he had forgotten to change his English boots. Sent to another farm, Muse was there when a group of revolutionary young German soldiers took over and released all the prisoners at the end of the war. Sailing back to England with a group of other free men, they all sang, "The End of a Perfect Day."

Also taken prisoner was Sgt. Edgar Hallyburton of Taylorsville, who was in the regular army and had seen service on the Mexican border. In Company F, 16th Infantry, he is considered to be the first American taken prisoner after the United States entered the war. In a prison camp on the Rhine from November 1917 until his release after the end of the war, he always helped his fellow prisoners. He organized them, divided food fairly, made rules to uphold their morale, and protected them from as much mistreatment as possible. One gets the picture of a tough, hardboiled soldier who earned the respect of the Germans and was thus able to protect the younger, less experienced men who were his fellow prisoners. Because of his achievements, General Pershing praised him for his "magnificent and noble conduct," President Wilson awarded him a Distinguished Service Medal, and other officers in the army wrote letters of high praise, commendation, and honor.

In the face of the difficulties and horrors of war, it was amazing that Americans kept the good spirits and high morale that they evidenced. This characteristic was especially welcomed by the Allies because after three long years of life in the trenches, the French and British were weary and disheartened. The Americans were full of confidence, sometimes even brash; they had come to do a job and get home; they were sure the job would be successfully accomplished; their spirit was thus encouraging and contagious to the war-weary Allies. A quotation from a letter home illustrates this ebullient spirit:

> Surely wish that our officers and Generals would turn our American troops loose and tell them to go into Berlin. Everyone is anxious to do something that will turn the tide—toward home. The people of the United States have an army, and one that they never need be ashamed of. The fellows here are *men*. . . . [B]ut if on the other hand I don't return, I am ready to die, and it will be the will of God. I believe he will take care of me.

Some men found a great thrill in fighting. As one said, "This country is *great* and the game of war is *greater*." Earl Griggs wrote in his last letter home, "Tell all the boys that they ought to want to be here on the fighting line otherwise they will never know what a great war this is." Homesickness was not allowed to interfere with the desire to get the job done. As one soldier expressed it, "I would like to have a mess of turnips and mustard [greens] for dinner today for a change, but no such luck, corn beef and beans for me, but I can manage a few months longer if we can only end this war our way." Most trusted in the protection of God, or were fatalistic about their chances of returning safe and sound. Describing the death of a friend, a soldier wrote:

> A German shell just blowed him to peaces about 20 yards from where I was standing you bet I thought of everything mean that I had every done when I first got on the lines But after I had bint on the[m] a few days I got so I did not care if one did get me.

A well-educated man expressed noble sentiments that many less well educated shared:

> If any of us had thought lightly of America before this war,—and many have— they should look at these boys—men from the top of their heads to the soles of their feet. Strength, courage, health, optimism, idealism, blaze from their faces, their muscles, their poses. We were not all bread and butter after all. An idea had enthroned us. A sublime impulse has transfigured us.

On the Battle Line

Although American troops received their baptism of fire in smaller engagements along various sectors of the front, they saw significant action beginning in the spring of 1918. With the surrender of Russia on the eastern front, Germany was able to divert nearly fifty divisions to a major offensive on the western front. In the Battle of Belleau Wood, which lasted for most of June, American marines fighting with French soldiers played a significant role in halting the German advance. In July the Germans made their last desperate effort to reach Paris, and at the Second Battle of the Marne American troops 100,000 strong led by Gen. John J. Pershing helped to halt them. Beginning in late September and lasting until November 11, the Allies and the Americans took the offensive and advanced with bitter fighting through the Meuse-Argonne area and finally into the Argonne Forest. North Carolina soldiers found themselves engaged all along this front.

The U.S. 2nd and 3rd divisions, which included a brigade of marines and some North Carolina men, were the first Americans engaged heavily at the front. Some of these troops had spent April and May 1918 in the relatively quiet Verdun sector when in June they received an SOS from the French near Château-Thierry. Eight thousand soldiers were rushed to that region. On the night of June 1, the 4th Marine Brigade under the command of Gen. James G. Harbord was placed at the front directly behind the beleaguered French. They dug in with bayonets, mess knives, and mess kits because they had no entrenching tools with them; once they were in place, the exhausted French fell back through them and the marines held the front line. It must have been a surprise to the Germans to find fresh Americans where they had expected exhausted French.

For five days the Germans attacked. On June 6 the marines counterattacked. The battle between the American marines and the Germans for Belleau Wood raged hotly for another ten days. Attacks and counterattacks resulted in slaughter on both sides with no significant gain in territory. By June 15 most German resistance had dissipated, but not until June 26 did the marines gain full control of the region. It was one of the most ferocious battles that Americans would fight in this war. Ray T. Moore said, "Since wars must be fought and men must go to fight them, I shall always regard it as a great privilege to have participated in this defense around Belleau Wood."

The 30th Division was assigned to the British and sent to the Ypres sector in Flanders, near the French-Belgian border. In August 1918, they were assigned to the Canal Sector, from Ypres to Voormezeele. On September 1, as directed, they advanced 1,500 yards, captured the Lankhof Farm, Lock No. 8 on the Canal, and the city of Voormezeele, all in Belgium. They took fifteen prisoners and captured two machine guns and thirty-five rifles. One man's diary described the attack on Lankhof Farm: "Our advance was made under heavy M.G. fire and near position subject to heavy M.G. and violent artillery and T.M. [truck mortar] fire throughout the day, seeming impossible at times to hold." The Americans held, however, and consolidated their position the next day. Only one man was killed, four wounded, and one missing. Col. Sidney W. Minor reported that the Americans made such a good showing that it was decided they were "too good to waste in sedentary warfare," so they were reassigned to the front near Bellicourt, France, just north of Verdun along the famous Hindenburg Line, rumored to be impregnable. Here they became part of the Somme Offensive.

The Germans had never been able to capture Verdun, but the French had never been able to push them back away from it. The St. Quentin Canal ran through the area, partly in a tunnel; concrete tunnels, blockhouses, and forts created a powerful defensive position for the Germans. The 2nd American Corps, with the 30th Division in the center, and under British command, faced three rows of German wire each forty feet deep, three rows of Hindenburg Line (heavily fortified trenches and concrete bunkers), and the southern end of the tunnel for the St. Quentin Canal. The 119th and 120th Infantry regiments were the frontline direct assault units, with Australians following through on their immediate rear. On September 27, food, ammunition, and guns went up to the front in long lines; roads were crowded with vehicles. More and more shelling took place as the big guns warmed up. The next day the big guns moved up nearer to the front. The men of the 30th Division came up past the engineers. "At sundown," noted Willard Newton in his diary, "lorries loaded with picks, shovels, axes, sign boards and white tape arrive in front of our dug-outs and unload."

Sidney W. Minor (1873–1945), commander of the 120th Infantry, 60th Brigade, 30th Division, American Expeditionary Forces, was born in Granville County and later lived in Durham, where he was president of the Durham Buggy Company in 1910. He was living in Virginia in the 1930 census. He received the Army's Distinguished Service Medal. Image provided courtesy of the North Carolina Museum of History.

The engineers were going to have a busy night. The lieutenant told them, "Don't stop if your buddie gets killed or wounded, but say tough luck and pass on."

At 1:00 A.M. on the morning of the attack, the 105th Engineers rose. With raincoats, mess kits, and a day's rations they marched toward the trenches with picks, shovels, tapes, sign boards and posts, rifles, bayonets, and ammunition. They laid the tapes and waited. At 5:00 A.M. the little guns started, and at 5:30 "everything broke loose." The 115th Machine Gun Battalion started firing at 5:50 A.M. The engineers moved forward filling in shell holes and removing destroyed wagons from the artillery road. When they reached the Hindenburg Line, they had to take cover for three hours in a shell hole. A tear gas shell hit nearby, and some of the men were affected.

They were allowed to return to their station to spend the night, while the infantry fought on. "The Infantry went over the top. The earth seemed to rock under the veritable rain of lead, iron, and steel. The Heavens were aflame with the flash of guns," wrote an infantryman. A member of the 115th Machine Gun Battalion reported:

> I have seen men of "A" Company during the firing mount upon the parapet in front of their gun, refill it with water, lean over the top and remedy a stoppage; stop and re-check their aim, or reset their aiming mark with as much ease and apparent self control as an old woman changes her knitting needles.

A dense fog and smoke from the barrage so clouded up the morning that men could see only six yards and had to fight on as individuals. An Asheboro man in "K" Company wrote home:

> Once a tank ran over me but I was in a shell hole. I got hit in the neck and dropped. It was shrapnel. . . . I lay under some tin all day. I couldn't holler because my vocal cords had been cut. Finally I was able to highball out of here and get help.

Newton wrote in his diary:

> Scores of dead Americans and Australians and Germans can be seen lying about the field, some covered with raincoats and overcoats, while others lie just as they fell. Walking wounded are going back in twos and threes, while those unable to walk are being carried off the field as rapidly as possible under the circumstances. Men with arms shot off, with slight shrapnel wounds in the face and slightly wounded in the body are being helped to the rear by German prisoners and by other men similarly wounded. Dead horses are lying here and there, but I fail to notice any wounded ones, for they are killed by their drivers as soon as they get hit so they can't travel.

Lt. James Graham Ramsay wrote:

> A corporal and I went over the top together and he was killed instantly. Our two platoons deployed and advanced to the first section of barbed wire about 200 yards from the top of the hill. We found the wire intact, but cut it with wire clippers and after crawling through in single file again deployed. At this time I was wounded in the thigh by shrapnel. The other platoon was unable to get through the first barbed wire entanglement. My platoon advanced to the second wire barrier and finding it also intact, we cut through it; but on

advancing to the third barrier which was within fifty yards of the machine gun nests, we found it also intact. Having lost seventy-five per cent of my platoon, I ordered them into the approach trenches at the side. About this time we were subjected to gas shell fire; and as my gas mask had been torn to pieces by machine gun bullets, it would have gone hard with me if Lieutenant Robert Riggs had not passed me his cloth mask. . . . After remaining in the advance post for half an hour, I was sent back to an evacuation hospital because of loss of blood. That afternoon the hill was taken by assault from the rear by our 3rd Battalion.

The main Hindenburg Line, the line that was supposed to be impregnable, was crossed by the 30th Division at 7:45 A.M. At 11:30 the men occupied Nauroy and finished cleaning up Bellicourt at 11:45. The 1st Battalion captured 10 officers, 800 men, and 60 machine guns. After a short rest, the 120th Infantry went back into the line on October 9, aiding in the attack on Brancourt

German prisoners captured by the 30th Division during the Hindenburg drive at Bellicourt, Aisne, France, October 10, 1918. Official AEF photograph.

and Prémont, farther beyond Bellicourt and the Hindenburg Line. John Otey Walker described the commanding officer of "G" Company in this attack, who "as usual, went in with sword in one hand and spade in the other—close on his heels came his orderly, Turner, with an SOS rocket which neither one knew how to use." After pushing forward five more miles, the men were moved back to Brancourt to rest. During its time in action (July–October 1918), the 30th Division lost 1,641 men killed in action; 198 were reported as missing; and 27 were taken prisoner. Another 6,774 were wounded.

A poem was written to celebrate the breaking of the Hindenburg Line by the North Carolinians.

The Boys That Broke the Line
by Thomas Mossette Lee, of Clinton

They fought like seasoned veterans, like warriors they fell;
They stormed the battlements of death; they charged the gates of hell;
And laid the haughty legionaires of Hindenburg supine;
And the world sang "Yankee Doodle" when the Yankees broke the line.

(The term "Yank" or "Yankee" was used for all Americans in this war.)

The Battle of St. Mihiel, September 12-15, 1918, also involved a significant number of North Carolinians. A small town in northeastern France, St. Mihiel was insignificant until Germany turned it into a stronghold, creating a bulge that disrupted Allied communication up and down the line of the western front. The attack, planned and executed by General Pershing, was a great success, in part because the Germans, having realized the indefensibility of the position in light of the Allied buildup, had begun to withdraw. However, Pershing's carefully detailed operational plan and the tenacity of small unit commanders on the battlefield were undoubtedly crucial to the final outcome.

The 113th Field Artillery, which belonged rightly to the 30th Division but had been detached to support the 89th Division, took part in this battle. Waiting behind the lines in late August 1918, they had watched planes and balloons overhead for nineteen days, signifying great activity.

On September 10 they moved up to the front, and the attack began on September 12. At 1:00 A.M. the artillery began, firing one million rounds of ammunition in four hours. They kept a protective or "rolling" fire in front of the advancing infantry. Men sent back for a 75-millimeter gun to help knock out a pillbox. Arthur Lloyd Fletcher, a member of the 113th Field Artillery wrote: "Up across the fields and through the woods on a dead run would come a gun section, the men clinging for dear life to the bouncing carriages and lying low over the necks of their horses." The gun would then be unlimbered, aimed, and fired at the pillbox, and then the men would dash away again to help at another spot. Fletcher wrote later:

> When deep trenches and wrecked roads and bridges confronted them . . .
> the horses were unhitched from the carriages and led, pulled and shoved
> across, while willing hands seized the guns and caissons and carried them
> over places that seemed to be impassable. . . . [O]n that memorable day the
> regiment did the impossible.

Other units containing North Carolinians that fought at St. Mihiel were the 117th Engineers and the 3rd Division, which had been organized at Camp Greene, Charlotte.

In the last great offensive, the Meuse-Argonne Offensive, units containing North Carolinians that were engaged included the 3rd Division, the 4th Division, the 117th Engineers in the 42nd Division; a portion of the 81st Division; and the 82nd or "All American" Division. The objective of this offensive, through a heavily fortified area that stretched from south of Verdun northward to the Argonne Forest, was the town of Sedan, a rail hub that, when put out of commission, would destroy the Germans' ability to resupply troops at the front and move troops easily from one sector to another. The attack began on the night of September 25. Attacks and counterattacks lasted for six weeks, with the Allies slowly gaining ground. By early November armistice talks were under way, but the fighting continued.

Only one day before the Armistice was signed, just east of Verdun, "K" Company, composed predominantly of North Carolinians and attached to the 81st Division, saw significant action. To reach the front line they marched over marshes, barbed wire, old trenches, a sunken road, up a steep hill, and over 400 yards of open shell-hit field. After ten minutes of rest, the whistle blew, and they went over the top. Gas shells came over. Planes shot at them. They had supposed the Germans to be withdrawing, but the information was wrong.

The men, however, went on and on, through a network of wire and concrete that the Germans had held for four years. They ran out of hand grenades, and the ammunition was getting short. From shell hole to shell hole they went, through thick undergrowth, capturing machine gun nests. Their advance had carried them five and a half kilometers, farther than any other company in the regiment. On guard all night in shell holes, they were relieved by fresh troops the next day. That day happened to be November 11. Allied forces controlled the high ground along the Meuse River and were completing plans for further advances when news of the Armistice arrived at headquarters.

Men of the 324th Regiment, 81st "Wildcat" Division, stand near the graves of their fellow soldiers who fell, in an ironic twist of fate, during the last three hours of the war on November 11, 1918. This image was taken at Manheulles, Meuse, France, on November 13, 1918.

The statistics of the war casualties are easy to read. From North Carolina 629 were killed in action; 204 died of wounds; 1,542 died of disease; and 3,655 were wounded but recovered. Reading statistics is different, however, from reading the letters written home to the parents of the dead. A descriptive letter tells a father of the death of his son Earnest:

We had been in the same platoon since getting to Camp Sevier, were togeather on the Flanders Front, and were side by side going over the top of Sept. 29th I will never forget that day nor him, he was one of the bravest men I ever came in contact with, on that day I saw him face two separate Enemy machine guns, capturing them both and capturing eight (8) prisoners, in the morning about eight o'clock he was slightly wounded in the right hip. I tried to get him to return to the rear but he refused to leave his men, we had no officer with the Platoon so it was up to he and I. . . . We lost him about nine am we had gained our final objective and were taking a smoke when a stray shell burst in our midst killing Earnest, Lieut McCullen and seven others. None ever spoke after the explosion. A piece of shrapnel went through Earnest heart, he never know what happened as he did not even make a sound.

Of the poems written about the dead, this one in memory of Capt. Ben F. Dixon, Company K, 120th Division, from Asheboro, killed in the battle of Cambrai on September 29, 1918, is one of the most moving. It is by Zoe Kincaid Brockman.

> Your company passed by today,
> O fearless one and brave,
> Above whose folded, quiet hands
> Quaint woodland blossoms wave,
> The blossoms of the Argonne wood
> That whisper to the dead,
> And twine the tiny snow-white cross
> Above your quiet head.

North Carolina troops, as individuals and as units, received many citations, awards, and honors. Some of the more significant ones included citations from Field Marshal Sir Douglas Haig to the 30th Division, plus thanks from the Australian Commander John Monash and appreciation from the mayor of Busigny for liberation from the Germans. Robert L. Blackwell of Hurdle Mills (Person County) of the 119th Infantry was the only North Carolinian to receive the nation's highest award, the Congressional Medal of Honor. When his platoon was almost surrounded, he volunteered to take a message for help, but was killed trying to get through. Brig. Gen. George W. McIver was cited for excellence in organization and training of his men as well as for his advance under inadequate support in the last three days of the war. A Distinguished Service Cross was awarded to Lawrence Stanfield for extraordinary heroism near Bellicourt, as well as to Ben F. Dixon, subject of the poem above. In all, 200 Distinguished Service Crosses and 12 Distinguished Service Medals were awarded to North Carolinians.

On November 11, 1918, the *Raleigh Times* carried this headline:

WILSON REVEALS TERMS ARMISTICE

The Associated Press article continued: "The greatest war in history ended this A.M. at 6 o'clock, Washington time, after 1,567 days of horror, during which virtually the whole civilized world has been convulsed."

The *Fayetteville Observer* (November 13, 1918) headed its paper, very simply,

THE ARMISTICE
Signed at Midnight Sunday—The Slaying of Human
Beings Is Ended in Europe at Last.

At 6:00 A.M. on that day the 321st Infantry Regiment had attacked at Châtillon and advanced three kilometers in dense fog. Lack of aerial observation prevented good backing from their field artillery. In a letter home, after describing the battle, a soldier said:

> At 11 o'clock we were partly in their last trenches. . . . all firing ceased and the Germans came over where we were and shook hands with us and talked as if there had never been any war at all. . . . I can't see how I came through it alive, but I am still living and doing well.

Col. Joseph Hyde Pratt who was at Amiens wrote in his diary:

> I went into the cathedral and to one of the chapels where I knelt before the altar and gave thanks to Almighty God for the cessation of hostilities. Tears of thankfulness would come and I did not try to check them.

Willard Newton was working on a railroad that morning and stopped for lunch. "While we are sitting along the track eating our lunch an old Frenchman, driving a donkey, rides up to where we are. He says, 'Allemand finis.' " Capt. Alan R. Anderson of the 81st Division wrote the following, which appeared in the *Charlotte Observer* (December 9, 1918):

Parades welcomed home soldiers after World War I. This celebration, on Fayetteville Street in Raleigh, 1919, was for the 113th Field Artillery. Soldiers march past the reviewing platform with a banner hung above that reads, "Welcome Home/Our Boys-Our Conquerors-Our Victors/War Behind You-Peace Before You/Struggle a Memory-Happiness a Reality/Welcome Back to Us./ Your Conquests have saved the World. Your Deeds have inspired Us. Our Hearts are filled with the Joy of It."

Honestly, I did not see much hope for us. The German had machine guns all through the fields—the heavy fog had saved us so far—but by 11 it was just lifting. I was lying behind my lines trying to get liaison with Capt. Angel, our new battalion commander. And just then, as I was waiting again to advance, here came the welcome news of peace. I can never tell you the experience—the feeling as I and all my men rose from the battlefield and looked around us. . . . How did I feel?—hardly at all.

On the night of November 11, "K" Company men were encamped in tents in the mud with raincoats and blankets for beds.

When darkness approached the German front lines from right to left were easily distinguished, for they, rejoicing over the ending of hostilities, illuminated the sky with rockets and flares of every imaginable color, which made a remarkable spectral beauty.

Another man recalled:

> It was as if "Recall" had been sounded at the end of a giant maneuver. No sound could be heard except men speaking in subdued tones. We were happy, of course, but our feelings were more of relief at having finished our job than joy. We were too close to the dead bodies of our comrades to have any desire to celebrate.

At home, Governor Bickett welcomed soldiers of the 113th Field Artillery with these words:

> When you were about to go forth to war,
> You stood before Carolina, the beautiful and loving
> Mother of us all, and in your hearts said,
> "Carolina, we, who are about to die, salute you."
> Today, Carolina, arrayed in happiness,
> Athrill with the joy of triumphant motherhood, cries,
> "O sons, who are about to live, Carolina salutes you."

The war had ended.

Between the Wars

November 11, 1918—the world was jubilant. The war was over; soldiers who had survived would be returning home; rebuilding could begin. President Woodrow Wilson, however, envisioned that much work remained. In January of that year he had outlined for Congress his vision of the postwar world in "Fourteen Points," an idealistic vision that included outlawing secret treaties, the end of colonial empires, self-rule for all people, disarmament, free trade, and freedom of the seas. Unlike the European allies, and especially France, Wilson did not support harsh treatment of Germany, realizing that such would produce only more bitterness. For Wilson, the most important of his Fourteen Points was the creation of a League of Nations, an international organization open to all democratic nations that would oversee the implementation of the treaty and would be empowered to resolve disputes between member nations in the future.

In December 1918, Wilson and his small delegation to the peace conference in Paris set sail for France on the *George Washington*, a former German liner. Attending the peace conference was a bold move on Wilson's part. Only President Theodore Roosevelt had left the country while in office, and then only to visit the construction area of the Panama Canal. However, Wilson firmly believed that he was destined to lead the European powers in the formulation of a world order that would reflect his vision. In this mission he was to be sorely disappointed. France wanted nothing to do with Wilson's determination to restrict the harsh treatment of Germany, and was not especially supportive of many other of Wilson's Fourteen Points. England was more moderate and often tried to find middle ground. One by one, Wilson yielded on his Points while clinging to the League of Nations. As a result, the Treaty of Versailles demanded harsh reparations from Germany that included payment of $33 billion in gold, forced disarmament, and loss of territory. In the end, Wilson sailed home with a treaty that contained very few of his Fourteen Points—but the League of Nations was part of the treaty, and on that part Wilson hung his hopes for the future.

Pictured (*left to right*) with Wilson (*far right*) are three prime ministers: Lloyd George (United Kingdom), Vittoria Orlando (Italy), and Georges Clemenceau (France) at the 1919 Peace Conference at Versailles. Image is in the public domain and credited to Captain Jackson, U.S. Army Signal Corps.

He quickly discovered, however, that Senate ratification of the treaty was going to be problematic at best. Some Republican senators opposed any sort of participation by the United States in the League of Nations, and many more opposed certain stipulations of that participation, particularly the requirement of mutual defense. They were not eager to position the nation to once again become entangled in a distant conflict. Wilson's effort to take his message to the people on a cross-country speaking tour ruined his already precarious health. Shortly after returning to Washington, Wilson suffered a massive stroke about which the nation knew very little at the time. Incapacitated both physically and mentally, Wilson was unable to fight further for ratification of the treaty. When the Senate approved an amendment that would require the president to receive approval from Congress before using U.S. troops on League business,

Wilson refused to accept this compromise and instructed his supporters to vote against the treaty. The United States never joined the League of Nations.

Meanwhile, the War Department had to formulate a demobilization plan that would return nearly two million servicemen to the United States in a timely manner, while remaining cognizant of both postwar occupation responsibilities and the impact on the U.S. economy. The rate of return was actually dictated by the relatively limited number of troop transports; over six months passed before most of the troops were back in the U.S. Industrial production, approaching its peak just as the war ended, slowed considerably with the end of orders from the War Department. Companies immediately began to shift production from war to peacetime needs; however, veterans seeking work in a slowing economy created problems in major industrial cities. In North Carolina, however, the situation was eased somewhat by an economy that remained strongly agricultural.

The War Department chose to maintain the huge surplus of equipment, including weapons and ammunition that had been produced during the war. While this decision appeared to be economically sensible, it meant that the military was slower than it should have been during the 1920s and 1930s to explore and invest in newer technology. The mind-set of most military and political leaders dictated that the U.S. would not again be involved in such a massive world conflict and that the current equipment would meet the needs of patrolling the border and quelling internal disturbances. Nonetheless, professional military education, including the continuation of ROTC programs, did receive funding. Neither the army nor the navy was particularly forward thinking about the potential for air power, despite enthusiasts such as Billy Mitchell who attempted to show that the role of the airplane could be much more important than simple reconnaissance. However, by the end of the 1920s, the army had organized a subsidiary branch, the Army Air Corps, and the navy did likewise with the Naval Air Service.

Of great concern to North Carolinians was the fate of the three training camps opened during the war—Camp Greene near Charlotte, Camp Bragg near Fayetteville, and Camp Polk near Raleigh. While Camp Polk had not yet been completed by war's end and had seen only limited duty with tank training, both camps Greene and Bragg had contained tens of thousands of men. Auxiliary services in each city provided employment opportunities for local residents, and apartments had sprung up to house the families of soldiers.

LOOKING EAST FROM ARMY HEADQUARTERS, DURING COMPLETION OF CAMP GREENE,
CHARLOTTE, N. C.

Camp Greene, named for Revolutionary War hero Nathanael Greene, could accommodate up to 60,000 men. Its construction played a significant role in the growth and development of Charlotte. Camp Greene was dismantled following the war's end. Color postcard courtesy of the North Carolina Museum of History.

Work ceased immediately on Camp Polk, and the area reverted to its former status—site of the state fairgrounds. Nor did the War Department think long about closing Camp Greene. While it had been an important training facility and a boon to the Charlotte economy, the hasty construction had generated major drainage and other problems that would simply not be cost effective to repair. Camp Bragg, however, was another story.

Located in a sparsely populated area of North Carolina near Fayetteville, Camp Bragg had been designated as an artillery training facility designed to accommodate six brigades. A nearby airfield (named Pope Field in honor of Lt. Harley H. Pope who crashed into the Cape Fear River in 1917 on a training exercise) provided training for airplane and balloon artillery spotters. Following the end of World War I, the War Department's consolidation plan brought artillery units to Camp Bragg from Camp McClellan in Alabama. In addition, it became a National Guard training camp. In 1921 the War Department debated closing Camp Bragg, but the current camp commander,

This photograph was taken in the Normandy Heights area of Camp Bragg ca. 1920. It shows the Second Section Gun Squad, led by Sgt. Joseph Jacob Douse, Battalion B, 21st Field Artillery 5th Division. Douse is fourth from the left. The photograph is from the estate of Margaret Rice Szczesny and was accessed via flickr on Kevin Borland's photostream and reproduced by permission.

Gen. Albert J. Bowley, convinced Washington otherwise. He invited Secretary of War John W. Weeks to visit the site, and undoubtedly pointed out to him all of the benefits of the area that had led to its selection in the first place—sparse population, southern location (for weather), and inexpensive and available land. As a result, on September 20, 1922, Camp Bragg became Fort Bragg, signaling that it had become a permanent military installation. Construction of more substantial buildings began almost immediately. By 1940, 5,400 troops were stationed at Fort Bragg. A year later, when it was increasingly apparent that the U.S. would become involved in World War II, that number grew to 67,000. During World War II it housed a maximum of 159,000 soldiers; infantry, field artillery, armor, and the 82nd Airborne all trained there. Currently, Fort Bragg covers nineteen square miles, spans parts of four counties, has two postal zip codes, and in March 2011 absorbed Pope Field.

The soldiers who returned home brought with them a vastly broadened perspective. They had not only been out of the state, but they had also served in England and in France. Many of them had been to Paris. They had formed friendships with British and French soldiers; some had married while overseas. While some returned to the familiar pattern of life they had left, others wanted more than to raise tobacco or cotton, or to work in the local mill. Their return coincided with a fascinating time in America, as a progressive spirit of reform that had emerged before the war collided with a stubborn resistance to change.

North Carolina's political leaders touted the state as one of the more progressive of the southern states. While the legislature chose not to support the issue of woman suffrage, it also declined to pass a bill prohibiting the teaching of evolution. Private, denominational institutions of higher education all raised funds for significant improvements based on standards set forth by the Carnegie Foundation for the Advancement of Teaching. The state legislature did likewise for the University of North Carolina in Chapel Hill, increasing appropriations from $155,000 in 1901 to over $2 million by the 1920s. Additional capital funds for both the Chapel Hill campus and the North Carolina College of Agriculture and Mechanic Arts (now North Carolina State University) led to facilities and services heretofore unknown in the state. Cameron Morrison, who became governor in 1921, worked cleverly with the legislature to secure the passage of two bond issues totaling $65 million that would lead to a modern highway system of over 5,500 miles. The state also provided additional operating funds for the State Board of Health and public schools. Nonetheless, many North Carolinians remained very traditional and were wary of social and cultural change.

In the immediate postwar years, the United States economy was relatively strong. While World War I decimated the economies of the major European nations and destroyed much of the infrastructure needed for recovery, the United States had ramped up industrial and agricultural production. Additionally, Europe's traditional trade patterns had been seriously disrupted. Following the war, the United States was able to fill much of the trade vacuum and supply the global demand for goods. North Carolina's economy mirrored this prosperity. Cotton prices rose to over 30 cents per pound by 1923; in 1929 cotton production generated $62.4 million in the state. The price of tobacco also rose to new heights, reaching 26 cents per pound by the mid-1920s and generating a crop worth a total of $88.6 million in 1929. Other than agriculture,

(*Left to right*) Locke Craig, Cameron Morrison, and Thomas Bickett all served a term as governor spanning 1913 through 1925. Morrison (1869–1953), governor, U.S. senator, and congressman, was an energetic supporter of higher education and an influential trustee at the University of North Carolina. He crusaded against lynching during the 1920s and helped organize the North Carolina Commission on Interracial Cooperation.

the primary industries in the state included tobacco processing, textiles, and furniture. In 1929, the value of cotton textiles produced in the state amounted to $317 million, and furniture manufacturing was estimated at $53.6 million.

As the 1920s moved on, however, the world economy began to sag. European nations imported more than they exported. Exacerbating the situation was the United States' trade policy, which was to increase tariffs. Consequently, European nations did likewise, which reduced somewhat the world demand for U.S. products. European nations except Britain had financed the war with paper money; with inadequate gold reserves, inflation grew. By 1922 Germany had completely defaulted on reparations payments. In 1924 a commission led by American Charles Dawes re-evaluated Germany's debt and urged nations to make loans to Germany. The United States did more by far than any other nation to follow these recommendations and stabilize the world economic situation, but ultimately it was not enough. The Great Depression, a worldwide phenomenon, completed the destruction of the house of cards that had been world peace and stability.

Americans had their lives turned upside down by the Great Depression. Investments were lost, jobs disappeared, and prices for agricultural products sank to new lows. Veterans of the Great War hoped that the federal government would pay early on the bonus that a grateful Congress had voted to give them. In 1924, Congress had approved payment of $1.00 for each day that a soldier served stateside and $1.25 for each day that he was overseas. However, this bonus was not scheduled to be paid until 1945. While at the time there was some grumbling about the lapse of twenty-one years before payment, by 1932 this grumbling had become a roar. In May nearly 15,000 veterans, some taking their families, went to Washington, D.C., demanding immediate payment. Known as the "Bonus Army," they built makeshift shelters from materials found at nearby junk piles and did their best to maintain orderly and sanitary camps while making their point. In June the House passed a bill authorizing immediate payment, but the Senate defeated it. The veterans refused to leave. In late July the city police attempted to remove the veterans, to no avail. President Herbert Hoover then turned to the army and in an irony that was lost on no one, current soldiers forcibly removed veterans from government property and destroyed the makeshift camp. Maj. Dwight D. Eisenhower, who witnessed the event, later wrote that "the whole scene was pitiful. The veterans were ragged, ill-fed, and felt themselves badly abused. To suddenly see the whole encampment going up in flames just added to the pity."

The Great Depression brought significant devastation to North Carolina's economy and its citizens. By 1932, a pound of cotton fetched only 6 cents and a pound of tobacco brought 8 cents. It cost farmers more to produce a crop than they could get at market, leading to massive foreclosures and mobility from country to town as people sought any type of work. While tobacco farmers fared poorly, the tobacco industry itself was less devastated by the Depression. Few of the 150,000 tobacco workers lost their jobs, and most of the companies actually reported profits during the 1930s. While exports of tobacco products dropped, manufacturers lowered prices, and domestic consumption increased. The textile and furniture industries, however, were not so fortunate. The textile output of 1932 dropped to $190 million, 75 percent of manufacturers reported losing money, and layoffs ballooned as factories cut back hours and even closed. Owners and workers battled one another over

Louis Steadman was one of several Charlotte businessmen who made trucks available for gathering supplies to be distributed to the North Carolina contingent of the "Bonus Army" in Washington, D.C. Image from the *Charlotte Observer* (July 28, 1932).

stretch-outs versus walk-outs and strikes. Violence was a customary result. Similarly, furniture production dropped in value to less than $27 million by 1932. Gov. O. Max Gardner kept the state solvent, which was more than many other states could claim, but doing so meant that the state did little to relieve the distress of its citizens.

New Deal programs, beginning with the inauguration of Franklin D. Roosevelt in 1933, provided work and relief. One of the most important of these programs in North Carolina was the Civilian Conservation Corps (CCC). Created during the era known as the First Hundred Days, the CCC was designed to provide work for millions of unemployed men in an effort to reclaim lands despoiled by soil erosion and excessive logging. Immediately upon passage of the bill, congressmen from throughout the nation began to petition for projects in their states. Many of North Carolina's congressmen had served multiple terms and thus enjoyed seniority that came into play as Congress wrangled over the types and locations of projects. North Carolina was well positioned to take full of advantage of this program, administered jointly by the Departments of Agriculture and the Interior. Newly established national forests such as the Pisgah and Nantahala, as well as the brand new

Great Smoky Mountains National Park, were perfect candidates for the type of conservation work envisioned for the CCC. The state's rapidly eroding beaches also fell into this category.

In the spring of 1933, enrollment into the CCC began. Many of the men were not quite sure of the work they would be doing, or where they would be doing it, but they were relieved to feel productive and knew that their $1.00 daily salary would feed their families. Assigned the task of setting up and organizing the hundreds of camps throughout the nation was the War Department. Gen. Douglas MacArthur devised an efficient organizational structure, and army officers assumed the responsibility of running individual camps, which operated similarly to training camps during World War I. Which agency would run the camps once men were conditioned was something of an issue since each agency wanted jurisdiction. Practicality settled the issue; camps would be run jointly by the military and the specific civilian agency supervising the work.

As Harley E. Jolley has noted, "Many locales in North Carolina, from the towering 6,000-plus-foot peaks of the Great Smoky Mountains, devastated by the ravages of the oriental chestnut blight and by wanton, mindless timbering, to the beaches of Cape Hatteras, viciously eroded by tide and wind, felt the healing hands of the Civilian Conservation Corps between 1933 and 1942." One of the most prominent and lasting memorials to this era is the Blue Ridge Parkway. Although it was originally slated only to cut across the extreme northwestern corner of the state, North Carolina congressmen convinced President Roosevelt of the benefit of locating the road along the crest of the Appalachians, running close to Asheville and connecting the Shenandoah National Park with the Great Smoky Mountains National Park. Construction of the roadway, as well as creating the adjacent recreational facilities and bountiful natural gardens, was shared by the CCC and the Works Progress Administration (WPA), along with the utilization of some contract labor. This enormous project was not completed until 1968; however, long before then visitors to the area were able to traverse large sections of it and marvel at the engineering feats required. Jolley indicates that "the landscape designers performed their work so deftly that motorists moving along the parkway at present find it difficult to believe that all the beauty they encounter is not simply Mother Nature's gift. . . . Rather, it is her bounty, richly fertilized and artfully planted—the crowning achievement of superb, purposeful design by

The New Deal programs, like the WPA and CCC, put many men to work who would later serve in World War II. This image shows CCC workers in western North Carolina planting trees to curb erosion, ca. 1936.

master landscape architects, aided by the diligent labor of CCC and WPA hands."

Roosevelt's New Deal put millions of people to work and significantly transformed the landscape of parts of the United States. In addition, the New Deal included regulatory legislation designed to prevent the sort of banking and investment practices that had done so much harm to the economy. It also sought to provide a measure of security for Americans through the Social Security Act and strengthened labor unions. However, far too many Americans remained untouched by New Deal programs, and the money spent, while enormous at the time, was inadequate to reverse the devastating impact of the Great Depression. Reversal would come, however, as the United States entered World War II.

Chapter 8

The Coming of Another War

O n Saturday, September 1, 1939, German tanks, troops, planes, and other mobile units crossed the frontier into Poland ostensibly to bring a halt to what Adolf Hitler had called "the barbarous persecution" of German people living in the Polish corridor. At eleven o'clock on the morning of September 3, Great Britain declared war against Germany to fight against the "evil things" of "brute force, bad faith, injustice, oppression, and persecution" in which Hitler had engaged; and at five o'clock the same day, France also declared war on Germany. World War II had begun.

What had brought about this war? Undoubtedly the provisions of the Treaty of Versailles, which left Germany so crippled and demoralized, played an important role. So, too, did the worldwide Depression that further deci- mated the economy not only of Germany but also of other major nations, including those inclined to make loans to Germany and those with whom Germany had traditionally traded. By 1930 the fragile Weimar Republic of Germany was nearing collapse, and members of the Nazi Party won elec- tion to the Reichstag. Political deal making continued to increase the power of the Nazi Party to the point where in January 1933, President Paul von Hindenburg had no choice but to appoint Adolf Hitler as chancellor. Hitler promised to make Germany strong again, to provide the nation its "rightful place" in the family of nations. Over the course of the subsequent year Hitler consolidated his power; the Third Reich was born.

The rise of militaristic leaders in Japan added to instability in the world. Japan had become a major industrial nation with an insatiable appetite for resources. China, politically weak and economically backward, had vast natural resources. In 1931 the Japanese government invaded Manchuria; the world watched and did nothing. The League of Nations, which was designed to prevent such conquests, wrote a note of protest to Japan, and the United States refused to recognize the puppet country of Manchukuo that Japan created; but Japan merely resigned from the League and became increasingly antagonistic toward the United States. Slowly, steadily, the

Japanese army increased its control over the western coastal area of China, hoping to entirely conquer that country. Japan dubbed its efforts an attempt to create a "Greater East Asia Co-Prosperity Sphere."

Another contributing factor to world instability occurred when the fascist dictator of Italy, Benito Mussolini, decided to avenge an old defeat of the Italian army by the natives of the African country of Ethiopia, and conquered that small country in the winter of 1935–1936. Again, the League of Nations reprimanded the aggressor country, and even considered boycotting Italy. When Mussolini threatened to blow up the Suez Canal if Italy were boycotted, the League of Nations again backed down.

Even in the throes of the Great Depression, England, France, and the United States were viewed by the rest of the world as the "have" countries. As the victors in World War I, they had rebounded from the devastation of the war. They enjoyed considerable international prestige, and their citizens had, relatively speaking, much better living conditions. Germany was at the opposite end of the spectrum. Also struggling were the many small nation-states that had at one time made up the mighty Austro-Hungarian Empire. Japan was a rising industrial nation, virtually unscathed by World War I, seeking additional resources to fuel its growth. Throughout the 1930s the Japanese army put many men to work, and equipment and ammunition orders kept factories humming. Hitler, with his power secured, at first secretly and then more openly began to rearm Germany. Eventually he would utilize this military might to implement his goals.

Because Germany had been completely disarmed in 1919, the nation had no "vintage" equipment. Thus military leaders invested in the latest technology to create an extremely modern force. The interwar years saw considerable advancements in both airplanes and tanks, which were in their infancy during World War I and hence used on a limited basis. The Germans devised plans for using planes to drop paratroopers behind the enemy lines as well as for target and saturation bombing. Airborne troops were entirely new, as were the great "dive bombers" with which Germany first experimented by sending some to help Generalissimo Francisco Franco in a civil war in Spain from 1936 to 1939. Entire towns in Spain disappeared as a result of these aerial attacks, the first time such destruction had been wrought. Tanks, meanwhile, rendered the horse and the foot soldier obsolete as the entire army became motorized. It could move so fast that its attacks came

The Stuka was a two-seat German ground-attack aircraft. This Junkers Ju-87 B2 is shown in flight on May 20, 1940, over France. Image from World War II Database website and reproduced by permission.

to be called "blitzkrieg" or lightning attacks. The navy did the same kind of planning. It built "pocket battleships" that were just as powerful as older ones but which took advantage of new inventions to save space and become smaller and faster. Submarines, whose value and vulnerability became evident during World War I, were also significantly modernized and built in large numbers. Although not easily predicted at the time, the war that began in Europe on that September morning in 1939 was destined to be the deadliest and most destructive war the world had yet endured.

While Americans were not oblivious to world events, most of them felt secure behind two oceans and were primarily concerned with recovering from the Great Depression. President Franklin D. Roosevelt, sworn into office in March 1933, had inaugurated the New Deal, a national experiment with policies to provide relief for those who were unemployed, to raise the incomes of the people, and to prevent future depressions. Even as Americans became increasingly aware of the rise to power of Mussolini and Hitler, many speculated that their policies would help their respective countries' economic recovery rather than lead them into war. Few paid close attention to the rhetoric, to the racism, to Hitler's call for *lebensraum* for the German people. Fewer still closely observed Japan.

If another war should come, Americans wanted no part of it. Naturally, they would defend their country if attacked, but they did not intend ever again to send soldiers to a foreign land to fight. This sentiment had been quite clear in the Senate hearings over the ratification of the Treaty of Versailles, and it did not dissipate with time. Isolationist feeling was so strong that in 1935 and again in 1937 Congress passed Neutrality Acts providing that if a war broke out, the president must prevent any American ships from carrying goods to the belligerent countries, and he must also warn all Americans that they traveled on foreign ships at their own risk. Public opinion polls at the time clearly showed that a majority of Americans did not favor intervention when one nation attacked another. Those who did favor some sort of action supported only economic and other nonmilitary actions, such as boycotts.

President Roosevelt, even while he was signing the various Neutrality Acts, realized that should a major war erupt it would be virtually impossible for a country as large and powerful as the United States to remain uninvolved. Other national leaders realized this, as well. The neutrality legislation was designed to keep America out of a war that had started the way World War I started. However, in 1939 circumstances were different, and the neutrality legislation had the effect of hurting America's friends instead of keeping the nation out of wars. In a number of speeches prior to 1939 Roosevelt forewarned the American people that they could not remain isolated much longer. National leaders remained anxious and uncertain as Germany annexed Austria, then the Sudeten region, then all of Czechoslovakia while Great Britain prime minister Neville Chamberlain's peace efforts seemed only to buy more time for Germany. When Germany invaded Poland, precipitating Britain and France to declare war on Germany, President Roosevelt issued a neutrality proclamation in a "Fireside Chat" on September 3, 1939: "This nation will remain a neutral nation, but I cannot ask that every American remain neutral in thought as well." Americans did not remain neutral in thought; they wanted England and France to win, but they did not wish to get into the war themselves. This was the feeling for the next two years, even as war was coming closer step by step.

Although Hitler's armies quickly overran Poland and Hitler signed a non-aggression pact with Russia that divided Poland with Russia, the war then seemed to come to a halt. The winter of 1939–1940, with no further military action, became known as "the phony war." Some assumed that Hitler was hopeful that his two enemies would decide to end the war now that Poland could not be rescued. Others mistakenly thought lack of further aggression on Germany's part indicated that the nation did not have sufficient forces to continue the war. France strengthened its great frontier defense wall, the Maginot Line, and felt secure behind its guns and concrete just as the United States felt secure behind two oceans. The American public relaxed. But when spring came and flying weather improved, the German armies unleashed an all-out war that quickly conquered Denmark, Norway, Holland, Belgium, and finally France. Mussolini entered the war on Hitler's side in order to get a slice of France. The dramatic fall of France in June 1940 awoke America to the fact that this was going to be a real war and not a phony one.

Germany hoped that Britain, now standing alone, would be amenable to a negotiated peace. While some sentiment for such existed in the country, newly appointed prime minister, Winston Churchill, rejected all peace feelers put forward by Germany, and other British leaders supported him. Hitler drafted a plan for an invasion of Britain that was quite unrealistic. Of much greater impact was what has become known as the Battle of Britain, an aerial assault that lasted from mid-July through October 1940. This bombardment considerably damaged Britain's infrastructure and took many lives, but it did not accomplish its objective of breaking the will of the British people. Witnessing the steadfastness of Great Britain as that nation alone faced and repelled the German assault, the United States provided increasing assistance. The Neutrality Acts tied the hands of the government, but President Roosevelt in mid-1940 cleverly proposed an exchange of fifty old destroyers for five naval and air bases located on British islands near North America. In March 1941 the president asked Congress to pass a Lend-Lease Act. This legislation provided England with wide access to America's war production capacity without requirement of immediate payment; the United States would loan or lease supplies to England that would be returned or paid for at the end of the war. Roosevelt compared this to lending a garden hose to one's neighbor if the neighbor's house had caught on fire.

A fierce fight broke out in Congress over the Lend-Lease bill. Some lawmakers felt that it would inevitably drag the United States into the war.

Clyde Roark Hoey (1877–1954) is seated between President Franklin D. Roosevelt (*left*) and Frank Porter Graham (*right*), president of the University of North Carolina, where Roosevelt received an honorary degree on December 5, 1938. During Hoey's administration, the state provided free textbooks for elementary schools, increased teacher salaries, expanded the highway system, reformed child labor laws, instituted parole reforms, and initiated the first advertising programs to attract tourists. Even though the governor did not support many of FDR's New Deal initiatives, in 1941 he supported Roosevelt's call for passage of the Lend-Lease Act.

Others wanted to run that risk, if risk it was, for the sake of gallant Britain and the democratic countries of the world that had been overrun by the Nazis. Democracy itself was at stake, they felt.

In North Carolina Lend-Lease was in general supported. In an address delivered at the fiftieth anniversary of Elon College on September 14, 1939, Gov. Clyde R. Hoey said that, "It is safer to sell supplies than to send men and if England and France can win this war that is our best security for peace." The *Wilmington Morning Star* was disturbed because the debate in Congress was going on so long that Britain might lose the war while America argued.

The *Charlotte Observer* did not fear that it would result in war; this paper stated that it was "a Declaration of the Will of the American People to underwrite whatever it takes to make victory for Great Britain as certain as it is humanly possible to be made." Senator Josiah W. Bailey of North Carolina made a notable speech supporting the bill, but Senator Robert R. Reynolds, a strident isolationist and apologist for Nazi aggression, opposed it. The bill became law in March 1941, at which time the editor of the *Charlotte Observer* said, "The ravings of the Nazi-Fascist press and spokesmen over enactment of the lend-lease bill serve to confirm the wisdom of the majorities that passed it through the Senate and House. Hitler and Mussolini are boiling with wrath."

Some of the fears of the isolationists were realized, however. From lending goods to England, it was but a short step to assuring their safe arrival through the submarine-infested waters of the Atlantic. American destroyers began to help the hard-pressed British navy by convoying merchant ships part of the way across the ocean and then turning them over to British destroyers. American planes flew on patrol over the Atlantic and reported by radio to British planes and ships if a submarine was spotted. In April the country of Greenland, which belonged to Denmark, was occupied by American forces to keep the Nazis from doing the same thing. The bases in Greenland were valuable for weather reports about flying conditions and for naval vessels that were convoying supplies to England. Given this increasing involvement of the United States in the Atlantic, it was a mere matter of time until an American ship was attacked by a German submarine. In May 1941, the *Robin Moor* was sunk in the Atlantic, the first American casualty in an undeclared war.

Realizing that he would be unable to defeat Britain directly, Hitler turned his attention to areas important to Britain, particularly northern Africa and the Balkans. Additionally, to fulfill his objective of *lebensraum*, in June 1941 he invaded Russia. Germany depended heavily on the Soviet Union for resources, particularly oil, and despite the nonaggression pact that Hitler and Russian premier Joseph Stalin had signed, Hitler did not trust Stalin. On July 22 German panzer divisions rolled across the Russian frontier, and another nation was brought into the war.

The United States had been very cool toward Russia since it became a communist state, not officially recognizing its government until 1933. Americans deplored Russia's taking half of Poland when Hitler invaded it, and also for fighting a war against Finland in order to gain more territory. After

Hitler's invasion of Russia, however, most Americans concluded that, for the moment, Russia was the lesser of two evils, and that with the United States' assistance perhaps the combination of Great Britain on the west and Russia on the east might eventually halt the Nazi armies. Many "armchair generals" recalled that Napoleon had been victorious until he committed the fatal error of invading Russia. "General Winter," they said, would prove smarter than Hitler, referring to the forbidding Russian weather. North Carolinians agreed that Stalin must be helped. As one newspaper editor expressed it, "The Kremlin is now on the side of the democracies and whatever the former relations between the United States and Russia, [it] would seem to have placed itself in a position to expect and receive our help." Another paper feared that "Hitler will attempt to persuade the American people that Britain has allied herself with communism" in an effort to keep aid from going to Russia. But, continued the newspaper, "The menace of the Soviet is far less than that of Hitler's Reich." The United States extended aid under the Lend-Lease Act to the Soviet Union, and American troops occupied Iceland in July 1941. When the ship *Reuben James* was sunk in October, American destroyers were ordered to "shoot on sight" any Nazi submarine, and merchant ships were instructed to arm themselves and were no longer restricted from sailing to belligerent ports. The Neutrality Acts, although never repealed, were clearly obsolete.

Hitler seemed invincible. His armies raced deeper into Russia; Rumania (later Romania), Yugoslavia, Greece, and British-owned Crete quickly fell. In North Africa, Nazi generals took the command away from the Italians and led their panzer divisions eastward toward Egypt to a point within seventy-five miles of the vital Suez Canal.

Halfway around the world, the war between Japan and China continued. Additionally, Japan moved to acquire more land and natural resources from the wealthy colonies belonging to the European countries that Hitler had overrun. Especially interesting to Japan were French Indo-China, the Dutch East Indies, and the British possessions of Hong Kong, Burma, and India. However, the United States opposed Japan's acquisition of either the territory or the natural resources of the friendly European countries that America favored. Although Japan preferred gaining this wealth without a war against the United States, the nation's leaders were not willing to cease war in China as the United States demanded. On the other hand, the United States did not want a war with Japan but was unwilling to see Japan seize other countries and then use their resources to subjugate China. The two countries began negotiations in order to avoid a showdown, but neither side was willing to give in on any vital point.

As negotiations seemed less and less likely to succeed, the United States adopted sterner measures, such as seizing Japanese property within U.S. borders, and Japan began quietly making war plans. The few leaders of Japan who desired peace were able to secure permission from their government for a last-minute diplomatic appeal. However, the special ambassador to Washington was unable to win any concessions. This failure led the militaristic leaders to believe that war was the only answer, and they set in motion their secret plan, "East Wind," which was designed to deal a knockout blow to the American navy in the Pacific and thus pave the way for Japan to seize much of Southeast Asia unhampered. On November 25, 1941, a Japanese task force sailed eastward from the Kurile Islands to carry out "East Wind."

The weekend of December 7 was a typical one at the Hawaiian naval base of Pearl Harbor. Because of fleet maneuvers, a great many naval vessels were concentrated at the base. Many officers and sailors had shore leave for Saturday night. Some were with their families who lived in Honolulu while others were engaged in various activities; a few were on ship duty. The same was true at Hickam Field, where only a few airplanes were flying the usual patrols. The newly invented radar was in operation only a few hours each day, and men were still learning its uses. American military leaders assumed that if trouble came with the Japanese, it would be in the form of sabotage, and provisions had been made for this eventuality. Another distinct possibility was an attack on Clark Field in the Philippines, so reinforcements were on their way there from San Francisco.

A young naval man and his wife from Rocky Mount were preparing breakfast in their little home near Pearl Harbor when they heard planes, guns, and explosions. They rushed out into the yard, thinking that a sham air battle was on. Somehow, it did not look that way. While the husband watched, his wife hurried to the radio where a frantic announcer was saying that the attack was real. As she returned to her husband with the news, he said, "I must report to my ship," the *Arizona*. The first wave of Japanese attack planes had swept over Pearl Harbor. An hour later came the second wave. Within two hours, the planes had destroyed or severely damaged 8 battleships, 3 light cruisers, 4 miscellaneous vessels, 188 airplanes, and important shore installations.

The Raleigh *News and Observer*, headline (December 8, 1941). Image courtesy of the State Library of North Carolina.

There were 3,435 casualties. Japan lost only 29 planes and fewer than 100 men. Their mission had been a complete surprise, and a significant success. However, as Japan would soon discover, this attack missed the aircraft carriers and their supporting vessels based at Pearl Harbor, which were not in port at the time. Cmdr. Norman M. Miller, USN, a North Carolina pilot who flew over Pearl Harbor a month later, reported:

> This was the end of January and the wreckage at Pearl was appalling. Broken ships and parts of ships lay everywhere in the harbor. Great patches of floating oil fouled the water, drifting sluggishly with the tide, clinging to the piers and blackening the shore. Reconstruction was under way, but the hundreds of men struggling to raise sunken ships and repair shattered ones, to clean up the piles of debris and bring order out of the apparently hopeless confusion, were like ants tunneling at a mountain.

An extra edition of the *Raleigh Times* (December 7, 1941) screamed in black letters:

JAPS MAKE WAR ON U.S.;
PACIFIC ISLANDS BOMBED

Said the *Asheville Citizen* (December 8, 1941):

JAPAN ATTACKS U.S. POSSESSIONS IN PACIFIC;
WAR PLANES BOMB PEARL HARBOR, HONOLULU;
CONGRESS AWAITS ROOSEVELT MESSAGE TODAY

In the *Wilmington Morning Star* (December 8, 1941), two lines proclaimed:

HONOLULU DEATH TOLL RISES IN JAP ATTACK;
U.S. DECLARATION EXPECTED BY NOON

On Monday, December 8, President Roosevelt addressed Congress and asked for a declaration of war against Japan. Within four hours the Senate, unanimously, and the House of Representatives, 388 to 1, voted for war. Three days later Germany and Italy, allies of Japan, declared war, and the United States responded on the same day without a dissenting vote.

North Carolina, as did the rest of the nation, stood squarely behind the country in the crisis. One writer cautioned that the state remain cool, yet "get behind the government's war machine with . . . every resource and every wish and every action." Another prophesied that "the conflict now launched shall be ended only when the yellow peril has been blotted from the Orient." The war in Europe and the war in the Far East had at last become one war, and the United States was in it for the duration.

Chapter 9

Military Preparedness

E ven before Pearl Harbor brought the United States into the war as an avowed belligerent, North Carolina had felt the impact of preparations for military expansion. By 1938 American military strategists realized at least the possibility of a two-ocean war and formulated a variety of responses to possible scenarios. Legislation authorized doubling the size of the fleet, including provisions for 11 new aircraft carriers and a total of 8,000 combat aircraft. In June 1940 Congress federalized the National Guard and three months later passed the Selective Training and Service Act, the first peacetime military draft in the nation's history. While this legislation increased the size of the army by approximately 500,000 men, such rapid expansion initially decreased the effectiveness of the army since many soldiers and officers were diverted to training duty. Nonetheless, by mid-1941 the army contained approximately 1.2 million soldiers, many of whom trained in North Carolina.

In January 1940, in anticipation of a Selective Service Act, North Carolina began training a staff to administer the draft. When the bill was passed the North Carolina delegates in Congress voted for it unanimously. By provisions of the law, all males between the ages of twenty-one and thirty-six were required to register. Unlike during WWI, this time exemptions were granted for certain types of jobs, for the clergy, for students, and for conscientious objectors. Servicemen could vote by absentee ballot and were guaranteed their rights to re-employment in their former jobs.

The local "draft boards," properly called Selective Service Boards, were composed of volunteers who did their best to be fair in all controversial cases. They worked without compensation for many hours away from their private businesses, were subjected to many criticisms both just and unjust, and doggedly struggled with reams of red tape and mountains of mimeographed directions that were difficult, and sometimes impossible, to understand. Their work was crucial to funneling eligible men into military service and, ultimately, to the front lines. When the first registration day was held on October 16, 1940, over 450,000 men registered in North Carolina, "with hardly a murmur of dissatisfaction or complaint," as Gov. J. Melville Broughton reported later on June 18, 1941, in a proclamation for the second registration day. From North Carolina a total of 258,000 persons served in the army; 90,000 in the navy; and 13,000 in the marines.

Over 50 percent of the North Carolinians who were drafted were deemed not physically capable of full military service; many of them served in the home guard or coastal watch. One such man had been working at the newspaper in Chapel Hill, but after he was inducted for limited service and trained at Fort Bragg, he served on Coast Guard duty at Fort Monroe, Virginia, for most of the war. In writing about the North Carolina soldiers with whom he served, he said: "They may not all be heavy weight grammarians, but they are fine men with whom to be initiated into the army way of life. They are friendly and unfailingly humorous and cheerful under trying circumstances. With such fellows around, it's impossible to whine and whimper when the going is tough." Similarly, a soldier from Winston-Salem wrote humorously to his family, "We have been getting up at 5:45 every morning lately and taking calisthenics before breakfast. We also have been getting an hour of close-order drill every morning. I don't approve of it, but, after all, what's one man's opinion." These men rendered important service to the nation, releasing those more physically able for duty overseas.

The necessity of training so many new men put a strain on the existing army, navy, and marine posts, showing clearly that additional facilities would need to be constructed. The incorporation of paratroopers and gliders into the military arsenal meant that at least some of those facilities would need large areas of ground where landings on enemy territory could be rehearsed. The climate of the South, as well as the availability of inexpensive land and the lower density of population, had led the government to locate many temporary camps in the region during World War I. In North Carolina, one of those camps, Fort Bragg, had become a permanent military installation and was destined to be the largest artillery post in the world. In addition, two large marine bases were created, Cherry Point and Camp Lejeune. Fourteen other bases of varying sizes were established within the state. Because of these numerous bases more fighting men were trained in North Carolina than in any other state.

Camp Lejeune was built because the Marine Corps was rapidly outgrowing its facilities at Quantico, Virginia, and Parris Island, South Carolina.

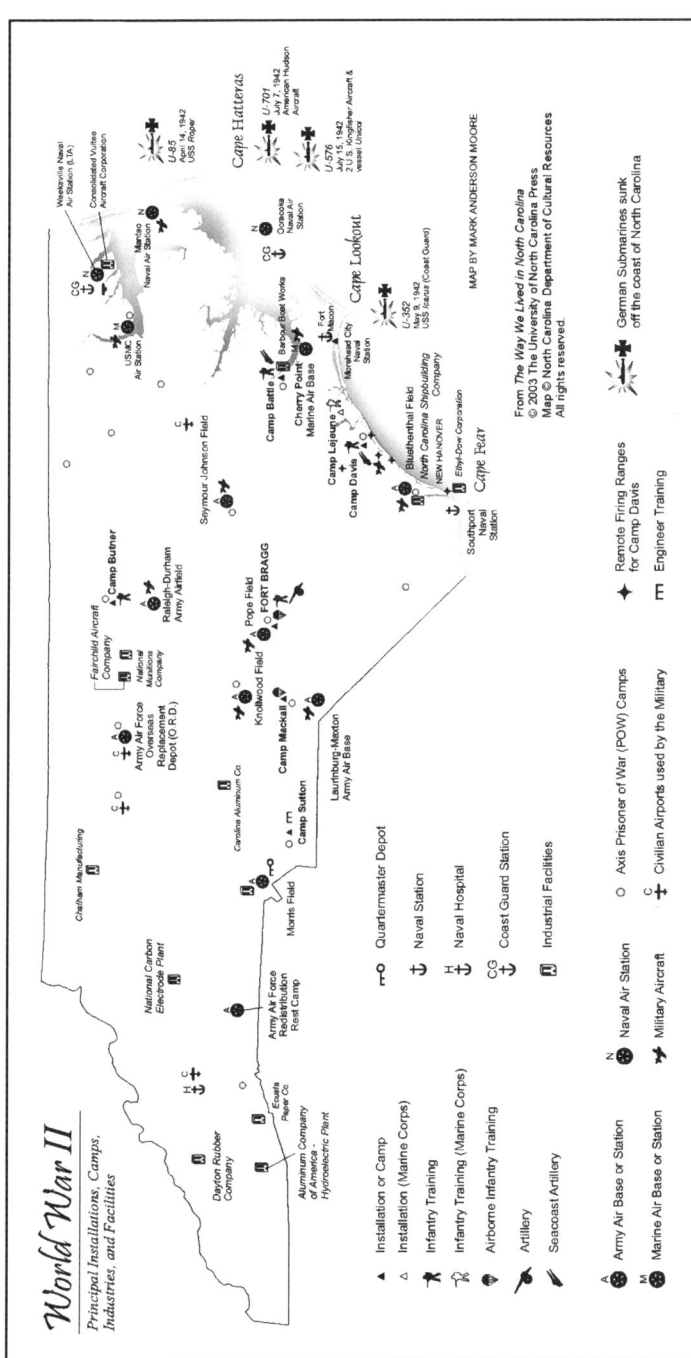

Map showing the principal military installations, camps, industries, and facilities during World War II in North Carolina. Map prepared by Mark Anderson Moore and reproduced courtesy of the North Carolina Department of Cultural Resources.

Military Installations in North Carolina during World War II

Name	Function	Origin of Name
Army Air Force Replacement Depot (Greensboro)	Self-explanatory	Self-explanatory
Camp Battle, New Bern	Infantry	Maj. Gen. Cullen A. Battle, Confederate States of America
Bluethenthal Field, Wilmington	Army Air Base	Arthur Bluethenthal, first Wilmington man to die in World War I
Fort Bragg	Artillery	Gen. Braxton Bragg, Confederate States of America
Camp Butner	Infantry	Maj. Gen. Henry Wolfe Butner, World War I
Charlotte Quartermaster Depot	Self-explanatory	Geographical location
Cherry Point	Marine Base	Geographical location
Coast Guard Station (Elizabeth City)	Self-explanatory	Self explanatory
Camp Davis	Infantry	Maj. Gen. Richmond P. Davis, World War I
Seymour Johnson Field	Army Air Base	Lt. Seymour A. Johnson of Goldsboro, navy pilot killed in March 1941
Knollwood Field	Army Air Base	Geographical location

The new base was approved in February 1941, and almost completed by August 1942. Where wild ducks and geese had once flown, simulated jungle warfare and beach attacks became commonplace. Unfortunately, small farmers as well as wildlife often paid the price for this rapid military expansion. Those in designated areas received eviction notices and minimal payments for family homesteads. Veterans of the South Pacific campaigns came to Camp Lejeune as instructors in ship-to-shore assault. Medics, specialists, Seabees, and Coast Guardsmen trained there, as did female marines. A section of Camp Lejeune, known as Montford Point, served as the training ground for approximately 20,000 black marines (the American military remained segregated until after World War II).

Military Installations in North Carolina during World War II

Name	Function	Origin of Name
Laurinburg-Maxton Army Air Base	Self-explanatory	Geographical location
Camp Lejeune	Marine Base	Lt. Gen. John Archer Lejeune, World War I
Army Air Force Redistribution Rest Camp, Lake Lure	Self-explanatory	Self-explanatory
Camp Mackall	Paratrooper training	Pvt. John Thomas Mackall, first paratrooper killed in North Africa
Morris Field	Army Air Base	Maj. Gen. William G. Morris, pilot in World War I
Naval Air Station (Elizabeth City)	Self-explanatory	Self-explanatory
Naval Convalescent Hospital (Asheville)	Self-explanatory	Self-explanatory
Pope Field	Army Air Base	Harley H. Pope, killed in 1919 in air crash at Fayetteville
Raleigh-Durham Army Airfield	Self-explanatory	Geographical location
Camp Sutton	Army engineers	Frank Howie Sutton, enlisted in Royal Canadian Air Force and killed in North Africa, Dec. 7, 1941

Among the women, Eugenia Lejeune, daughter of Lt. Gen. John Archer Lejeune for whom the camp was named, earned her commission there in November 1943. In 1944 Dutch marines were trained at Camp Lejeune for their deployment to Central Malaysia to free that country from the Japanese.

Camp Lejeune was also the training site of the "devil dogs" for canine warfare. The marines had encountered the enemy use of dogs in small skirmishes in Central America, primarily as an alert mechanism. By the advent of World War II, a group of marines had expanded significantly the possibilities for the use of dogs in warfare. Doberman pinschers, german shepherds, and even labrador retrievers were trained as messengers, sentries, and scouts.

Montford Point Marines

On June 25, 1941, President Roosevelt issued the Fair Employment Act, which prohibited government agencies from refusing employment to anyone because of race, creed, color, or national origin. This order was the first presidential decree issued on race since Reconstruction. As a result, African Americans were allowed to be recruited and enlist in the U.S. Marine Corps. Recruiting began June 1, 1942, when the first black recruits received basic training at Camp Montford Point at Camp Lejeune in Jacksonville, N.C.

Despite the new policy against discrimination, segregation was still evident. Not only were the men barred from white training grounds, in many cases they were also kept out of battle once they completed basic training because they were considered unfit for combat duty.

At Montford Point, over one thousand men were housed in prefabricated housing described as cardboard huts that could hold as many as forty men. They also endured mosquitoes and sweltering heat in this swampy, remote location.

Black recruits were not allowed to enter the main base at Camp Lejeune unless accompanied by a white marine. Nonetheless, many Montford Point Marines blamed the unfair treatment on local citizens instead of on the Marine Corps. Railroad tracks divided white residents from the camp. Business and restaurant owners frequently treated them like second-class citizens and denied them service. Some were arrested and charged with impersonating a marine, since most policemen had never seen an African American in uniform. When traveling by train, they were segregated and could not buy food and beverages. In addition, bus drivers gave priority to white passengers, by state law, which left the African American marines without transportation back to camp.

Despite continued discrimination, by mid-1943 all drill instructors at Montford Point were African American. Willie James McDonald, 85, said, "Being from North Carolina, I was used to segregation. The drill instructors were much more demanding than others to make sure that we were good Marines. They made certain that they made us proper Marines. It was tough but we survived."

Between 1942 and 1949, nearly 20,000 men trained at Montford Point. They eventually saw action and service on the Mariana Islands (Saipan, Tinian, Guam) and in Peleliu, Iwo Jima, Okinawa, Japan, and China. Upon learning about the heroism of these men, Lt. Gen. Alexander A. Vandegrift, Commandant of the Marine Corps, announced, "The Negro Marines are no longer on trial. They are Marines, period."

In late 2011, the U.S. House and Senate unanimously approved recognition of the original Montford Point Marines. On November 23, President Obama signed a bill that would award these men a specially designed Congressional Gold Medal in honor of their sacrifice and service to their country.

At a ceremony held June 27, 2012, around 400 living Montford Point veterans, 32 from North Carolina, were awarded the nation's highest civilian honor. In attendance were Joseph B. Walker of Durham and James Wilson of Wilmington. "I hate to use the word overdue . . . but it's time," said Yoder Faulkner, 81, who was raised in Winston-Salem. James Robert Simpson, 88, of Fayetteville, said of his achievements, "I'm proud . . . to be part of history for sure."

A February 2011 article in *Leatherneck* magazine sums up the history of the Montford Point Marines: "The Montford Point Marines fought with courage, served honorably, and won the respect of those who served with them. They accomplished everything that was expected and asked of them. They helped to change history by demonstrating racial harmony on the chaotic beaches and battlefields around the world."

Background: Three African American U.S. Marine Corps recruits running the obstacle course at Montford Point Camp, Camp Lejeune, N.C., April 1943. Image from the National Archives. The obverse (*left*) design of the medal features three Montford Point Marines in varying uniforms with a training scene filling the lower portion. On the reverse (*right*) is a scene of Montford Point Marines in formation during training. The obverse was designed by Michael Gaudioso, and the reverse was designed by Don Everhart, both based on official Marine Corps photographs. Images from http://coinupdate.com.

Sgt. Raymond G. Barnosk is training a german shepherd for duty. These marine "devil dogs" carried messages and first-aid supplies, located wounded soldiers, and accompanied marines in landing operations and sentry duty. U.S. Marine Corps photograph provided courtesy of the North Carolina Museum of History.

While the dogs were trained to detect enemy presence and to attack if necessary, the marines considered the dogs too valuable for such a risk. Marine dog platoons first went into action in 1944 and were utilized exclusively in the Pacific. A number of these dogs were cited for outstanding performance in the assault on Bougainville Island in 1943. For example, "Jack" conveyed a vital message, despite wounds, after telephone lines had been cut; "Cookie," credited with ten Japanese alerts, took a message through intense fire for four miles to inform his command post that "All hell is breaking loose."

The third large base in North Carolina was Cherry Point, the Marine Corps air station. Construction began in August 1941, and the base officially opened in May 1942, although marines had arrived as early as December.

The long stretches of beach provided excellent practice areas for simulated landings, while the ocean from Bogue Banks to Hatteras made live target practice possible for fighter planes. The pilots not only learned to fly, but they also studied the use of small arms and hand grenades, how to dig foxholes, and how to fight with knives, bayonets, and their bare hands. The Third Wing of Marine Aircraft went from Cherry Point to the Pacific. The first squadron of Mitchell medium bombers and the first fighter squadron of F7F Grumman twin-engine fighters both trained at Cherry Point. Some notable servicemen stationed there during the war included Lt. Col. John Lucian Smith, Congressional Medal of Honor winner, who shot down nineteen enemy planes in the Solomon Islands and Col. Walter L. J. Bayler, who was the "last man off Wake Island" on December 21, 1941, and was one of two officers who accepted the Japanese surrender of Wake Island on September 3, 1945.

Of the nonpermanent installations, those with unique and specialized training facilities included Camp Davis, the first antiaircraft camp in the country. It housed 60,000 at its maximum capacity and often attracted considerable attention with the giant balloons tethered around the base. Additionally, Camp Mackall was the second largest center for airborne soldiers, and Camp Butner served as a combat training camp for the infantry where gas attacks, camouflage, and river crossings were rehearsed. In Greensboro the Army Air Force leased 650 acres from Cone Mills to serve as a basic training base. Eventually this camp became an overseas replacement depot as the war took its toll on American soldiers.

Long before the attack on Pearl Harbor, military maneuvers took place in North Carolina. In October 1938 a joint antiaircraft exercise involving both army and navy personnel was staged near Fort Bragg. The purpose of this exercise was to test the system of observation and information relay relative to strength, speed, and direction should enemy planes be sighted.

In the fall of 1941, large-scale military maneuvers involving over 400,000 men were conducted in North Carolina and South Carolina. Gen. Hugh Drum led 196,000 Blue troops from North Carolina in an attack against Camden, South Carolina, which was defended by the Red army. The Reds had fewer men but had two armored divisions. The Blue army stopped the tanks and won the contest, an experience that was undoubtedly of great value in North Africa and in Europe later against Nazi tanks. Other similar maneuvers were held from time to time as fresh groups of men were trained. So many men from Massachusetts were among those engaged in the 1941 maneuvers that Gov. Leverett Saltonstall and the entire House of Representatives of that state sent thanks to the State of North Carolina for its southern hospitality.

Along with the servicemen came many wives and children. Some regular army or marine personnel who were assigned quarters at the permanent posts were able to have their families with them, but many men were stationed in North Carolina temporarily with no provisions for housing their families. Their wives had to do the best they could to find a room, a tiny apartment if they were lucky, or a house that could be shared with another wife or family in the same predicament. Citizens of many towns opened their homes to these women, mostly young and often just married, sometimes with babies, usually a long way from home, lonely and frightened. These young women were in the main willing to put up with almost any conditions in order to be with their husbands until they were shipped overseas. Then they would gather up their belongings and children and return home to wait for the end of the war. Three young women who lived in one house came back very despondent one evening; they had gone to Fort Bragg to see their husbands at the usual time and place, but no one had come, and there was no message. They told their landlady that if the same thing happened the next day, they would know that the army had shipped the men out without allowing them a chance to say good-bye.

Women were not drafted but they were encouraged to volunteer for service in the army, navy, and marines as enlisted personnel and officers, as well as in the specialized services of nursing and medicine. At first known as the Women's Army Auxiliary Corps (WAAC) and later Women's Army Corps (WAC), these women worked as cooks, bus drivers, teletypists, weather observers, aircraft mechanics, control tower specialists, parachute riggers, aerial gunnery instructors, and hospital technicians. Female pilots often ferried planes across the Atlantic or from one base in Britain to another. In October 1943, as part of a recruiting campaign for the army, a mass induction of WACs was held on Capitol Square in Raleigh following a military parade. The army had asked North Carolina to recruit 105 WACs to serve as hospital technicians. Given a three-month window to raise the quota, the state filled that number in one month. Women who had perhaps never been out of the South found themselves in faraway places of the world. One corporal, who had been a bookkeeper at a hotel in Winston-Salem before the war, served

Women were urged to join the Women's Army Auxiliary Corps (later referred to as WAC), and active recruiting campaigns were carried on regularly.

at Hollandia, New Guinea; at Leyte, Philippines; and also at Manila before returning home. She wrote in a letter what many young women must have felt, "I am ready to get in civilian clothes and a nice evening dress and eat some nice fresh vegetables."

North Carolina colleges and universities went to war also. At the University of North Carolina, training for Navy Pre-Flight and Navy V-12s was begun. At Duke University, the navy established an ROTC program, and the army set up a Finance School. Another Army Finance School was at Wake Forest College. Davidson College had an Air Force training program, and Bowman Gray School of Medicine trained doctors. Agricultural and Technical College trained soldiers. At North Carolina State College in Raleigh a school of diesel engineering for the navy was begun, and Army Air Cadets had their pre-flight instruction there. The army also established Air Corps training at Elon College. Elon students and Professor Alonzo Hook began the Aeronautics Club, designed to prepare students for flight training upon graduation. Dr. Hook earned a private pilot's license and bought a small plane so that his students could experience flight firsthand. At the women's colleges, the classes in mechanical drawing, photography, and mathematics were crowded, while the students organized defense councils, Red Cross knitting and sewing groups, first-aid courses, and war bond sales.

The National Guard units of the state were called into active service immediately, leaving no provision for home protection against riots, sabotage, or enemy landings. The State Guard was therefore created, consisting of 44 companies of 50 men each. These companies were organized into a brigade commanded by Gen. James W. Jenkins of Henderson, under the state Adjutant General, J. Van B. Metts. Its purpose was to handle riots and disasters and to cover areas where sabotage was deemed likely. Members were between the ages of thirty-eight and fifty, plus younger men who had been rejected by the regular armed forces on grounds of health. An example of the service rendered by the State Guard was its help in fighting a great forest fire in western North Carolina in 1942. In a March 14, 1944, proclamation during North Carolina State Guard Week, Governor Broughton said that the State Guard had "rendered prompt and effectual service" in a number of "critical situations."

Because of the major training encampments in North Carolina and its shipbuilding and other industries, sabotage was a major concern. A Counter Fifth Column Plan was worked out in 1943. People known as "Fifth Columnists" were secret sympathizers or supporters of the enemy who engaged in espionage, sabotage, or other subversive activities within the defense lines or borders of a friendly nation. There were two dangers to fear from a Fifth Column: that which would occur behind the lines in case of an invasion; and that which would result in sabotage of industrial plants and installations. The former was not a significant problem, as an actual invasion was highly unlikely. Sabotage was, however, an ever-present threat, and elaborate precautions were taken to meet this threat should it materialize. Every military post was assigned certain critical areas or installations to protect. The three critical areas in which everything was to be guarded were Manteo, Elizabeth City, and Wilmington. The types of war production plants and installations that were to be guarded in other areas were electric power dams and plants, munitions plants, chemical plants, shipbuilding companies, and textile mills. In addition, key highways and railroad lines, especially bridges that were very vulnerable, were to be guarded. The routes to be taken by armies, evacuees, and others were carefully plotted on maps and sent to all military posts and directors of civilian defense. Fortunately, none of these elaborate plans ever had to be put into effect.

These enormous military installations had a positive effect on business in North Carolina. The men stationed in the state spent money on recreation, food, transportation, and clothing. Their families who joined them added to the income of the local citizens. The federal government used local carpenters and masons to build the new camps, and purchased some of its lumber and brick from within the state. Other industries profited as well, primarily shipbuilding, but also textiles.

Large numbers of people suddenly moving into an area brought problems as well as economic benefits. Overcrowding in housing was one such problem, jamming hotels and motels. Bus and railroad facilities ran at full capacity, and grocery stores and other stores had difficulty keeping up with the new demand for their products. Problems also arose in small towns that had only one motion picture theater and several thousand men who wanted to go to the movies at the same time. Still another problem was that of public health. Local health authorities had to educate the citizens, inspect many more eating places and hotels, inoculate more people than ever before, and cooperate with the health officials at the military posts.

And, just as during World War I, vice soon became an issue. Excitement was in the air, a sort of "Eat, drink, and be merry, for tomorrow we may die"

Soldiers dance at an unidentified YWCA (probably in Raleigh) on May 9, 1941. Image provided courtesy of the North Carolina Museum of History.

attitude. Gamblers were attracted to camp areas because many servicemen had little on which to spend their pocket money except amusement, since their shelter, clothing, and food would be supplied even if they should gamble away their paychecks. High-stake gambling games, both inside and outside the military posts, often resulted in crime. Prostitution was the second such problem that sprang up near all of the encampments. Post commanders worried not only about the moral issue but also about the very real possibility of the spread of venereal disease.

Both the federal government and the state did their utmost "to keep our State and its communities free from degrading influences and practices." Governor Broughton, in his biennial message to a joint session of the Senate and House on January 7, 1943, stressed educational conferences that supported public health personnel and law enforcement officials in their efforts to keep the state as free from such problems as possible. Thankfully, North Carolina never became nationally notorious for vice and crime.

The Arsenal of Democracy

The United States, the only major industrial nation among the Allies not subject to enemy bombing raids and destruction, became the chief "arsenal of democracy." Even before the United States officially entered the war, plants began converting to the manufacturing of guns, ammunition, planes, tanks, and ships. Additionally, the demand for such items as uniforms, shoes, tents, radios, mess kits, C rations, roast beef, bread, buttons, shoestrings, paper, wristwatches, bombsights, and walkie-talkies brought employment to Americans throughout the nation. Every factory, every farm, every man, woman, and child were needed to make enough goods in a short enough time to defeat the Axis powers.

In the second half of 1940 the defense boom began. The federal government awarded $10 billion in contracts, primarily to shipyards and aircraft plants. The War Production Board and its many subdivisions assumed responsibility for national planning. By the beginning of 1944 America was turning out more than double the output of all the Axis countries combined. Many of the new factories were in formerly agricultural regions, such as the Pacific Coast and the South. The landscape of the South changed radically as farmers left their small farms to work in defense plants, and more and more factories dotted the landscape where previously there had been cotton fields or pine barrens. Many a man or woman who had never done anything but "chop cotton" learned to rivet the fuselage of an airplane or to install a complicated electrical circuit in an instrument panel.

The United States spent $2 billion directly in North Carolina for the purchase of manufactured goods, made by nearly one million men and women. No essential war production was delayed for even an hour, reported Governor Broughton, by strikes or controversies. The coveted Army-Navy "E" Award, for excellence in production, was won by twenty-eight North Carolina firms, some of them more than once. Among the items manufactured in the state were rockets, bomb clusters, radar components, airplane assembly, ships, tent twill, woolen blankets, towels, shoestrings, and polo shirts. One plant produced pigeon coops for the Signal Corps. When briar pipe bowls ceased to come from Italy and France, a substitute first discovered during World War I came from the mountain laurel roots in western North Carolina.

One of the greatest of all the wartime industries was shipbuilding. The North Carolina coast was geographically suited to this business with its many inlets, rivers, and harbors protected by the Outer Banks. Elizabeth City ship-yards built submarine chasers, and mine sweepers were made at New Bern. Morehead City and Southport became naval repair stations. Wilmington's new shipyard had nine ways and employed over 20,000 people, many of whom came from far away seeking the work. Cargo and troop transport ships launched at this time, dubbed "liberty ships," were named after famous North Carolinians or for cities and counties that had bought an unusually large num-ber of war bonds. The first liberty ship launched at Wilmington was on December 6, 1941; it was named the *Zebulon B. Vance* in honor of the state's Civil War governor. More than 40 others were built in the next year, with a final total of 243. Others were named the *John Merrick*, the *Donald W. Bain*, the *Cassius Hudson*, and the *Addie Bagley Daniels*. Fifty-seven counties were also honored by having ships named for them.

The cotton textile industry was also of vital importance. Working three shifts, North Carolina mills doubled their payrolls. Cannon Mills in Kannapolis specialized in camouflage cloth and bandages, and in addition produced the yarn needed to manufacture 15 million machine-gun belts. In Winston-Salem, the P. H. Hanes Knitting Company focused on underwear. Overall, 70 per-cent of North Carolina's textile output—including blankets, towels, hosiery, clothing material, work suits, uniforms, and tent fabric—went to the armed forces. One federal agent commented that "so wide is the variety of produc-tion . . . that every soldier and sailor in the service of the Nation either wears or carries some article manufactured in North Carolina."

Mineral production became another valuable contribution of North Caro-lina to the war effort. For over fifty years Spruce Pine had been the center of mica mining. Used as an insulator in radio tubes, mica was in great demand. While mining in the mountains was expensive, high prices during the war made it profitable to reopen old mines and prospect for new ones. Before the end of the war, half of the mica mined in the United States came from North Carolina. Another valuable mineral used to harden steel, tungsten, came from Vance County. This source was critical since before the war much tung-sten had been imported from Europe. Other minerals from North Carolina included manganese, olivine (when crushed into sand was used to cast objects

The liberty ship *Zebulon B. Vance*, built in North Carolina, was later converted to a hospital ship and renamed the *John J. Meany*.

in aluminum), and spodumene (an important source of lithium). At Kure Beach the Ethyl-Dow plant made all the tetraethyllead used in the war.

Forest products were also in great demand. The United States Forest Service estimated that North Carolina timber could produce 1,656,000,000 board feet of lumber and 600,000 cords of pulp-wood annually without devastating the vital resources. This timber eventually became veneer, furniture, and paper.

Perhaps the greatest contribution that North Carolina made to the war effort, however, was its agricultural production, or as Commissioner of Agriculture Kerr Scott put it, the state's "food, feed, and fibre." The normal demand for food increased exponentially by the demands of men and women in service, of the Allies, and of refugees from countries overrun by Germany and Japan. At the same time, there was a shortage of labor because a great many able-bodied farm workers were in active military service. Some deferments were possible, but the shortage of labor was a real hardship. Nevertheless, North Carolina was able to double its wheat production, increase its peanut crop from 250 million to 374 million pounds, raise its Irish potato poundage from 6 million to 9 million, and also to increase its output of sweet potatoes and hay. This tremendous effort was made possible by the cooperation of state and federal agencies with the farmers, by assignment of manpower to help at harvest time, by the use of high school students, and by sheer patriotism. Perhaps the most interesting farm laborers were prisoners of war. North Carolina contained a number of small prisoner of war camps, and prisoners could volunteer to harvest crops for a very modest remuneration.

Increasing the state's food production for the war effort also required that citizens grow at least some of their own food. North Carolina State College gave away seeds of twenty-two different kinds for each family of five to plant a victory garden. Automobile mechanics volunteered their services to repair tractors and other farm machinery. The tobacco crop was left in the fields until all the cotton, hay, and peanuts had been harvested. The Farm Manpower Commission had adopted as its general slogan, "No Idle Labor, No Idle Land, No Idle Machines." Although a shortage of gasoline impeded the marketing of such perishable crops as strawberries, squash, and cucumbers, on the whole the program of farm production was successful. In 1944, for instance, the cash received for North Carolina farm crops was over $610,000,000.

Without a doubt, the war ended the Depression in North Carolina. Factories ran full tilt, mining was reinvigorated, timbering provided significant employment, and construction boomed as the thousands of new people who arrived needed places to live. Shipbuilding and related industries restored the coastal economy. Agricultural production tripled. Soldiers on the many military bases had at least small amounts of discretionary funds to spend, and North Carolinians who had scrimped and saved for so long could now afford a night at the movies. Yet in the midst of this prosperity, some concern lingered as to what would happen when the war ended.

Chapter 11

Daily Life in Wartime

Just as it did during World War I, war altered significantly the way in which Americans lived their daily lives. Men went to fight; women and children did their best to maintain a home life and keep up morale. Many state governments struggled, having to do more with less. Jobs, however, became plentiful, and women joined the ranks of workers in traditionally male roles. Rationing had a larger impact than during World War I, as did the fear that the enemy might be able to attack the U.S. mainland along either coast. Therefore, on January 1, 1942, the Rose Bowl was moved to the East Coast. The very next day North Carolinians turned their attention from football to the business of war.

In 1942 sports writer Paul Gallico quipped:

> That was the spring when women took to wearing slacks in the street (a great blow to the human race), old toothpaste tubes had to be turned in for new ones, men's trousers were commanded to be cuffless, and a radio comedian named Bob Hope began to play soldiers' camps around the country. . . . That was the spring we first heard about sugar rationing, with gasoline rationing to come. Ice cream was reduced to ten flavors, and civilian suffering really hit its stride when the War Production Board banned the use of metals for asparagus tongs, beer mugs, spittoons, bird cages, cocktail shakers, hair curlers, corn poppers, and lobster forks. New York blacked out, and for days we talked about how beautiful the great city looked stark and naked, silhouetted against the moon and the stars.

This humorous quotation illustrates the fact that many civilians first understood the reality of war with shortages of items to which they were ordinarily accustomed, such as metal containers, and with foods such as sugar, meat, and butter. The government implemented rationing and price controls to ensure that available supplies were spread among the general public and that wealthy or unscrupulous individuals could not "corner the market" on such items. The Office of Price Administration, known as the OPA, held jurisdiction over both rationing and price controls.

The Rose Bowl

Fear of an attack on the West Coast, seemingly a real possibility in the aftermath of Pearl Harbor, hit home in North Carolina in an unusual way. Duke University was scheduled to play Oregon State in the 1942 Rose Bowl. Students were excited about the possibility of a train trip to Pasadena with a side stop at the Grand Canyon. However, Gen. John L. DeWitt was dismayed by the lack of blackout and other preparations on the West Coast and recommended that the game be canceled. Duke University quickly responded with an offer to host the game, after confirming with Governor Broughton that this change of venue would not hamper North Carolina's military preparedness efforts. Some questioned whether or not Oregon State would agree to make the long trip, but the team had never played in the Rose Bowl and eagerly boarded a train for the East Coast. For the only time in its history, the Rose Bowl was played outside Pasadena. The university scrambled to borrow bleachers from neighboring colleges, boosting the seating capacity of its stadium from 35,000 to 55,000. Governor Broughton promised good weather, but the day was rainy and cold. Oregon State had not been able to bring its band, so the Southern Conference arranged for a composite band to perform. Linwood S. Inscoe, a freshman at North Carolina State College at the time and a trumpeter in the band, remembered the invitation to play. Band members from all teams in the Southern Conference were welcome, as long as they would return early from Christmas vacation to practice before the big New Year's Day event. William Robert Smith, a freshman trumpeter from Davidson College, remembered the thrill of being in the stadium that day, even if it was a soggy mess. At the end of the day, the heavily favored Blue Devils lost to the Beavers, 20–16. It was not, however, the end of contact

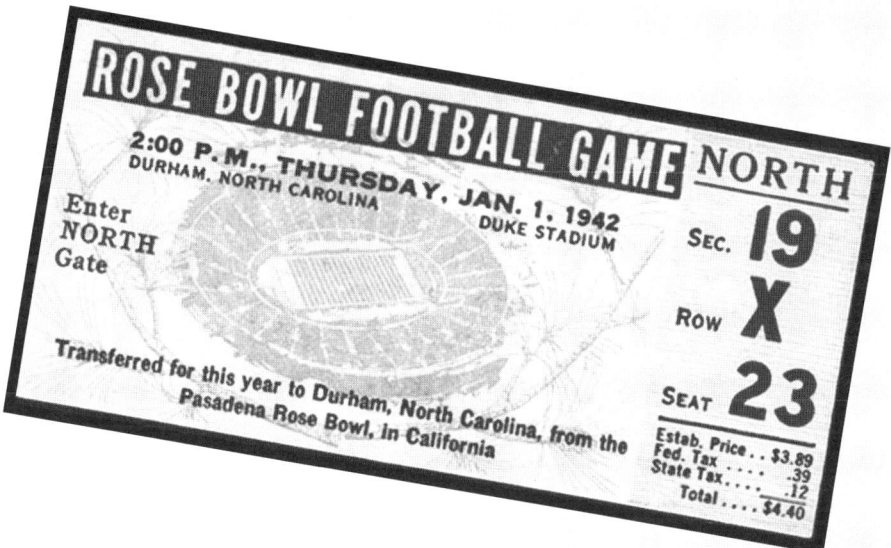

ROSE BOWL FOOTBALL GAME NORTH

2:00 P.M., THURSDAY, JAN. 1, 1942
DURHAM, NORTH CAROLINA   DUKE STADIUM

Enter
NORTH
Gate

Transferred for this year to Durham, North Carolina, from the
Pasadena Rose Bowl, in California

SEC. **19**

ROW **X**

SEAT **23**

Estab. Price . . $3.89
Fed. Tax 39
State Tax 12
Total $4.40

The only Rose Bowl game held outside California was played in Durham on January 1, 1942. After the game was canceled because of growing fears that the West Coast would become the target of enemy bombing, Duke offered to host the game, and Oregon State accepted. Image of ticket provided courtesy of the North Carolina Museum of History.

between some members of these teams. Frank Parker, a guard for Oregon State, later recognized and rescued Duke quarterback Charlie Haynes who had been severely wounded on the Italian front. Wallace Wade, the Duke coach, shared a meal during the Battle of the Bulge with Stan Czech, a tackle for Oregon State. Jim Smith, an end for Duke, met up with a marine in a bar in Panama who had played for Oregon State.

Mileage was rationed through C Stamps. A gas ration sticker was affixed to a vehicle's front windshield so the reverse side was visible to the occupants. This offered an opportunity to give tips to the driver and passengers: "Is this trip really necessary? Share your car. To save tires, drive under 35." The national maximum *Victory Speed* was 35 miles an hour, and driving clubs or carpools were encouraged. The main idea was to conserve rubber, not gasoline. Image from the Library of Congress, Prints and Photographs Division.

Shortly after Pearl Harbor, every civilian received a book of ration stamps, bearing alphabet letters but no other identification. From time to time, as critical shortages were recognized, announcements indicated that one E Stamp, for instance, would thereafter be required for each purchase of a certain item. These announcements were generally made unexpectedly to prevent individuals from rushing out ahead of time to stock up on the scarce item. Some people stocked up anyway; sugar was one product that would almost certainly be scarce, and some people stored enough sugar in their attics to last the duration of the war. An interesting sidelight on sugar rationing resulted when individuals who began to request large quantities of extra sugar for canning purposes were suspected of operating illicit whiskey stills, which in many cases was true. The announcement concerning the rationing of shoes occurred on a Sunday afternoon over the radio, to go into effect the next morning. One result of shoe rationing was the development of "play shoes," which did not use much critical material, such as leather, and which have been popular ever since.

Coffee was hard to obtain, even with ration stamps; and cigarettes were so scarce that the most appreciated gift a serviceman could take a civilian hostess was a carton of cigarettes from the Post Exchange. The weekly share of meat for an adult was two and one-half pounds; substitutes such as cheese, eggs, dried beans, soybeans, and peanut butter became a larger portion of the American diet.

Particularly scarce were gasoline and rubber tires, which were needed for the new mobile warfare. Among the first casualties of the war in North Carolina were the rural filling (service) stations, which were, as Gov. R. Gregg Cherry later described them in a January 9, 1946, address to the N.C. Oil Jobbers Association, "a sad sight with their windows boarded up and with grass growing around the door." Tires were recapped when they became worn, and people started carpools to ride to work in order to save gasoline and wear and tear on their irreplaceable cars. The car that a family had in 1941 had to last for the duration of the war, as did other heavy goods such as refrigerators and washing machines. Scarce materials could not be spared for such luxuries when tanks and planes were needed at the front.

Rationing boards enforced the regulations concerning shortages, heard appeals in hardship cases, and checked prices in stores. In a December 27, 1943, address to commemorate the second anniversary of the rationing program, Governor Broughton praised the men and women who donated their time to the work on these boards. He called it a "difficult and important, though frequently a distasteful and unpleasant task." Posters and other propaganda materials encouraged housewives not to patronize any "black market" stores, that is, stores that sold goods without demanding ration stamps or that charged prices higher than those set by the OPA. The housewife's pledge was, "I pay no more than top legal prices. I accept no rationed goods without giving up ration stamps." Families were encouraged to grow victory gardens, to raise a pig or chickens for themselves, and to can all the food at home that they could. In North Carolina in 1944, no less than 28 million quarts of food were canned, 30 million pounds of meat cured, and 8 million pounds of fruits and vegetables dried by homemakers for home consumption. The city of Raleigh had 4,000 victory gardens in 1945. The combination of local gardening and the lack of gasoline for distant transportation encouraged the development of strong auction produce markets at Hendersonville, Boone, West Jefferson, and Spruce Pine selling

Food Prices and Ration Points

Food	Price	Ration points
Apples	33¢/2 pounds	20 points
Bisquick	37¢/box	18 points
Bread	10¢/loaf	0 points
Bugles snacks	19¢/box	5 points
Butter	22¢/pound	20 points
Cake mix	18¢/box	18 points
Cheerios	14¢/box	7 points
Cheese	35¢/pound	12 points
Coffee	24¢/pound	42 points
Coke	5¢/bottle	10 points
Cookies	22¢/box	22 points
Corn	13¢/can	18 points
Crackers	19¢/box	5 points
Eggs	35¢/dozen	0 points
Flour	66¢/10 pounds	18 points
Grits	9¢/box	3 points
Ground beef	27¢/pound	0 points
Jelly	24¢/jar	40 points
Lemon juice	27¢/bottle	9 points

Source: *News and Observer* (March 1943). In addition to ration stamps, a point system was used.

snap beans, cabbage, and potatoes. The effects lasted beyond the war, and a new truck farming industry developed in the mountains.

In addition to the reduction of civilian consumption of scarce goods, metal and rubber drives collected items that would ordinarily have been thrown away. Estimates suggested that the average family discarded 36 "tin" cans per month, which for the entire nation would add up to a total of 1,250 tons of tin and 123,750 tons of No. 2 steel per month. Special weeks were set aside to encourage the saving of such scrap metal. Scrap iron

Food	Price	Ration points
Luncheon meat	33¢/pound	0 points
Margarine	17¢/pound	2 points
Mayonnaise	20¢/jar	0 points
Milk (evaporated)	9¢/can	1 point
Noodles	5¢/box	18 points
Orange juice	19¢/can	0 points
Peanut butter	25¢/jar	9 points
Popsicles	29¢/box	22 points
Potatoes	39¢/10 pounds	0 points
Rice	10¢/pound	3 points
Sausage	35¢/pound	0 points
Shrimp	53¢/pound	12 points
Soup	9¢/can	10 points
Spinach	15¢/can	18 points
Steak	40¢/pound	13 points
Strawberries	28¢/pound	0 points
Sugar	31¢/5 pounds	80 points
Syrup	23¢/jar	80 points
Tomato juice	10¢/can	20 points
Tuna	24¢/can	6 points

Sugar, syrup, coffee, and jelly required the most number of points because of their scarcity.

was collected in similar fashion, and people turned in every available pound of scrap rubber, from rubber bands and hot-water bottles to old tires, at the nearest filling station. Citizens were also urged to conserve electricity. Governor Broughton asked North Carolinians to use 10 percent less electricity, coal, telephone service, and bus service in 1943, so that war industries and servicemen would have more resources available to them. Most civilians, after experiences of standing for hours on trains or buses because of crowded conditions, preferred to stay home as much as possible.

Photograph showing a Raleigh scrap drive, probably taken by Robert L. Maxey, who worked for the *News and Observer*. Notice the billboard that encourages people to "Get in the Scrap."

A second way in which Tar Heels felt the war at home was in appeals for financing the war. The income from taxes is never sufficient to support a war; therefore, the government has to borrow money from citizens and banks by selling bonds. These were variously called war bonds, victory bonds, and war loans. The bonds came in different denominations, from $25 up; small ones were designed for the wage earner and large ones for banks and corporations. Schoolchildren bought war stamps and pasted them in books; when a book was filled, it could be exchanged for a bond. Since people like to know where their money is going, the government established a plan whereby bond purchasers could designate how their money would be used. For instance, in 1945 the women of North Carolina sold $600,000 in bonds and paid for a Boeing B-29 superfortress bomber. In 1944 North Carolina led the nation in the purchase of ambulance planes (a total of 14) through the sale of "E" bonds. The teachers and children of the public schools raised $43 million in eight drives that purchased jeeps, airplanes, and tanks; they received national recognition for this large sum. In fact, North Carolinians exceeded all quotas for bond drives during the war, some by twice the amount requested.

Still another way in which the daily lives of citizens were affected was in the matter of defense. The Office of Civilian Defense was a national agency that enrolled men and women for protection of the nation in the event of air raids or other attacks like those England was experiencing. Beginning in March 1942, volunteers were organized and trained for such duties as plane spotting, fire fighting, ambulance driving, first aid, and similar activities. Since North Carolina was a coastal state and there was some fear that German planes and submarines might attack the eastern seaboard, for nuisance value if nothing else, the work of civilian defense was extremely important. The army finally assumed the enforcement of defense regulations in eastern North Carolina, not

Students from Burton Elementary School in Durham held monthly drives where they contributed coins to buy bonds.

The Raleigh air raid siren was typical of those installed across the state to warn of the approach of enemy planes. Air raid drills were held so that people would be prepared in case of an attack. This image is dated January 17, 1942.

because volunteers had not done a good job but because the government felt that a tighter organization was required for safety.

Most of the work of civilian defense centered around possible air raids and sought to make it difficult for enemy planes to locate cities for bombing. At first "dim-outs" were required every night near the coast, in order to make as little light as possible. People could not be on the beaches after dark. Neon lights and traffic signals especially, which could be seen from long distances, were turned off at sunset. At certain times "blackout" conditions were demanded, during which window shades were to be drawn, cars were to pull off the road and turn off lights, railroad trains were to pull down shades on passenger cars and substitute white lanterns for their taillights, and factories could not operate night shifts unless satisfactory blackout conditions could be maintained. These regulations existed for a distance of 200 miles inland and were in effect until November 1943. By that time coastal attacks seemed unlikely, although the Outer Banks continued dim-outs as a matter of protection to coastal shipping. Persons not obeying dim-out and blackout regulations were arrested and fined by the courts.

Air raid drills occurred frequently as far inland as Clinton, Dunn, Fayetteville, Goldsboro, Roxboro, and Southern Pines. A steady two-minute blast from the siren meant to black out one's home or business but to continue activities. This was the "blue" signal. The next one, or "red" signal, meant to take shelter. A repeat of the "blue" meant that it was safe to leave the shelter, and the "white" signal was the all clear, at which lights could be turned on again. A typical air raid drill was a surprise one held in Durham on September 1, 1943. The signal was given by the military over the telephone to the air raid center at 9:10 P.M. Within 3½ minutes, the firemen had reported for duty. Camp Butner was notified within 9 minutes. Within 29 minutes, all personnel were on duty at the center, and the State Guard had been mobilized with one lieutenant and 35 men ready; within 39 minutes the Welfare Services were on duty. Camp Butner was completely blacked out. This was considered a highly successful drill, especially since it was a total surprise to all the civilians involved.

Public schools were mobilized also. Physical fitness became an important daily activity. Civil defense instruction, first-aid classes, and war vocational instruction became part of the curriculum. Schools made every effort to maintain standards of instruction, although it was difficult because many teachers joined the military. A pamphlet entitled *What Can I Do?* offered many ways that students could help to win the war. Suggestions included keeping strong by eating the right kind of food, getting enough sleep, and exercising in the open air; being careful not to waste anything and to take care of clothes, toys, and bicycles since new ones would not be possible during the war; being useful at home by running errands, babysitting, making small repairs, mending, and saving scrap; being useful in school by studying to understand the war; being useful in the community by distributing literature and posters, planting a victory garden, serving as a playground helper, and welcoming children of new families who came to work there in a war industry. In Winston-Salem boys and girls organized a Junior Commando complete with military insignia and ranks for the purpose of salvaging scrap.

This group of fifteen students show off their 4-H posters created to celebrate "victory gardens." This ca. 1943 image provided courtesy of the Green 'N' Growing Collection (The History of Home Demonstration and 4-H Youth Development in North Carolina), Special Collections, North Carolina State University Libraries.

Patriotic songs that had been written by many students throughout the nation were published in a booklet. One of them was written by four girls in Lenoir High School. To the tune, "This Is the Army, Mr. Jones," the first verse was:

> This is Stamp Day, Mr. Jones,
> You've got to buy some stamps and bonds:
> You've wasted money, but this is war,
> And you won't waste it now, any more.

A popular radio program was "Victory Quiz," with students as participants. It was conducted like a spelling bee. Typical questions included: If you have a worn out copper teakettle, one old roller skate, and a rusty bedspring in your attic, what's the best possible thing you could do with them? When a boy or girl is sixteen, what office can they register with during the present times to help our country? If your home is in a target area, what should you do? In ways such as these, North Carolina schools went to war.

View of a USO club building in Rockingham (Richmond County) in the 1940s. The northeast wing of the building later served as a library and Saturday night dances were held there in the 1950s.

Still another way the daily lives of North Carolinians were affected by the war was in helping servicemen and their families who were temporarily in the state, primarily by establishing a USO club or its equivalent. These initials stood for United Service Organizations, which was a combination of the efforts of the YMCA, the YWCA, and many more such organizations to provide wholesome entertainment, recreation, food, sympathy, and help for the thousands of men and women who were far from home. Due to the many military bases in North Carolina, the work of the USO was extremely important and very much needed. There were 103 units in 47 communities, a number exceeded only by seven other states. In addition, 38 communities sponsored their own similar clubs, such as the one at Aberdeen that was located in a converted bank in the center of town. It had a large main lobby, a snack bar, a kitchen, a check room, a writing room, a library, an office, and shower and rest rooms. Service personnel came there from Camp Mackall, Laurinburg-Maxton Army Air Base, and Fort Bragg when they had leave. During its existence it served

489,358 individuals, whose three chief problems were food, housing, and recreation. An extension was later set up at Aberdeen Lake.

Besides the regular work of the USO, from time to time special efforts were made to entertain foreign servicemen, such as 500 officers and men from the English ship *Formidable*, which was in port at Norfolk in October 1941. They were given a five-week holiday at Crabtree Creek Park (now Umstead State Park) and were entertained frequently by people in Raleigh and Durham during that five weeks. There was also a need for recreation on the military reservations, as many men did not have the privilege of regular weekend passes. Dances were sponsored on the posts, and busloads of young women, well chaperoned, went from nearby areas to be junior hostesses. The work of the USO was financed by contributions collected in the name of the United War Fund. North Carolina gave over $4 million, in addition to which the state spent another $3 million on locally sponsored programs. Only fifteen states in the Union gave more than North Carolina.

To further build the morale of white sailors and civilians, the B-1 Band, an all-African American unit, was established by the U.S. Navy in early 1942. Up to that time, blacks in the navy had only served as cooks. The band was made up of the best African American musicians in North Carolina. Many of the forty-four men came from North Carolina A&T College in Greensboro. Just like their white counterparts, they went through standard naval training in Virginia and were stationed in Chapel Hill. They faced discrimination by the very audience they were supposed to entertain, but because of their talent they eventually gained acceptance. The band presented concerts on military bases, at community and naval events, at ship launchings, during war bond drives, and at dances across the state. They were the first blacks in the navy to be recognized for their talent, and their accomplishments helped ensure that future African American sailors could serve in jobs that had previously been reserved for whites.

In addition to entertaining U.S. and foreign servicemen, North Carolinians sometimes saw prisoners of war (POWs), although the government kept their presence and numbers secret. Over 400,000 German, Italian, and Japanese soldiers were imprisoned in the United States. Eventually North Carolina had a total of seventeen base and branch camps. The first POWs to arrive in the state were sailors rescued from a German submarine that sank off North Carolina's coast on May 9, 1942. They were interned at Fort Bragg. However, as more

B-1 Band members from North Carolina A&T College in Greensboro were stationed in Chapel Hill. This image was taken on the steps of their barracks.

POWs arrived, the government realized that many smaller locations would be preferable to one or two large ones, thereby reducing the opportunity for plotting escape. These camps dotted the state from Hendersonville in the west to a great many locations in the east. Many of the POWs, as allowed by the Geneva Convention, worked outside of the camps. While they could not be employed directly in war industries, they were widely used in agriculture and the timber industry. They were paid the same as civilian workers, but kept only eighty cents per day that they could use for personal purchases in the camp. The remainder of their pay supported the facilities provided in the camps. During the course of the war, twenty-nine POWs held in North Carolina attempted to escape, but only one was successful. By early 1946 no POWs remained in the state.

The crew of the *U-352*, sunk off the Outer Banks, became the first German POWs confined in the United States. They were initially imprisoned at Fort Bragg, where this May 1942 U.S. Army photograph was taken.

Not only were foreign-born POWs interned in camps, but foreign-born civilians were also housed temporarily in similar living conditions. In 1942, the Immigration and Naturalization Service took into custody a number of German and Japanese civilians, primarily businessmen and their families. A total of 264 people, many of whom were children, were housed in the Assembly Inn in Montreat for approximately six months.

As the war progressed, North Carolinians generously answered the call for aid to refugees in Europe. When Hitler invaded Russia, many people fled their homes and were in need of clothing to stave off the cold Russian winter. A campaign to "Share Your Clothes with Russians" was successful.

The Church World Service Center at Windsor, Maryland, received one shipment from the state of 56,000 pounds of clothing and 11,000 pounds of food. Through a special showing of the movie, *This Is the Army*, the sum of $50,973 was collected for relief, the second highest in the Southeast. King George VI of England awarded the King's Medal for "Service in the cause of freedom" to sixteen North Carolina women for volunteer work they had done in this and other fields.

Throughout the war, maintaining civilian morale was always an issue never far from the surface. It was perhaps easier for men under arms to have a high morale, certainly so if they had enough to eat, were well trained, and thought they would win. But civilians many times became frustrated; they did not see how they could contribute to the war; they had to sit at home when they would have preferred action; they waited weeks and months for letters from loved ones; they did without goods when black marketers had plenty. It was therefore important to help civilians realize that every action of theirs was either helpful or detrimental in winning the war. Posters, radio programs, speeches, propaganda of all sorts, were directed toward civilians to keep their morale high, to insure that they were not careless and thus detrimental to the cause, and to encourage them to work as hard as possible to defeat the Axis powers. From time to time the governor announced a "day of dedication." In a June 23, 1943, proclamation, Governor Broughton declared July 5, 1943, as such. Churches observed special days of prayer. Songs were written to encourage a cheerful spirit, such as this one by Carrie-Lewis Simpson of Raleigh:

> Old Glory floats o'er land and sea,
> We'll keep our home and country free,
> United we march together,
> Our flag will wave forever,
> With courage we will meet the foe,
> Our faith will guide us as we go,
> We're marching again on to victory,
> Fighting to hold liberty
> Out on the sea, high in the air,
> Over the land, we'll all be there. . . .

The Office of Civilian Defense pamphlet titled, *What Can I Do?*, expressed it this way:

> War changes the pattern of our lives. It cannot change our *way of life*, unless we are beaten. The kids still play baseball in the corner lot—but they knock off early to weed the victory gardens, cart scrap paper to the salvage center, carry home the groceries that used to be delivered. The factory whistle blows—but it calls three shifts of workers instead of one. The daily paper still has comics, but it's the front page that carries the answer to the urgent question "how are we doing?" All over America there's a new tempo, a new purpose, *a new spirit.*

Governor Broughton, in an address to the state legislature on January 7, 1943, spoke for all North Carolinians when he said:

> It is our privilege to be living in the most challenging period of our national existence. We may well take pride in the fact that North Carolina in this emergency, as in all previous national crises, is living up to its highest traditions. As we gather here to deliberate about matters of fiscal and domestic concern we cannot be unmindful of the fact that tens of thousands of our young men are on the blazing fields of action. Many of them will not return. To those who do return and in loving memory of those who do not may we be able truthfully to say, "We, too, have kept the faith!"

Governing a State in Wartime

When the United States entered the war, J. Melville Broughton was governor, Josiah W. Bailey and Robert R. Reynolds were the United States senators, and the congressmen were Graham A. Barden, Herbert C. Bonner, Alfred L. Bulwinkle, William O. Burgin, Jerome B. Clark, Harold D. Cooley, Robert L. Doughton, Carl P. Durham, John H. Folger, John H. Kerr, and Zebulon B. Weaver. These same men served until the beginning of 1945, so that for the majority of the war they were North Carolina's leaders. In addition, the census of 1940 showed an increase in population in the state, which entitled it to an additional congressman. Former governor Cameron Morrison was elected to this position in 1942 and, to succeed him, Joseph Wilson Ervin in 1944. Since many of these men, although not Morrison or Ervin, had served in Congress for many years, they held important committee posts. Doughton was chairman of the powerful Ways and Means, Durham was on Military Affairs, Burgin on Foreign Affairs, Kerr on Appropriations, and Cooley on Agriculture. With the exception of Senator Robert R. Reynolds, North Carolina's national lawmakers supported preparedness and aid to the Allies in the period before Pearl Harbor. All of them supported the war effort when war finally came. Senator Bailey, whose term expired in 1942, was very popular and won another term over his opponent, Richard T. Fountain, a man whom he had defeated once before.

In spite of the all-out war effort, Governor Broughton and his administration did not neglect the fields of health, education, and welfare. Health care conditions in North Carolina were very poor. Thirty-four counties had no hospital; the state ranked near the bottom in comparison with the other states in the number of doctors and hospital beds per 1,000 people. Governor Broughton appointed a commission to study the needs of the state in this field. Recommendations included expanding the medical school at the University of North Carolina from two years to four years of training and building an adequate hospital there. The commission also recommended that an extensive system of smaller hospitals be built throughout the state. The medical school

NORTH CAROLINA ELECTION RESULTS			
	1940	1942	1944
Governor	Broughton	Broughton	Cherry
U.S. Senator	Bailey★ Reynolds★★	Bailey Reynolds	Bailey Hoey
Congressmen			
1st District	Bonner	Bonner	Bonner
2nd District	Kerr	Kerr	Kerr
3rd District	Barden	Barden	Barden
4th District	Cooley	Cooley	Cooley
5th District	Folger	Folger	Folger
6th District	Durham	Durham	Durham
7th District	Clark	Clark	Clark
8th District	Burgin	Burgin	Burgin
9th District	Doughton	Doughton	Doughton
10th District	Bulwinkle	Morrison	Ervin
11th District	Weaver	Bulwinkle	Bulwinkle
12th District	(not in existence)	Weaver	Weaver

★Serving a six-year term to which he was elected in 1936.
★★ Serving a six-year term to which he was elected in 1938.

and Memorial Hospital at Chapel Hill later became a reality, but the erection of a system of smaller hospitals lagged for many years. The mental hospitals of the state received larger appropriations, new facilities and equipment, and were placed under the direction of a consolidated board.

Educational improvement was so extensive that it might be compared to the work of Charles B. Aycock, governor of North Carolina from 1901 to 1905 and a former school board chairman and county school superintendent. He oversaw major adjustments in the way in which money was distributed so that poorer counties had the opportunity to improve significantly the quality of their schools, a measure that, in time, had extensive positive ramifications for the education of all North Carolinians. Although the nation and the state were facing war, North Carolina expanded on this foundation. The legislature mandated a nine-month school term statewide. It voted for the largest increase in teachers' salaries in any one year up to 1943 and equalized pay for white and black teachers. The twelfth grade was added in 1941, and a retirement program for teachers was inaugurated. At Belmont the first state-owned vocational training school was established, foreshadowing the rise of the community college system after the war. North Carolina State College, a land grant institution, received significant new support. Its dairying school was strengthened with the purchase of 600 acres of land for cattle and dairy needs; Reynolds Coliseum was erected; and several new buildings, such as the Bureau of Mines building and the diesel engineering building, were constructed. An engineering foundation was begun and the textile foundation increased to $750,000. These foundations supported research projects and provided scholarships for students. For adult and general education, the state appropriated $100,000 for aid to public libraries, especially rural ones. The first direct appropriations for art and music were made, later leading to the establishment of the North Carolina Symphony and the North Carolina Museum of Art.

By watching income and expenditures carefully and by taking advantage of the additional taxes afforded the state because of the influx of military personnel and new war industries, North Carolina's government was prosperous during the war. Although the Highway Fund suffered because gasoline rationing reduced the sale of gasoline, and hence the resultant taxes, surpluses built up in other areas so that the state was in the best financial condition in its history. Some citizens wanted to spend this money promptly. Others, led by Governor Broughton and his successor Governor Cherry, believed it wiser to conserve this money in order to cushion the shock of postwar adjustment. For instance, if money were saved with which to build roads after the war, the state would be able to improve the highways and also to employ men who might otherwise be out of jobs when the war factories closed. This conservative view prevailed, and the postwar reserve fund accumulated $20 million to make the transition to peacetime economic life smoother.

All was not smooth sailing during the Broughton administration, however. In 1942 a scandal came to light in the State Revenue Department. A field tax collector was arrested on information from a taxpayer, a true bill returned against him by the Wake County grand jury, and a full-scale investigation launched. The investigation determined that $16,500 had been embezzled or misapplied. Before the investigation and resultant court cases were over, ten persons were imprisoned, others dismissed, and the system of collecting taxes and auditing the results was overhauled.

Much worse than this, however, was a scandal in the administration of the State Hospital for the Insane at Morganton. The exposure of bad conditions there was begun by Tom P. Jimison, a former minister, lawyer, and newspaper columnist, who spent thirteen months there after committing himself to the hospital on the advice of his physicians. Following his release, he documented his observations and experiences as a patient in a series of sixteen articles that were widely published in newspapers throughout the state, including the *Charlotte News* and the *Greensboro Daily News*, beginning in January 1942. Jimison was already well known to North Carolinians as a reformer. He had written a number of articles on various social conditions and received statewide publicity as a lawyer for the defense during the trials that resulted from the Gastonia labor strikes. Jimison began by describing the antiquated methods of commitment, in which a person was placed in jail and treated like a criminal rather than an ill person. He described the "prison-like" atmosphere of the hospital, the secretiveness of action by the staff, the ignorance of the attendants, the poor food, and the occasional brutality. In one of his concluding articles, published on February 6, 1942, he said, "I cannot believe that the people of North Carolina are content to have their sick and helpless neighbors herded in such

Observation of bad conditions for patients at the State Hospital for the Insane at Morganton led to significant reform in the treatment of mental illness.

an asylum, fed on fatback and dried beans, . . . worked like convicts, and then furnished with such a small staff of physicians that many of them cannot have the proper medical attention when wracked with physical pain and suffering."

As a result of the shock caused by these articles, Governor Broughton appointed a five-member Board of Inquiry plus a special counsel and a psychiatrist. This board held hearings in several parts of the state and heard testimony from former patients, relatives of patients, and others who had insight into the conditions at the institution. It quickly became clear that conditions were indeed bad. Some of this testimony revealed that patients were hit by attendants who then told relatives that the patients had fallen. One man testified that he was "beaten and stomped" by an attendant. A woman reported that she was committed with no legal action at all. Others charged outside interference with the operation of the hospital on the part of certain Morganton businessmen. There was only one physician for each 425 patients, whereas the national average was one physician for each 248 patients. Not more than six nurses or attendants had had previous training, and therefore most of the attendants were ignorant. Some of them "diagnosed" the patients' troubles themselves and behaved accordingly. The money allowed for food was only $51 per patient per year, plus about $20 worth of farm produce raised at the institution. On the other hand, accounts of cockroaches were grossly exaggerated; only three were found after an exhaustive search. Additionally, at least some of the stories of brutal treatment were made up by the patients.

The board uncovered enough evidence, however, to prove that reforms were needed at the Morganton State Hospital and probably at others as well. Recommendations included better pay to the staff, a young and aggressive psychiatrist as head of the staff, a change in state laws to prevent wrongful commitments, improvement in the variety of food, rebuilding to eliminate fire hazards, additional staff to provide better care, and an immediate cessation of all mistreatment of patients. Improvements began at once. A new dietitian provided better food; new equipment for the kitchen and farm was purchased; and window screens were installed. Legislation was passed to create a consolidated board for all mental institutions to eliminate any possible local interference, as charged at Morganton. While implementation of these recommendations did not occur all at once, North Carolina was on a new pathway for the treatment of mental illness.

A horror of another kind was the great munitions explosion near Selma in March 1942. A truck carrying munitions collided with a car on the highway and caught fire. The result was so spectacular that several hundred spectators gathered to see the wreck. Two hours after the accident had occurred, the 30,000 pounds of black gunpowder and hand grenades on the truck exploded "with a thunderous roar," as witnesses reported. One eyewitness said that everything turned dark for a minute and then fires began to break out all around, lighting up "a dim scene of destruction." Buildings were wrecked, including the Tarlton Hotel, which was leveled. A crater the size of a freight car was torn in the concrete highway, and remains of the truck were strewn for a mile and a half. The stained glass windows of the Methodist church in Selma were shattered. Ambulances from surrounding towns and hospitals were filled with the injured. Six people were killed, including the two drivers of the truck; fifty were injured. Damage estimates, both in Selma and in Smithfield, three miles away, totaled approximately $500,000.

This photograph of the scene of the munitions explosion near Selma, in March 1942, shows the terrible destruction caused by the disaster.

The year 1944 was significant politically in North Carolina because the presidential election coincided with the gubernatorial election. In addition, North Carolinians would choose one senator and all twelve congressmen. Most people assumed that President Franklin D. Roosevelt would be renominated by the Democrats and subsequently reelected. However, the current vice president, Henry A. Wallace, had come under considerable criticism, and with President Roosevelt's obvious poor health, party leaders searched for a running mate who would be more widely acceptable. Since North Carolinians were proud of the work done by Governor Broughton, the state's Democratic leaders decided to nominate him for the position. It is customary for states to nominate a "favorite son" for the vice presidency as an honor to the man, with little expectation that he will actually be chosen. In this case, however, many thought that Broughton had as good a chance as any other candidate, and he decided to make a real effort to capture the nomination. His campaign committee received $6,000 in donations and printed a brochure for distribution at the convention that outlined his career and pointed out his excellent qualities. In spite of the fact that black delegates refused to support any southern candidate and that organized labor also took a stand against southerners, Governor Broughton ran sixth of 16 nominees on the first ballot. On the second ballot he yielded his support to Senator Harry S. Truman, the choice of President Roosevelt. In this process, however, North Carolina gained considerable recognition for Governor Broughton on the national level. Ultimately, the presidential campaign was a quiet one in the state, and North Carolina cast its votes for President Roosevelt and Vice President Truman rather than for the two Republican candidates, Thomas E. Dewey of New York and John W. Bricker of Ohio.

The senatorial campaign was not much more exciting than the one for president. While Senator Bailey had easily been reelected in 1942, Senator Reynolds, whose seat was up for reelection in 1944, was another story. By the mid-1930s he had fallen out of favor with the Democratic Party. His extreme isolationism, combined with his support for Gerald L. K. Smith (an avowed fascist) and his partial ownership of *The Defender*, an anti-Semitic paper, led party members to seek another Democrat to oppose him in the 1938 primary. Reynolds won that election, but in 1944 the Democrats were determined to be rid of him. Former governor Clyde R. Hoey was interested in running, as was former governor and congressman Cameron Morrison.

Dr. Ralph McDonald, a professor at the University of North Carolina who had run unsuccessfully for governor in 1936 against Hoey, was a favorite candidate of a number of newspapermen who hoped he would enter the race for senator. He decided to run for governor instead. Reynolds toyed with the idea of running as an Independent, but he finally gave up the plan. The Democratic primary in May, therefore, offered only two important candidates for the position, Clyde R. Hoey and Cameron Morrison. Other names on the ballot were M. L. Ritch, Arthur Simmons, and G. Y. Newton. Hoey won the nomination overwhelmingly, polling 211,049 votes to Morrison's 80,154, with the other three candidates receiving far fewer votes. In November Hoey defeated the Republican candidate A. L. Ferree by a vote of 533,813 to 266,037.

The race for governor was "one of the bitterest campaigns the State has ever seen," according to the Raleigh *News and Observer*. Three men sought the Democratic nomination in the May primaries: Olla Ray Boyd, well known as a hog caller in eastern North Carolina but not a force in the campaign; Major R. Gregg Cherry of Shelby, a World War I veteran; and Dr. Ralph McDonald, formerly professor of radio at UNC.

Cherry, orphaned at an early age, was raised by his uncle in Gastonia. He graduated from Trinity College (now Duke University), earned a law degree at Trinity, and set up a practice in Gastonia. During World War I Cherry was part of the 115th Machine Gun Battalion of the 30th Division and rose to the rank of major. Much of his support came from those who thought that he would understand the problems of returning veterans when World War II was over. He had served in every state legislature from 1931 to 1944, and was Speaker of the House in 1937. In April 1944, he announced that he would campaign on a platform of twenty planks, including the following: to raise teachers' salaries, to provide schooling for returning GIs, to strengthen the public welfare system, to create a four-year medical school at the University of North Carolina, to extend to the farmers better electrical service through the Rural Electrification Administration (REA) and through better telephone service, to maintain through state money any city streets over which state highways ran, to help war veterans, and to reduce state taxes. Financially he did not believe the state could reduce its spending because of postwar needs. Cherry was supported by the coastal counties, former gubernatorial candidates A. H. "Sandy" Graham and W. P. Horton, and the "old guard" of the Democratic

R. Gregg Cherry (1891–1957), after being elected governor in 1944, guided North Carolina through the end of World War II and the postwar period of adjustment.

Party. The same political leaders who supported Hoey for the Senate tended to support Cherry for the governor's chair.

McDonald had announced a year in advance that he would run for governor, resigning his position at the university at that time. He was a political liberal and strong supporter of President Roosevelt and the New Deal. When he had run unsuccessfully against Clyde Hoey in 1936 for the position of governor, he had given the old guard "the awfullest fright" since Redemption days, according to one newspaper, by coming within 3,000 votes of winning. He opened his campaign with a rally in Winston-Salem on April 11, 1944, at which time he presented these platform planks: to increase farm income, to provide a higher wage level, to secure better health and hospital facilities, to procure better schools and roads, to persuade more industry to come to North Carolina, and to offer more and better state services. His greatest support came from the North Carolina Education Association, of which he was then vice president, and from liberal Democrats.

One of the main issues was a purely political one—the professional politician versus the amateur. Many observers believed that if only a few people voted in the primary, the better-organized professionals would carry the day, and Cherry would win. If, on the other hand, a larger turnout than usual was the case, indicating that people were protesting the control over state politics by the professionals, McDonald had a good chance to win. A second major issue was that of state finances. The program put forward by McDonald was very expensive, yet he also favored a repeal of the sales tax. Several attacks on the sales tax had been made since it was first levied during the Great Depression, including one by McDonald in 1936 when he almost defeated Governor Hoey. To Cherry, however, it seemed impossible to expand the state's services and at the same time repeal the sales tax. As the war drew nearer to a close, he believed that the state should prepare for a loss of revenue with the closing of war industries, while at the same time needing to spend money to help returning veterans and to prevent a depression. To him, this was no time to repeal the sales tax. McDonald's campaign was the last real effort made to abolish the sales tax, although the law has since been amended numerous times.

Although the campaign was at first fairly quiet, with both men making speeches and attending rallies in various parts of the state, it became very heated after the meeting of the State Democratic Convention in Raleigh on May 4. During the last three weeks, bitterness and ugliness became standard fare. In an open letter appearing prominently in the May 25, 1944, issue of *The Dispatch* (Lexington), Cherry was accused of insulting some veterans of World War I at a state convention of the American Legion. It was alleged that Cherry snobbishly referred to one delegate as "nothing but a private" and called his home chapter "one of the little and inconsequential posts of the State." This was hotly denied by the Cherry forces. McDonald also accused the Broughton

"Nothing but a Private!"

Frankly, Mr. Cherry, whom do you think fights those bloody wars anyway? When "D-Day" comes, whose names will be first, second, third, fourth, etc., on the list of casualties? Will it be the Privates, or, gallant and brave as they may be, only the Majors, Colonels and Generals?

What kind of a Governor do you think you would make for the returning Privates, their fathers, mothers, wives and sweethearts? If you lacked respect for him as a soldier, how could you respect him, or be willing to serve him, when he comes back here as an ordinary citizen?

I am a Legionnaire, Mr. Cherry, a Past Commander of my Post. But this is not a quarrel between us legionnaires, nor is it simply a protest against your dragging the Legion into politics against the plain provisions of our Constitution, which you swore to uphold. Those are involved, to be sure, but it goes far beyond that! In fact,

Your conduct on the occasion referred to indicates your fundamental thinking, your basic attitude toward those who come from the country, and small country towns; toward those you consider "little and inconsequential," whether they be Privates, ordinary citizens, or mere members of the Legislature while you were Speaker.

It goes to the heart of the quest our men and women—so many of them be Governor of our State at a time whenion of whether a man like you ought to Privates—may be returning, God willing, to their businesses, their homes, to take up again the broken thread of their lives.

It goes to the heart of the question of whether a man like you ought to be Governor of a State that has so many of us "little and inconsequential" people in it.

With scads of money at your command, I have been informed that you have canvassed North Carolina thoroughly for the absentee votes of our men and women in the armed forces; you have had letters and blanks printed and mailed at the same time indicating that you were instrumental in providing them with a ballot, and asking that they vote for you. I believe, however, there are enough of us "little and inconsequential" citizens, enough of us Legionnaires, also fathers, mothers, sisters and wives of the members of our armed forces now fighting alongside of Valentine, to see that we do not lose in North Carolina what they are fighting and dying for over there. **

Yours truly,

Robert Dennis.

This excerpt from an open letter written by Robert Dennis, a former post commander of the Rocky Mount American Legion, was used in a smear campaign against Cherry and appeared in *The Dispatch* (May 25, 1944).

administration of certain illegal "rocking chair deals" in connection with acquiring needed stocks for the Board of Alcoholic Beverage Control. The governor defended this action. Some observers believed that this resort to what is popularly called "smear tactics" by the candidate indicated his fear of losing and was a last-ditch effort to defeat his opponent. Whatever the reason, the tactics did not work.

On primary election day Cherry received 185,027 votes, McDonald had 134,661, and Olla Ray Boyd had 2,069. Following this victory Cherry then won the general election in November and was inaugurated as governor in January 1945.

In addition to national and state elections, two other events made 1944 an unforgettable year for North Carolinians. One was a severe epidemic of infantile paralysis, or polio, which the state had not experienced since 1935. A total of 878 cases were reported in 1944, which preceded an even worse epidemic in 1948. July, August, and September were the worst months. At Hickory on July 1, 45 polio patients were in the hospital. A second iron lung was borrowed from Salisbury, and a therapist from Warm Springs came to provide additional help. Hickory was hit hardest, with 452 cases between May 30, 1944, and March 1, 1945. Charlotte was next, with 111 cases, and Gastonia third, with 85. North Carolinians contributed $100,000 for emergency treatment, while the National Foundation for Infantile Paralysis gave another $100,000. Although the number of cases was high, the mortality rate was lower than in past years because of help from the National Foundation. The disease was still raging so strongly in September, however, that the State Board of Education voted to postpone the opening of all public schools by one week, despite concerns on the part of some individuals that the decision should have been made locally.

Finally, three tropical storms hit North Carolina in 1944. The first one, on August 1, lashed Carolina Beach, causing thousands to evacuate to Wilmington. Winds did not reach hurricane force, however, although $2 million in damage from wind and water occurred at Carolina Beach, Wrightsville Beach, Morehead City, and New Bern. The second storm, a real hurricane, struck in mid-September in the Nags Head area. A Coast Guardsman said, "It was an unusual hurricane, lasting only three-quarters of an hour, but if it had been longer I believe every building on the island would have been washed away. . . ." One person was killed. The road near New Inlet was washed away, while the road from Elizabeth City to Manteo was blocked in two places. Winds reached a speed of 120 miles per hour, and 141 houses were moved off their foundations at Avon, Buxton, Hatteras, Rodanthe, Salvo, and Wave. The electricity was off for ten hours. Jamie Styron of Ocracoke became a hero when he rescued an eighty-eight-year-old man who was unconscious on a sand dune in the midst of the tidal wave. The Miami Hurricane Warning

This oil painting by Louis Barberis depicts the Coast Guard cutters *Jackson* and *Bedloe* arriving off the coast of North Carolina during the Great Atlantic Hurricane to escort the torpedoed liberty ship *George Ade* on September 13, 1944. A total of forty-eight men from the Coast Guard lost their lives in the storm. Image from http://www.d7.uscgnews.com and reprinted by permission.

Office, predecessor to the National Hurricane Center, called this storm the Great Atlantic Hurricane, which appears to be the first time that a hurricane was named. The third storm took a path across the interior of the state but did very little damage. Winds at Southport were clocked at only 65 miles per hour. Only Avon was evacuated. These three storms marked the beginning of a cycle of years in which North Carolina suffered many hurricanes because of changing locations of the winds of the upper atmosphere.

During the war years, North Carolinians' lives changed dramatically. The demands of war increased industrial and agricultural production, providing much needed employment in factories and a boon to farmers. The Depression was soon only a memory. Governor Broughton led the state government not only in meeting all of the demands of the war as requested by the federal government, but also by paying attention to nonwar issues such as the care of patients in mental hospitals and the state school system. While the state's revenue increased significantly, the governor and legislature chose a conservative approach to using the treasury's surplus, realizing that postwar adjustments would require as yet unanticipated expenditures. People adjusted their lives—they drove less, changed their diets, and learned how to "do and make do." For many North Carolinians, their thoughts were often less on their own situation than with their family, friends, and neighbors who were actively part of the United States military.

Chapter 13

On the Battlefronts

Even before entering the war, the U.S. was shipping food and war matériel to the Allies. After December 7, 1941, these shipments increased greatly and soon included troop transports as well. An essential role for the United States was that the "arsenal of democracy" be able to ship enough supplies to Great Britain, Russia, North Africa, and Australia to win the battle of logistics. Likewise, German submarines were determined to wreak havoc in the Atlantic shipping lanes. In the Battle of the Atlantic, merchant ships and their escorts on the side of the Allies moved doggedly toward Europe against submarines on the side of the Axis powers. The Battle of the Atlantic was fought in Arctic waters on the route to Murmansk, Russia; in the cold North Atlantic off Greenland and Iceland; and in the Caribbean and central Atlantic off the coast of the southern United States, including North Carolina.

Hoke Norris wrote in the Raleigh *News and Observer*, "Take a liberal helping of sea-water, add blood and oil and fire, and you have the recipe for the grim, secret battle which was fought off the Dare County coast between the planes and ships of the United States armed services and the lurking submarines of Nazi Germany." Although the government attempted to keep the sinkings secret so that Germany would not know of its success, it was not possible to conceal from the coastal inhabitants the explosions at sea, the oil and debris on the beach, the flames against the eastern sky, or the men "horribly wounded and burned" who were taken to local hospitals for emergency treatment. A tanker was torpedoed so close to Southport that "thousands of residents of Wrightsville and Carolina beaches heard the explosion and saw the flames." There were only 11 survivors. When the *City of Atlanta* and a Latvian steamer were sunk the same night, the submarine surfaced and threw its searchlight on "the helpless sailors struggling in the icy water." Seventy-seven died on the first ship and 57 on the second. A total of 287 people perished off Hatteras alone, so that it was nicknamed "Torpedo Junction." Tankers carrying oil from Texas were the most frequent targets. Governor Broughton said, "Not since the War of 1812 has any foreign enemy approached so closely to

A variation of "Loose Lips Sink Ships," this propaganda ad, and many like it, appeared in magazines and match covers to deter people from spreading gossip about military activities off the coast of North Carolina. This image was taken from http://www.the-stuffofwar.com/2009/12/world-war-ii-magazine-ad-zip-your-lip.

the shores of North Carolina." In addition Nazi submarines laid mines in the waters off the chief seaports. Mine sweepers daily cleared the channels. At one time Wilmington harbor was closed for a week while a search for mines was conducted. Although mines were found at Charleston, South Carolina, and at other places, none were discovered in North Carolina waters.

With sightings of such disasters so close to land, it took no time at all for rumors to spring up that in the dead of night crewmen from the German U-boats came ashore. While no one claimed to have actually seen a German, many people "knew someone" who had found a German newspaper on a theater seat. Quite a few individuals reported seeing suspicious people lurking about and strange signals passing from land to sea. One rumor suggested that Alice Hoffman was refueling German submarines from the dock of her home in Salter Path. Since the water depth in the sound at this point was approximately six feet, it seems illogical that anyone would entertain such a notion. However, the power of fear is strong. Between January 1942 and May 1943 the FBI investigated over 500 such reports, all of which were unsubstantiated false alarms.

The fight against the submarines was conducted on land, on sea, and from the air. On land, strict blackouts were designed to prevent ships from being silhouetted against the light and thus rendered "sitting ducks" for the Nazis. From 6:15 P.M. to 7:15 A.M., except for longer hours in December, all citizens within 20 miles of the coast were required to turn off all outside lights, to black out the upper half of their automobile headlights, to run only on parking lights with six or fewer candle-power bulbs in them if they would be visible from the sea, to keep off the beach at night, and to embark or land from a boat only at recognized landings. These regulations were difficult to enforce, especially in the summer when many people went to the beaches. At Harker's Island, for instance, the initial roadblock at the end of Highway 70 proved to be no barrier at all to cars that people drove out on the beach with their lights burning. Soon enough the roadblock was so reinforced that "nothing less than a small tank" could get through. Numerous people were arrested in Morehead City and Beaufort for violation of blackout regulations. One of the civilian defense officials made an inspection trip by boat from Wrightsville Beach on June 5, 1942. In his report he pointed out that "The night was very dark. Distant storm clouds in the west made a good background for the looms observed." These "looms" were glowing patches in the sky caused by light from towns

189

View of men on the U.S. Coast Guard charger *Spencer* setting off depth charges in search of a German U-boat. Image provided courtesy of the U.S. Coast Guard.

and cities. The purpose of the inspection trip was to spot the looms and then to tighten enforcement of the blackout. On this trip the inspector found no looms from Topsail Inlet to Masonboro Sound. Red and green traffic lights showed, however. Camp Lejeune and Camp Davis had looms, and there was too much light from those camps down the coast to Wilmington. Continuous efforts sought to correct situations such as these.

Another way to reduce the number of sinkings was to patrol the sea in small craft. The Coast Guard used trawlers, yawls, and cutters for this duty. A typical trawler carried 28 men who patrolled for eight days at a time, then spent two days resting in port before sailing again. The *Icarus* captured a Nazi submarine by dropping a pattern of depth charges and forcing it to the surface, then bringing the 33 crewmen ashore as prisoners. Other submarines were destroyed under water. The total number sunk by depth charges is not known, but this method of attacking submarines was, overall, not particularly effective. The Coast Guard also used planes to watch for submarines. Planes could drop depth charges themselves, or radio for ships to do so. In one dramatic instance, a plane spotted the Coast Guard yawl *Zaida* in trouble and rescued its crew after a 27-day ordeal.

During the height of the sinkings, Governor Broughton paid a visit to the coast to make his own observations. Upon his return he wrote in a March 26, 1942, letter to Secretary of the Navy Frank Knox saying, in part: "After a personal visit just completed and upon the basis of reliable reports I am definitely of the opinion that the defenses against submarine depredations certainly in the North Carolina coastal areas are wholly inadequate and frequently inept and that there is a shocking lack of coordination between army, navy, coast guard, and air forces." He continued by saying that the German submarines were "menacing our coastal waters with impunity, causing tremendous tanker losses and overrunning the hospital and medical facilities on the eastern coast of North Carolina. . . ." As a reminder of the toll taken by German submarines, many sites of sunken ships are still marked on the fishing maps used in those waters.

The height of the danger off the North Carolina coast occurred during the first months of 1942, before the United States Navy implemented the convoy system. Early in that year Admiral E. J. King, commander of the U.S. Atlantic Fleet, had said that implementation of a convoy system along the eastern seaboard of the United States would have to wait until more escort ships became available. However, by May of that year shipping losses had become intolerable. General George Marshall, chief of staff of the U.S. Army, questioned King's decision on convoys when he wrote to King: "I am fearful that another month or two will so cripple our means of transport that we will be unable to bring sufficient men and planes to bear against the enemy in critical theaters to exercise a determining influence on the war." King got the message and implemented a convoy system along the eastern seaboard. By the summer of 1942 the success of German U-boats declined significantly. At the end of the period of extreme danger, 4,000 seamen had lost their lives. In his biennial message to the General Assembly on January 7, 1943, Governor Broughton aptly said, "The winged messenger of death on land or sea has already saddened the homes and hearts of hundreds of our citizens, and the end is not yet."

Not all Tar Heel naval interests were centered off the coast. Some men were on the Murmansk run, at least four of whom received Russian medals for heroism in getting supplies to the Soviet Union through icy northern waters. At least one North Carolinian was stationed in Greenland to protect the North Atlantic convoys. "Arthur," as he signed himself, wrote home: "So far I find that the cold affects me little. Greenland feels no colder than North Carolina. It hasn't been as cold here as it was that December I went to the Smokies." This probably did not remain true for very long, however. Also, Rabbi Alexander Goode, who was assigned to the 333rd Airbase Squadron in Goldsboro, gave his life along with three other chaplains, George L. Fox, Clark V. Poling, and John P. Washington, when a German submarine struck the USS *Dorchester* in February 1943, as it was transporting over 900 soldiers to England. These four chaplains struggled to organize the soldiers as the ship was sinking rapidly. They gave their life vests to others and perished with 672 men who were unable to escape in time. All four chaplains were awarded the Distinguished Service Cross and the Purple Heart in 1944. In 1948, a postage stamp was issued in their honor, and in 1951 Grace Baptist Church in Philadelphia dedicated a chapel to them. A onetime only posthumous Special Medal for Heroism was authorized by Congress and awarded to their families by President Eisenhower on January 18, 1961. The special medal was intended to have the same weight and importance as the Medal of Honor.

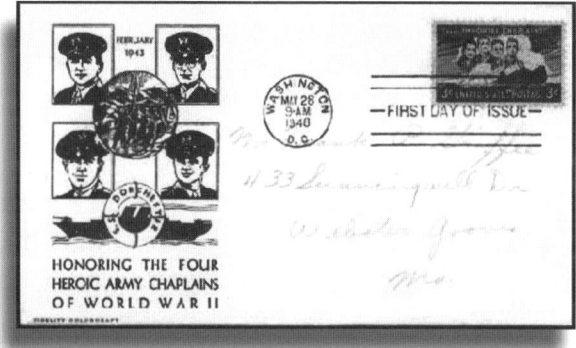

The image on the stamp was adapted from a design by Louis Schwimmer, head of the Art Department of the New York City branch of the U.S. Post Office Department. This postcard was franked on May 28, 1948, the first day the issue was authorized for use. The stamp was unique because, unlike most commemorative stamps, this one was issued less than ten years after the men died. Image from http://www.sossi.org/scouters/chaplains.htm.

In the summer of 1941, before Pearl Harbor, a group of nurses from Charlotte sailed to England to volunteer their services. After being there a short while, they were transferred to Iceland and finally to Africa where they set up a tent hospital. The medical care that they gave and the surgery performed there were little short of miraculous, according to the newspaperman, Ernie Pyle, who visited them. More than 700 patients at a time were cared for by a staff of 400 working in a veritable city of 300 tents pitched in the stubble of an oat field.

In addition to nurses, more than 350,000 women played crucial roles in the military during World War II. Though much of the work allowed men to go to the front lines, the women themselves endured enemy attacks, captivity, danger in training and action, grueling work schedules, and time away from family. In addition to the WAACs mentioned earlier, women served in four other branches: SPARS were part of the Coast Guard; WAVES were the Women Accepted for Volunteer Emergency Service in the Navy; WASPs were Women's Air Force Service Pilots; and women served in the Marine Corps Women's Reserve.

On July 30, 1942, the Marine Corps Women's Reserve was established as part of the Marine Corps Reserve. Its mission was to provide qualified women for over two hundred different jobs, including radio operators, photographers, parachute riggers, drivers, aerial gunnery instructors, control tower operators, auto mechanics, and telegraph operators. In North Carolina, Marine Corps women reservists served at Camp Lejeune and Cherry Point.

Women's Air Force Service Pilots (WASPs) were organized in reaction to the increased need for pilots following the attack on Pearl Harbor. Even though many people dismissed the idea of women flying planes, they successfully flew supplies, delivered new aircraft to air bases, and taught air cadets. WASPS were stationed at two facilities in North Carolina, the Asheville Weather Wing headquarters and Camp Davis Army air field, near Holly Ridge. At the Asheville Weather Wing headquarters, WASP personnel flew planes that ferried non-flying personnel, transported documents and cargo, and helped establish routes and weather flights. At Camp Davis they flew radar deception missions, night target-towing missions, and tracking missions.

From their formation in 1943 until their dismissal in December 1944, WASPs flew nearly 60 million miles for the Army Air Forces. Pictured here, *left to right*, are Viola Thompson, Mary Clifford, and Lydia Lindner, WASPS, Target-towing Squadron, Camp Davis, Holly Ridge, November 1943.

England was home base for many soldiers in the Army Air Corps (forerunner to the Army Air Forces, USAAF) as part of the strategic bombing initiative against Germany. England's approach was to attack major cities in an effort to strike at enemy morale. The United States preferred precision bombing aimed at industrial and military targets. In general, then, the USAAF made the daylight runs, and the Royal Air Force (RAF) made the night runs. This duty was extremely hazardous, for the heavy B-17 bombers, while powerfully armed, were not easily maneuverable. By late 1943, when the USAAF put a high performance engine and two disposable fuel tanks on the P-51 Mustang, the B-17s had escort planes to divert the attention of the German fighters. The Mustangs now had the range to accompany the B-17s deep into German territory, and they were superior to German fighters in both speed and maneuverability.

The largest number of Tar Heel soldiers in any one operation of the war was the 30th Division, called the "Old Hickory Division." This division had served in World War I, was then given the status of a National Guard unit between the two wars, and was called back into service on September 16, 1940. The men were originally all from North Carolina, South Carolina, and Tennessee, the three states associated with General Andrew Jackson, "Old Hickory" himself. This division landed on the Normandy beaches in the great invasion of France five days after D-Day on June 11, 1944. Commanded by Maj. Gen. Leland S. Hobbs, it was called "the work-horse of the western front," because it saw action in almost every major engagement. It spearheaded the breakthrough at St. Lo, smashed the Siegfried Line, marched 180 miles in 72 hours to race into Belgium, and pushed on across Germany to meet the Russian patrols at the Elbe River on May 8, 1945. This division was one of the most highly decorated of all United States units; in addition to thousands of individual awards to servicemen, the Belgian government awarded the Fourragère of Belgium to the entire division.

Two other infantry divisions containing many North Carolinians were the 4th and the 80th, also fighting in Europe. The 8th Infantry of the 4th Division was the first surface unit to hit Utah Beach on June 6, 1944. The 4th Division swept the Cotentin peninsula and broke through the left flank of the German Seventh Army as it moved toward Paris. The troops of the 4th were the first Americans to enter Paris, August 25, 1944, having yielded first place in the liberation of the city to the French forces. The 4th then moved through Belgium and encountered stiff resistance in Germany in the Battle of the Hurtgen Forest, which lasted from September 1944 to February 1945. The 4th, however, was removed in December and sent to reinforce the Allies in the Battle of the Bulge. Beginning in January, the 4th Division was part of the Allied force that moved ever deeper into Germany. On May 2, it reached Miesbach, in Bavaria. Shortly thereafter it was returned to Camp Butner for rest in anticipation of reassignment to the Pacific theater of war. However, the Japanese surrendered before the 4th left Butner.

The men of the 80th Division sailed for England on July 4, 1944, aboard the *Queen Mary*. They landed on Utah Beach on August 2, 1944, and remained a stalwart unit of Gen. George Patton's army until the war ended. They fought from France across southern Germany to Bavaria and Austria. They released prisoners in the notorious German concentration camps like Buchenwald.

The Memphis Belle

The loss of both planes and lives was significant. Between November 1942 and February 1943, 80 percent of the bomber group based in Bassingbourn, England, was lost. In an effort to improve morale, the USAAF decreed that with the completion of 25 missions, a crew would go home. Who would be the first to fly 25 successful missions? By May 1, 1943, the *Memphis Belle*, a B-17 commanded by Capt. Robert K. Morgan of Asheville, clearly had an opportunity to do just that. Named for Captain Morgan's girlfriend, a native of Memphis, the *Memphis Belle* flew her first mission on November 7, 1942. Her successful return on May 1, 1943, was mission number 22—only 3 to go. On one mission the plane's tail was hit and caught fire; Morgan dove 5,000 feet to extinguish the flames, and the B-17 flew home with half a tail. But with quick repairs she flew on. The USAAF saw a golden opportunity for positive publicity and sent a film crew, along with director William Wyler, to the plane's home base of Bassingbourn to be on hand for the twenty-fifth mission. On May 17 the *Memphis Belle* departed for Loriet, France, to attack U-boat pens on her twenty-fifth mission.

Wyler's depiction of the return of the *Memphis Belle* from this mission was an anxious one. As planes from the squadron arrived in the skies over Bassingbourn, all eyes watched for the first sight of the *Memphis Belle*. Other planes limped in, the wounded carried away to medical attention. "There she is," came an excited cry. And in a completely unauthorized but understandable maneuver, the *Memphis Belle* buzzed the landing strip and circled the field once before putting down.

That was Wyler's version; it made for good cinema. But, as Morgan said, "that was a little bit of show-biz." On that day, all twenty-four of the B-17s that had taken off from Bassingbourn returned; no airman was wounded. "It was like we'd had an angel covering us that day," Morgan wrote. As the *Memphis Belle* neared the field, the tower radioed instructions to circle until all other planes had landed. Finally, the *Belle* was authorized to land; the portion of the film where Morgan buzzes the landing strip and then circles the field one more time before putting down, however, is entirely accurate. "I gave it [the field] a grass-cutting you couldn't get these days with a Lawnboy. Somebody said I knocked over a flagpole, but I didn't. I was way too low for anything like that."

Wyler hastened to complete the documentary film, Memphis Belle: *A Story of a Flying Fortress*, and get it out into theaters. On June 8, Captain Morgan (soon to become Major Morgan) and crew flew the *Memphis Belle* back to the

The *Memphis Belle* crew shown at an air base in England after completing twenty-five missions over enemy territory on June 7, 1943. (*Left to right*): Tech. Sgt. Harold P. Loch, top turret gunner; Staff Sgt. Cecil H. Scott, ball turret gunner (from Arapahoe); Tech. Sgt. Robert J, Hanson, radio operator; Capt. James A. Verinis, co-pilot; Capt. Robert K. Morgan, pilot (from Asheville); Capt. Charles B. Leighton, navigator; Staff Sgt. John P. Quinlan, tail gunner; Staff Sgt. Casimer A. Nastal, waist gunner; Capt. Vincent B. Evans, bombardier; and Staff Sgt. Clarence E. Wichell, waist gunner. Both images from Airforce Image Gallery http://www.historylink101.com/ww2-planes/aa-memphis-bell.htm.

United States for a 31-city war bond tour. In his memoirs, Morgan recounts his departure from Asheville Regional Airport after a brief stop on their tour. He wrote that he said to his co-pilot, "I think we'll just drive up over the city and give them a little goodbye salute." According to Morgan, he then traced the route of Patton Avenue toward downtown Asheville and flew between city hall and the courthouse, buildings separated by a distance of only about 50 feet, lowering his left wing in a 60-degree bank. The USAAF weather detachment, housed in city hall, complained to the Pentagon but was ignored.

After the war, the city of Memphis purchased the *Memphis Belle* for $350. The plane sat outdoors on display and suffered both from the elements and vandalism. The city made numerous efforts to raise funds to restore the plane, but was unsuccessful. Currently the *Memphis Belle* is undergoing restoration at the National Museum of the United States Air Force near Dayton, Ohio.

The 80th Division also took many prisoners of war. Other interesting smaller units included Field Artillery Battalions (113th, 540th, 541st, and 690th); Engineers (105th and 175th); the 252nd Coast Artillery; and the 105th Medical. The 65th General Hospital in England was sponsored by Duke University and staffed by many men and women trained in North Carolina.

North Carolina also made its contribution to the war through the United States Navy. Forty-one vessels were named for North Carolina, the largest being the famous battleship. In addition, there were three escort carriers, named *Bogue*, *Core*, and *Croatan*; and thirty-seven transports, gunboats, tankers, and miscellaneous ships in the Pacific theater of war. The battleship *North Carolina*, commissioned on April 9, 1941, fought in almost fifty engagements in the Pacific. In the fighting in the eastern Solomon Islands, near Australia, in August 1942, the ship was part of a task force that included the carrier *Enterprise*, the heavy cruisers *Portland* and *Atlanta*, and six destroyers. The *North Carolina* fired so many guns that another ship radioed to her, "Are you on fire?" Nearly a dozen enemy planes plunged into the Pacific Ocean as a result of her accurate fire. In this battle the losses suffered by Japan were so heavy that the nation deferred further attacks for seven weeks to recuperate. On September 15, 1942, a Japanese torpedo hit the *North Carolina*, but she was able to limp into port for repairs and soon rejoined her unit. Nine times she shelled enemy territory, the heaviest being on Iwo Jima; other islands shelled included Nauru, Roi, Namur, Saipan, Hitachi, and Okinawa twice. When Roi and Namur were attacked on January 31, 1944, the fleet was the greatest ever assembled in history, with more firepower than had been employed in the famous naval battle of Jutland. In all, the *North Carolina* logged over 300,000 miles; at the end of the war only 10 men had been killed in action and 67 wounded. For a short time after the war the ship was used as a training vessel. In June 1947 she was decommissioned and remained inactive for fourteen years. When North Carolinians learned in 1957 that she was destined for the scrap heap, they initiated the successful "Save Our Ship" campaign.

Early in the war, during the retreat from the Philippines, at least one North Carolinian served in Motor Torpedo Boat Squadron Three. The majority of Tar Heels in the Pacific, however, were in the marines. Indeed, the fighting on the Pacific Islands may well be called, "the Marines' War." In the battle for Gavutu on Guadalcanal Island, Major Robert H. Williams of New Bern was one of the first marine casualties, killed while leading the first wave of

USS *North Carolina* (BB-55) ("Showboat") was the fourth ship in the United States Navy to be named in honor of the Old North State. She was the first new-construction battleship to enter service during World War II, participating in every major naval offensive in the Pacific theater, and became the highest decorated U.S. battleship of the Second World War with fifteen battle stars. Image provided by the U.S. Navy, 1946.

troops storming a steep hill. At Lae, New Guinea, in September 1943; at Cape Gloucester, New Britain, in December of the same year; in landing attacks on the Admiralty Islands, Tar Heel marines were there. The 81st (Wildcat) Division was in the attack on the Palau Islands, easily conquering its assignment of Anguar, in 1944. Pilots flew Flying Fortresses (B-17s) attacking Rabaul in the Bismarck Archipelago, and they flew planes that sank 22 Japanese ships in a battle in the Bismarck Sea. Paratroopers were there also. When North Carolinians in the 11th Airborne rescued other Tar Heels from an internment camp on Luzon in February 1945, after they had been abandoned by their Japanese captors, there was a joyful reunion.

Let's bring the *REAL* **U.S.S. NORTH CAROLINA** *HOME!*

Special Opportunity to North Carolina Students!

HELP SAVE OUR STATE'S GREAT SHIP...
RECEIVE AN ADMISSION TICKET FOR JUST 10¢

If every member of the student body of the school contributes as much as 10c to the Battleship fund, every student in the school will receive an admission ticket to the U.S.S. North Carolina Battleship Memorial that will be valid until January 1, 1965. Make arrangements for your school to be listed on the permanent roster aboard the ship of schools that contributed 100% to bringing home the famous U.S.S. North Carolina. Money must be accompanied by a statement from School Principal stating that all students in school during 1960-61 term have contributed, or had contributed for them, as much as 10c to the Battleship Fund, care of Governor's Office, Raleigh, N. C.

This special opportunity is open only to elementary schools and high schools in North Carolina and will be withdrawn at the end of drive for funds.

The U.S.S. North Carolina is scheduled to be demolished for scrap on July 1 1961 unless sufficient funds are raised to establish her as a memorial and educational exhibit.

A Great Ship is Ours for the Saving!

In 1961 students in schools across the state donated their nickels and dimes to have the USS *North Carolina* moved from dry dock to Wilmington to become a museum. The campaign was a huge success, and on October 2, 1961, the ship was moored across the river from downtown Wilmington. Image of this poster provided courtesy of the North Carolina Museum of History. *Background*: Image of the battleship courtesy of the Battleship *North Carolina*.

"Save Our Ship"

Hugh Morton, former publicity manager for North Carolina, persuaded Gov. Luther Hodges to convince the navy to hold off on scrapping the USS *North Carolina*. Saving the ship, though, would cost $100,000 to prepare a new site, $100,000 to condition the ship for display, and $50,000 to tow her to a new site. At a total of $250,000, that was the equivalent of about $1.8 million in today's dollars.

Hodges suggested to Morton that instead of using state funds, all North Carolinians should be involved in the effort. Those who donated $100 (about $725 today) would earn a certificate and lifetime free admission to the ship. Incoming governor, Terry Sanford, suggested that they involve schoolchildren, so every student who contributed ten cents received one pass for free admission. Morton, along with Wayne Jackson at WRAL-TV in Raleigh, developed the "Save Our Ship" promotional television program, which aired simultaneously on prime time across the state. From Wilmington to Charlotte, newspapers called the USS *North Carolina* "our ship." As a result of this statewide effort, the Save Our Ship campaign raised nearly $330,000, about $2.4 million today. Of the 1.1 million North Carolina schoolchildren, 700,000 donated at least one dime.

Once the money was raised, a decision had to be made regarding her location. Officials decided to berth her at Wilmington, a safe position far enough from the ocean. On September 25, 1961, the *North Carolina* left New York City, and tugboats hauled her home. On October 14, 1961, the USS *North Carolina* opened to the public, and more than 5,000 people visited her. The *North Carolina*, at her permanent home in Wilmington, serves as a memorial to the state's veterans and as a floating historical museum of World War II.

One man formerly employed by Liggett and Myers Tobacco Company accepted a Camel cigarette from his rescuer and said, "I hope the boss will not take this as an act of disloyalty." After the freeing of the island of Eniwetok from Japanese occupation, a North Carolinian from Chapel Hill was appointed Legal and Civil Affairs Officer to assist its inhabitants in readjusting their lives. Eventually, the native inhabitants of Eniwetok were removed from the island so that it could become an atomic bomb testing range.

Many Tar Heels received decorations for bravery. The achievements of five of these war heroes illustrate the deeds of others. Capt. Charles P. Murray of Wilmington won the Congressional Medal of Honor. In December 1944 he was leading his platoon on a reconnaissance mission in the Vosges Mountains where they discovered a German unit of approximately two hundred men. Murray radioed for artillery support, but the shots landed off-target. Deciding not to send his patrol against the much larger enemy unit, he climbed to a high vantage point and lobbed rifle grenades into their position, disabled a truck, and fired automatic rifles as fast as the men below him could load and pass them up. His troops maneuvered a mortar into position and fired at the remaining enemy. As the Germans scattered, Murray and his men initiated a pursuit that resulted in the capture of ten men. An eleventh approached the Americans and tossed a grenade that resulted in eight pieces of shrapnel penetrating Murray's leg. Despite his wounds, Murray refused to allow his men to kill the prisoner; he organized them into a defensive position before turning over command of the unit.

Comdr. Norman Mickey Miller of Winston-Salem, a graduate of the United States Naval Academy, Annapolis, was leader of Liberator Squadron VB-109 in the Central Pacific, a search and patrol squadron of 15 planes. He developed and perfected an "incredibly effective low-level type of attack" with which in eight months of duty his plane the *Thunder Mug* sank or damaged 66 enemy ships. He was the first to attack, at treetop altitude, the inner fortress islands of Iwo Jima, Chichi Jima, and Haha Jima. He was the most decorated aviator in the navy, earning the Navy Cross (second only to the Medal of Honor), six Distinguished Flying Crosses, six Air Medals, a Purple Heart, and two Letters of Commendation. In his letter of commendation, Commander in Chief of the U.S. Pacific Fleet Admiral Chester Nimitz wrote, "It is enough to say that the enemy will be glad you have left the forward area. Congratulations on an outstanding tour of combat duty. Well done." Miller died of tuberculosis in 1947 and is buried at Arlington Cemetery.

Corp. Hubert Douglas Crotts of Siler City was awarded the British Distinguished Service Medal by King George VI and the Navy Cross for heroism in dashing up and down a reef at Tarawa under heavy fire in order to locate a path through water-hidden craters to enable marine tanks to land safely. He was also awarded a Purple Heart for wounds he received on Saipan. Following the war Crotts earned a B.A. in History and English from Lenoir-Rhyne College and an M.A. in History from the University of North Carolina in Chapel Hill. He taught for many years in the Charlotte-Mecklenburg School System. Crotts died on February 9, 2011.

Oscar F. Peatross of Raleigh received his commission as Marine Second Lieutenant in February 1941. He entered the Pacific theater with the 2nd Marine Raider Battalion. As a company officer, he received the Navy Cross for his actions on Makin Island. He also earned the bronze star for his actions at Guadalcanal, Bougainville, and Iwo Jima. Peatross also saw service in Korea and Vietnam. He retired in 1971 with the rank of major general, having been decorated fifteen times.

George Preddy, a native of Greensboro, was a barnstormer prior to the outbreak of the war. He was unable to pass the navy's physical fitness test, but managed to do so for the Army Air Corps. He first served in the southwest Pacific, flying out of Australia. In July 1943 he was transferred to England and flew fighter escort missions in a P-51 Mustang. On December 25, 1944, his plane was shot down by friendly fire. At the time, he was the highest-ranking American Ace.

The Congressional Medal of Honor was awarded to three men from North Carolina who served in World War II, in addition to Captain Murray of Wilmington: Sgt. Max Thompson of Canton; and two who died in action, Sgt. Ray E. Eubanks of La Grange and Cpl. Henry F. Warner of Troy.

From North Carolina a total of 4,088 men and women were killed in action. The State contained 2.66 percent of the population of the United States; it furnished slightly less than its share of servicemen and women, 2.33 percent. It lost more than its share to death, 3.01 percent. When the battle flags and guidons of the National Guard units that had served in the war were presented to the State of North Carolina in 1946, Governor Cherry spoke words

George Preddy and his plane, *Cripes A'Mighty 3rd*. Image provided courtesy of the Greensboro Historical Museum.

that were appropriate not only for the National Guard but also for all those who fought on land, sea, and in the air, in the Atlantic, Africa, Normandy, and the Pacific. On November 11, he said:

> We know who was at the Hindenburg Line of September 29, 1918; we know who was on the beachheads of Normandy in 1945 [*sic*]; we know who was at the Battle of the Bulge in the same year; and we shall not forget that the North Carolina National Guard in the 30th Division and other units was there, and the blood of its soldiers seasoned the soil of every such battle and many others I cannot mention here. With a record such as this and with the hope that they will inspire our citizens to greater cooperative effort for our great nation, I accept, on behalf of North Carolina, these sacred battle flags and guidons as commemorative of the service of the soldiery equal with the bravest that North Carolina has yet produced.

Victory and the Future

While 1941 and 1942 proved to be very difficult years for the Allies, by mid-1943 the tide had turned. The German Sixth Army, which had invaded Russia in the fall of 1941, was trapped and defeated at Stalingrad by February 1943. The Russian winter and the seemingly inexhaustible supply of Soviet soldiers doomed the German army. Likewise, the early Axis success in North Africa was halted and then reversed in 1943. Allied forces, led by Gen. Dwight D. Eisenhower and including U.S. soldiers as well as Sherman and Grant tanks, began streaming through ports in French Morocco and Algeria in November 1942. The push across North Africa was long and difficult, but it also took its toll on the Axis forces. On May 13, near Tunis, the last Axis forces surrendered, and approximately 170,000 soldiers became prisoners of war. In July Allied forces landed in Sicily, which fell in slightly more than a month. In September combined British and American forces landed in Italy. Here the rapid successes slowed down, for although the Italian government surrendered, the Nazi armies refused to do so, and they fought tenaciously every inch of the way up the Italian peninsula. Some of the bloodiest fighting of the war took place in Italy at such places as Anzio beach and the monastery of Monte Cassino. Rome fell on June 4, 1944, just two days before the Normandy invasion.

The great invasion of France began on D-Day, June 6, 1944, with the American and British forces landing on five separate beachheads on the coast of Normandy. In July the slow inch-by-inch fighting through the Normandy hedgerows came to an end with a breakthrough at St. Lo, followed by a swift drive to Paris that ended with a triumphal entry into the city on August 25. The German army escaped, however, and retreated to its Siegfried Line to make a stand on the boundary between France and Belgium. Allied commanders had optimistically hoped that the war would be over before winter came, but it settled down to a hard struggle along the borders of the Nazi homeland. At Christmas season a counterthrust by the Germans resulted in the famous Battle of the Bulge, which ended victoriously for the Allies and subsequently opened a path to the Rhine River. By the end of March the last great drives were under way, with the British, French, and Americans pouring to the east while the Russian troops drove steadily toward the west, crushing Germany between them. On May 8, Germany surrendered unconditionally.

The Asheville Times headlined it thus:

WORLD WAR II ENDS IN EUROPE
WITH UNCONDITIONAL SURRENDER
OF GERMANY TO ALLIED POWERS

The *Hickory Daily Record* reported:

GERMANY UNCONDITIONALLY
SURRENDERS TO BIG THREE
40 MILLION CASUALTIES OF WAR

The *Concord Tribune* proclaimed:

PEACE IS NOW OFFICIAL

but it recalled one of the many sorrows of the war in its next headline:

DAY OF TRIUMPH WAS DENIED
ROOSEVELT WHO DIED AT JOB

As the war had progressed, pictures had shown an increasingly frail Roosevelt. He retreated to Warm Springs, Georgia, whenever he could, and it was there, on April 12, 1945, that he died. Americans mourned the death of Roosevelt and lined the train tracks to catch a glimpse of his flag-draped coffin as the train slowly made its way from Georgia to Washington. Vice President Harry S. Truman became president at one of the most challenging moments in U.S. history. Less than a month later, Americans celebrated V-E day (Victory in Europe day) passionately but briefly, for the war in the Pacific remained to be won.

At the height of its expansion in early 1942, Japan controlled Pacific islands that nearly touched the mainland of Australia, embracing the island groups between Japan and the southern continent, as well as much of eastern China and what was known then as French Indo-China. While the United States proclaimed a "Europe First" policy, in fact American military strength was fairly evenly divided between the European and Pacific theaters. The marines and the navy provided the majority of the force in the Pacific and were able to counter Japanese aggression sooner than Japan had expected. While the attack on Pearl Harbor had proved devastating, it had not destroyed the Pacific-based aircraft carriers or their support ships, which had been at sea when the attack had occurred. The Battle of the Coral Sea in May 1942 marked a shift in momentum as the U.S. forces stalled a Japanese attack that, if successful, would have opened the door to Australia. Then one month later, at Midway, U.S. forces inflicted disaster on the Japanese fleet that restored the naval balance of power in the Pacific and ended Japanese expansion. The next two years were grueling for the marines and the navy in what has been termed the "island-hopping" campaign; gradually though, Japanese strongholds in the Mariana and Caroline islands were eliminated, clearing the way to regain control of the Philippines and then to move on Japan itself.

The United States and Britain disagreed over the importance of China. Roosevelt hoped that aid to China would shore up Chiang Kai-Shek's government and that the Chinese army would be able to push back the Japanese. He also argued for an Allied invasion of Burma to open up a supply route into China, since Japan controlled the Chinese seaports. Eventually this supply route was opened, but by that time U.S. advances in the Pacific had lessened the importance of China, and Roosevelt had become disillusioned with Chiang.

Following a major naval battle in Leyte Gulf in October 1944, the door to the Philippines was open. By early December troops were ashore in the southern islands, and in January control of the main island of Luzon, along with Clark Field, had been secured. Yet the Japanese homeland still had to be conquered. One of the popular cartoons of the time showed Japan as an octopus, some showing American forces cutting off one arm after another without being able to kill the body. The Allies believed that the final conquest of Japan would require an invasion like that on the beaches of Normandy, only more difficult because the attack would have to be launched from a greater distance. At a significant meeting of the Big Three (United States, Great Britain, and Russia) at Yalta in February 1945, Russia agreed to declare war on Japan within two or three months after the surrender of Germany. America and Britain believed that Russian help would be invaluable in the final assault in the Far East.

This memorable and effective image appeared in various media. There is no mistaking which side of the war the viewer would want to be on, given the octopus with its vile characterization of the Japanese. Image provided courtesy of the U.S. Marine Corps.

The incredibly costly struggles for Iwo Jima and Okinawa heightened concerns about the potential military nightmare of an invasion of Japan itself. However, that invasion would not occur. Throughout the war American and British scientists worked feverishly on the Manhattan Project, charged with developing an atomic bomb. By May 1945, the team knew that it was close, and President Truman learned of this potentially devastating weapon. On July 16 a fireball in the desert of New Mexico announced success, and Truman, on July 26, sent an ultimatum to Japan to surrender or face "complete and utter destruction." By the deadline of August 3 Truman had received only a vague reply, which he and his advisers interpreted as a refusal of unconditional surrender. On August 6, therefore, a B-29 bomber, the *Enola Gay*, dropped an atomic bomb on the city of Hiroshima. Thomas Ferebee, from Mocksville, was among the crew. At 8:15 A.M. he opened the bomb bay doors and released an atomic bomb nicknamed "Little Boy." Sixty percent of the city was destroyed immediately, and perhaps as many as 100,000 people died instantly. Many more perished in the subsequent days and weeks, as the power of lingering radiation took its toll. *The Report of the United States Strategic Bombing Survey* described it thus:

> A single atomic bomb, the first weapon of its type ever used against a target, exploded over the city of Hiroshima at 0815 on the morning of 6 August 1945. Most of the industrial workers had already reported to work, but many workers were enroute and nearly all the school children and some industrial employees were at work in the open on the program of building-removal. . . . The explosion came as an almost complete surprise, and the people had not taken shelter. Many were caught in the open, and most of the rest in flimsily constructed homes or commercial establishments. The bomb exploded slightly northwest of the center of the city. Because of this accuracy and the flat terrain and circular shape of the city, Hiroshima was uniformly and extensively devastated. Practically the entire densely or moderately built-up portion of the city was leveled by blast and swept by fire. . . . The surprise, the collapse of many buildings, and the conflagration contributed to an unprecedented casualty rate. Seventy to eighty thousand people were killed, or missing and presumed dead, and an equal number were injured.

Japan still refused to surrender, so on August 9 a second bomb was dropped, this time on the city of Nagasaki. Frantic negotiations began, and on August 14 the Japanese government agreed to surrender. On September 2, 1945, aboard the battleship *Missouri* in Tokyo Bay, the formal documents were signed.

On the morning after Hiroshima was destroyed, the headlines read:

TERRIFYING NEW ATOMIC BOMB LOOSED ON JAPAN
WEAPON EXPECTED TO HASTEN ENEMY SURRENDER

Although the Elizabeth City *Daily Advance* was quite blasé about the new bomb and said editorially that "if it should befall that these evil islands are blown off the map we can comfortably forget about the entire matter," most

Enola Gay bombardier Thomas Ferebee after the dropping of the atomic bomb on Hiroshima. This image was uploaded to Wikipedia by the son of the photographer, Ted H. Lambert. Image from NCpedia.

thoughtful people realized that a terrible new force had been unleashed in the world. The *Asheville Citizen* editorialized: "The bombing of Hiroshima has introduced into the world an element of naked power, almost too great to comprehend, whose usefulness both for the good and bad must figure in every human calculation." Wrote the *Wilmington Morning Star*, "One cannot contemplate the speedier victory obviously to be won in Japan because of our atomic bombs, without trembling for the future, unless the powerful nations upon which rests the burden of maintaining peace are prepared to prevent another war by means not yet discovered."

The day following the attack on Nagasaki, the headlines read:

TRUMAN WARNS JAPS TO FLEE FROM BIG CITIES
AS DEBRIS FROM ATOM BOMB BLANKETS NAGASAKI

On August 14, an extra edition of The *Durham Herald* told the news to a waiting world:

PEACE!
IT'S OVER — JAPS QUIT

Yet, as President Truman warned, "The peace in the Far East is yet to be
won." Governor Cherry concurred in an August 20 address, "We Must Keep
the Peace," saying, "In a universe of nations so closely integrated by the mar-
vels of transportation and communication and so constantly threatened by
bigger and better engines of destruction, our only alternative is international
law, openly arrived at and collectively enforced. No other sure way remains.
We who love peace must be willing to sacrifice in order that it may be real
and everlasting."

The war was over. Close to 350,000 North Carolinians had served directly.
In addition, countless more had trained in the state's military bases, and the
citizens of the state had more than done their part on the home front with
conservation and rationing. Farmers had met all of the challenges presented to
them despite labor shortages and the difficulty of acquiring new machinery.
Likewise the expansion of the mining industry generated minerals in support
of war production.

Even with the war in progress, North Carolina did not lose focus on internal
development. Governor Broughton served for most of the war, from January
1941 to January 1945. During his time in office, and with the cooperation of
the state legislature, the State Board of Education was begun. The State Board
of Correction and Training also emerged at this time, providing for better
care and training for those in the prison system. Another significant achievement was the completion of a survey of North Carolina's mineral resources
and the establishment of a related research laboratory at North Carolina State
College. As early as February 1943, Governor Broughton spoke in terms of
reconversion of the state from a wartime basis to one of peace. He hoped to
retain many of the war industries, installations, and prosperity, while recognizing the possibilities of a severe economic dislocation and possible depression

when victory came. His first progressive step was the recommendation of a North Carolina Aeronautics Commission to take advantage of the 64 airports in the state and to keep in step with other southern states that had created such commissions. By March 1944, veterans were returning at the rate of 1,500 per month. The State Department of Labor expanded by adding special veterans' service divisions at Asheville, Charlotte, Greensboro, Greenville, and Raleigh to supplement the one in Fayetteville. Many veterans had gone into service directly from school, never having held regular employment; others had learned new skills in the armed forces and did not wish to return to their former work. Thus, many veterans needed assistance in finding work. These veterans' divisions aided thousands of returning service personnel, all at no charge to the individuals.

In addition to returning veterans seeking work, cutbacks within the state meant that unemployment was the biggest worry of reconversion. In June 1944, the Office of Civilian Defense began reducing its organization to a minimum size, cutting down on the air raid warning system and the employed staff. A large war plant closed in July as United States production outstripped its need and the federal government began canceling orders. Camp Davis was scheduled to close shortly. Many industries, such as textile and furniture plants, had made few alterations in order to furnish wartime supplies; but others that would not be able to make a profit without wartime orders and brand new industries were expected to cut back and thus further increase unemployment. The North Carolina State Planning Board, with headquarters at Chapel Hill, began to study ways to enable industries to remain in operation in the state.

Following his inauguration in January 1945, Governor Cherry continued to concentrate on the problem of reconversions, the more so as it became apparent each day that Germany was nearing defeat. In his inaugural address the governor proposed vocational schools set up by the state to supplement the federal GI Bill of Rights, which would enable veterans to continue their education that had been interrupted by the war or to return to school for additional or new training. Governor Cherry's reasoning somewhat missed the mark, for he assumed most of the men would prefer to learn a trade rather than return to finish high school or college. Actually the reverse was true. Returning veterans produced a great surge in enrollment in the state's consolidated university system; the first community colleges were not established until 1957.

Governor Cherry and the General Assembly also continued to advance the state's educational system. A new textbook adoption law provided free books through the 8th grade and minimum rent for the subsequent four grades. Compulsory school attendance to the age of sixteen was now required, and salary increases had been granted to teachers as well as to other state employees. This legislature continued the work of the previous administration by setting up a State Hospital and Medical Care Program and a Veterans Commission. Both Broughton and Cherry realized that the closing of military installations would leave behind empty buildings; they recommended that counties and cities could convert these buildings into schools, hospitals, and libraries if they would move quickly enough to acquire the properties. For instance, a portion of Camp Butner, just north of Durham, became a hospital for people with mental illnesses. The U.S. Navy retained a lease on a portion of Camp Davis that extended to Topsail Island. In this relatively remote (then) location, the navy, the Kellex Corporation, and Johns Hopkins University erected facilities to study the firing and passage of experimental rockets. Although this project was soon moved to New Mexico, North Carolinians were proud of pioneering in flight once again.

It was in the financial field, however, that Governor Cherry and his legislature gave the state a wise and sound administration. With the years of prosperity, North Carolina had acquired a backlog of funds to cushion the end of the wartime boom. With this money, the state paid off $51 million of debt, set up a road-building fund of $80 million, and held in reserve $20 million for other needs, all of which represented a statesmanlike accomplishment. One final achievement of the 1945 legislature was the requiring of licenses for foster homes, in order to protect the children of the state who needed care in healthy surroundings with suitable foster parents.

Governors Hoey, Broughton, and Cherry, while advocates of full cooperation with the federal government during the time of Depression and war, expressed concern about the expanding role of the national government. As early as January 26, 1937, Hoey, speaking to the national governors' conference, September 14, in Atlantic City, N.J., warned that states must safeguard their rights or expect "assumptions of authority by the Federal Government." Broughton, in 1943, at a Council of State Governments meeting in Baltimore, Md., stated that "If Thomas Jefferson were alive today . . . he would doubtless be greatly disturbed by the vast powers which the Federal government

Operation Bumblebee

In 1940, the Applied Physics Laboratory (APL) was organized at Johns Hopkins University to work on antiaircraft shells. In 1943, after navy ships were hit by German air-launched glide bombs and anti-ship missiles, attention turned to the development of a guided missile to intercept aircraft beyond the range of gunfire. APL proposed a supersonic ramjet-propelled missile that could carry a 600-pound warhead with a range of 11 miles. It would use radar guidance and some form of homing system to steer it to the target. Kamikaze attacks provided further incentive for guided missile development, as did Germany's V-2 rocket assaults on France and England in 1944.

In early 1945, the code word "Bumblebee" was given to the top secret project. Supposedly the name came from a wall hanging in the Office of Scientific Research and Development titled, "The Bumblebee Cannot Fly." "According to recognized aero technical tests, the bumblebee cannot fly because of the shape and weight of his body in relation to the total wing area. BUT, the bumblebee doesn't know this, so he goes ahead and flies anyway."

In January of 1945, there were no facilities for testing supersonic ramjets. An abandoned Coast Guard Station in Island Beach, N.J., was quickly developed into a field test site. Eventually, in June of 1946, the flight program was moved to a remote area on Topsail Island in North Carolina. The U.S. Naval Ordnance Test Facility became the first permanent ground for missile testing in March of 1947. It operated until July 28, 1948.

During its span, an estimated 200 experimental rockets were fabricated, taken to the launch site, and fired off the coast. The site incorporated structures designed and built for specific uses related to the assembly, firing, monitoring, and perfecting of experimental ramjet missiles. Seven observation/instrument towers were erected, and a portion of the concrete launch pad is still visible near the Jolly Roger Motel at Topsail Beach. The buildings associated with the testing—the Assembly Building, Facility Control Tower, and Observation Tower No. 2—are the only aboveground resources that remain and give evidence of the top secret project going on in eastern North Carolina following World War II.

Background: Observation Tower No. 2 is an unaltered example of the seven towers erected on Topsail Island. Image from the National Register of Historic Places.

has appropriated from the states." In his inaugural address on January 4, 1945, Governor Cherry echoed the same theme of cooperation in time of war, but continued by stating that "the Federal republic owes us the duty of recognizing the functions and the duties not expressly assigned to the republic." As William S. Powell has astutely noted, the governors were prophetic. "Power, once yielded, can be regained only through great effort, and the states lacked the unity necessary to recover what they had lost."

Clashes between state and federal governments would come soon enough. Many of the issues, including the expansion of federal spending into areas long considered states' purviews and civil rights, were born of the changing times during World War II. Nonetheless, the state of North Carolina was justifiably proud of the role that its citizens had played in World War II, and with the government on sound financial footing, looked hopefully to the future.

Additional Reading and Selected Sources

North Carolina

Lefler, Hugh Talmage, and Albert Ray Newsome. *North Carolina: The History of a Southern State.* Chapel Hill: University of North Carolina Press, 1963; third edition, 1973.

Link, William A. *North Carolina: Change and Tradition in a Southern State.* Wheeling, Ill.: Harlan Davidson, Inc., 2009.

Powell, William S. *North Carolina through Four Centuries.* Chapel Hill: University of North Carolina Press, 1989.

Ready, Milton. *The Tar Heel State: A History of North Carolina.* Columbia, S.C.: University of South Carolina Press, 2005.

World War I

Arnett, Alex Mathews. *Claude Kitchin and the Wilson War Policies.* Boston: Little, Brown & Co., 1937.

Clarke, Ida Clyde. *American Women and the World War.* New York: D. Appleton and Company, 1918.

Cooper, John Milton, Jr. *Walter Hines Page: The Southerner as American, 1855–1918.* Chapel Hill: University of North Carolina Press, 1977.

Daniels, Josephus. *Our Navy at War.* New York: George H. Doran Col, 1922.

_____. *The Wilson Era: Years of War and After, 1917–1923.* Chapel Hill: University of North Carolina Press, 1946.

Ferrell, Robert H. *Woodrow Wilson and World War I, 1917–1921.* New York: Harper & Row, 1985.

Fletcher, Arthur L. *History of the 113th Field Artillery 30th Division.* Raleigh: The History Committee of 113th F. A., 1920.

Hendrick, Burton J. *The Life and Letters of Walter H. Page.* 2 vols. New York: Doubleday, Page & Co., 1922.

Hyams, Charles W. *Sergeant Hallyburton, the First American Soldier Captured in the World War.* Moravian Falls, N.C.: Dixie Publishing Co., 1923.

Johnson, Clarence Walton. *The History of the 321st Infantry with a Brief Historical Sketch of the 81st Division*. Columbia, S.C.: R. L. Bryan Company, 1919.

Lyons, Michael J. *World War I: A Short History*. Englewood Cliffs, N.J.: Prentice Hall, 1994.

McConnell, James R. *Flying for France: With the American Escadrille at Verdun*. Garden City, N.Y.: Doubleday, Page and Company, 1917.

Marshall, R. Jackson, III. *Memories of World War I: North Carolina Doughboys on the Western Front*. Raleigh: N.C. Department of Cultural Resources, 1998.

Murphy, Elmer A., and Robert S. Thomas, *The Thirtieth Division in the World War*. Lepanto, Ark.: Old Hickory Pub. Co., 1936.

Muse, Benjamin. *Tarheel Tommy Atkins*. New York: Vantage Press, 1963.

New York Times Sunday Magazine, October 28, 1917. "Barring Sex Diseases from the American Army." Pp. 6–7

Public Letters and Papers of Thomas Walter Bickett, Governor of North Carolina 1917–1921. Raleigh: State of North Carolina, 1923.

Rockwell, Paul Ayres. *War Letters of Kiffin Yates Rockwell, Foreign Legionnaire and Aviator, France, 1914–1916*. Garden City and New York: The Country Life Press, 1925.

Stokesbury, James L. *A Short History of World War I*. New York: William Morrow and Company, Inc., 1981.

Sullivan, Willard P., and Harry Tucker, comp. *The History of the 105th Regiment of Engineers . . .* New York, George H. Doran Company, [1919].

Swinton, Col. E. D. "The 'Tanks'." Reprinted from *The World's Work*. New York: George H. Doran Company, 1918.

Van Hise, Charles Richard. *Conservation and Regulation in the U.S. during the World War*. Washington, D.C.: Government Printing Office, 1917.

Walker, John Otey. *Official History of the 120th Infantry "3rd North Carolina" 30th Division, From August 5, 1917, to April 17, 1919*. Lynchburg, Va.: J. P. Bell Company, 1919.

Between the Wars

Davis, Anita Price. *North Carolina during the Great Depression: A Documentary Portrait of a Decade*. Jefferson, N.C.: McFarland & Company, Inc., 2003.

Jolley, Harley E. *"That Magnificent Army of Youth and Peace:" The Civilian Conservation Corps in North Carolina, 1933–1942*. Raleigh: North Carolina Department of Cultural Resources, 2007.

World War II

Baker, Blanche Egerton. *Mrs. G. I. Joe.* Raleigh: Graphic Press, 1951.

Carraway, Gertrude S. *Camp Lejeune Leathernecks.* New Bern: Owen G. Dunn, 1946.

Cheatham, James T. *The Atlantic Turkey Shoot: U-Boats off the Outer Banks in World War II.* Greenville, N.C.: Williams & Simpson, Inc., 1990.

Corbitt, David Leroy, ed. *Public Addresses, Letters, and Papers of Joseph Melville Broughton, Governor of North Carolina, 1941–1945.* Raleigh: Council of State, 1950.

_____. *Public Addresses and Papers of Robert Gregg Cherry, Governor of North Carolina, 1945–1949.* Raleigh: Council of State, 1951.

Dembo, Jonathan. *A Life of Duty: The Autobiography of George Willcox McIver, 1858–1948.* Charleston, S.C.: The History Press, 2006.

Dew, Stephen Herman. *The Queen City at War: Charlotte, North Carolina, during World War II, 1939–1945.* Lanham, N.Y., and Oxford: University Press of America, 2001.

Jordan, Joye E. *The Wildcat Division.* Raleigh: State Department of Archives and History, 1945.

King, Spencer B. *Selective Service in North Carolina in World War II.* Chapel Hill: University of North Carolina Press, 1949.

Lyons, Michael J. *World War II: A Short History.* Englewood Cliffs, N.J.: Prentice Hall, 1989.

MacGregor, Morris J. *Integration of the Armed Forces, 1940–1965.* Washington, D.C.: Government Printing Office, 1981.

Miller, Norman M., and Hugh Cave. *I Took the Sky Road.* N.p.: Wildside Press, 2001.

Morgan, Robert and Ron Powers. *The Man Who Flew the* Memphis Belle*: Memoir of a WWII Bomber Pilot.* New York: Dutton, 2001.

Pyle, Ernie. *Brave Men.* New York: Henry Holt and Company, 1944.

_____. *Here Is Your War.* New York: World Publishing Company, n. d.

Stokesbury, James L. *A Short History of World War II.* New York: William Morrow and Company, Inc., 1980.

Journal Articles

Billinger, Robert D., Jr. "Behind the Wire: German Prisoners of War at Camp Sutton, 1944–1946." *North Carolina Historical Review*, LXI (October 1984), 481–509.

_____. "Enemies and Friends," *Tar Heel Junior Historian*, Spring 2008.

Breen, William J. "The North Carolina Council of Defense during World War I, 1917–1918." *North Carolina Historical Review*, L (January, 1973), 1–31.

Burbach, Corporal H. J. "Six Days on the American Firing Line." *Forum*, LIX (May 1918), 536–544.

Diary of Colonel Joseph Hyde Pratt. Reprinted from the *North Carolina Historical Review*, I (January, April, July, October, 1924) and II (January, April, 1925).

Lucas, John Paul. "Food Production and Conservation in North Carolina. *The Training School Quarterly* Oct-Nov-Dec 1917. (Published by East Carolina College)

Mattox, Henry E. " 'Chariots of Wrath': North Carolinians Who Flew for France in World War I," *North Carolina Historical Review* (July 1996): 287–308.

Winter, Richard. "Hot Springs, North Carolina—A World War I Internment Camp," *North Carolina Postal Historian*, v. 27, n. 1, Winter 2008.

Internet Resources

The following websites contain a wealth of information about North Carolina and the state's involvement in World War I and World War II:

http://docsouth.unc.edu

http://earlyaviators.com

www.aviation-history.com

www.ancestry.com

www.archives.gov/research/military

www.arlingtoncemetery.net

www.archives.ncdcr.gov

www.army.mil

www.d7.uscgnews.com

www.80thdivision.com/

www.history.ncdcr.gov

www.ncmuseumofhistory.org

www.oldhickory30th.com

www.presidency.ucsb.edu

www.uscg.org

www.vmi.edu

Specific Internet Articles

Kiffin Rockwell

"Kiffin Rockwell: The Carolinas' First Lost Hero in WWI."
http://docsouth.unc.edu/highlights/rockwell.html
"Kiffin Rockwell, Fearless Pilot of World War I."
http://www.ncmuseumofhistory.org/collateral/articles/Kiffen.Rockwell.pdf

Memphis Belle

www.memphisbelle.com

www.nationalmuseum.af.mil/factsheets/factsheet.asp?id=6740

Montford Point Marines

"In History: Black Montford Point Marines Are First to Serve during WWII," by Ebony Chambers.

www.empowermagazine.com/in-history-black-montford-point-marines-are-first-to-serve-during-WWII

"The Right to Fight: African-American Marines in World War II," by Bernard C. Nalty."

www.marines.mil/Portals/59/Publications/The%20Right%20to%20Fight%20African-American%20Marines%20in%20World%20War%20II%20

"World War II Montford Point Marines: Honoring and Preserving Their Legacy," by Coral Anika Theill.

www.mca-marines.org/leatherneck/article/world-war-ii-montford-point-marines-honoring-and-preserving-their-legacy

Operation Bumblebee

"History of the Talos Missile" by Phillip R. Hays.

www.okieboat.com/Talos%20history

The Rose Bowl

"The Durham Rose Bowl, 1942."

http://library.duke.edu/uarchives/history/histnotes/rosebowl.html

The Spruce Squadrons

"The U.S. Army Spruce Squadrons in the First World War," by Bob Swanson. www.swansongrp.com/spruce.html

World War I

Graham, J. R. *Tar-Heel Record (In the Great World War)*. Charlotte, N.C.: World War Publishing Co., [1921].

http://docsouth.unc.edu/wwi/graham/

Scott, Emmett J. *Scott's Official History of the American Negro in the World War*, 1919.

www.gwpda.org/wwi-www/Scott/ScottTC.htm

Sistrom, Michael. "North Carolinians and the Great War: The Impact of World War I on the Tar Heel State."

http://docsouth.unc.edu/wwi

Tate, Mabel and Naomi Neal. "Women and the War in North Carolina."
http://docsouth.unc.edu/wwi/tate/menu.html
"Wildcats Never Quit: North Carolina in World War One."
http://www.archives.ncdcr.gov/wwi/info.htm
World War II
"North Carolina at Home and in Battle in World War II." http://www.
ncmuseumofhistory.org/workshops/WWII/Home.htm

Miscellaneous

"North Carolina's World War II Experience," PBS Video, 2011
North Carolina Manual for 1941, 1943, and 1945 (contains information on state
government during the war years)

Newspapers and Periodicals

Asheville Citizen
Asheville Times, The
Carolina Magazine, The
Charlotte Daily Observer
Charlotte News
Charlotte Observer
Concord Tribune
Congressional Record, The
Daily Advance (Elizabeth City)
Daily Industrial News
   (Greensboro newspaper)
Dispatch, The (Lexington
   newspaper)
Durham Herald
Durham Morning Herald
Everything (Greensboro
   newspaper)

Fayetteville Observer
Greensboro Daily News
Hickory Daily Record
Independent, The (magazine)
Leatherneck (Marine Corps magazine)
News York Times
News and Observer (Raleigh)
Pinehurst Outlook
Raleigh Times
Sandhill Citizen (Southern Pines)
Tribune (New York)
Trinity Alumni Register (Duke)
Washington Progress
Wilmington Morning Star
World's Work, The

Index

Busigny, France, 111
Businesses. *See* Industry/industries; Manufacturing
Businessmen, 37, 41, 177
Butner, Henry Wolfe, 140
Buxton, N.C., 184

C

C stamp: pictured, 158
CCC. *See* Civilian Conservation Corps
California, 157
"Call for Volunteers," (proclamation), 20
"Call to Prayer, A" (proclamation), 39
Camden, S.C., 145
Camp Battle, 139, 140
Camp Bragg, 47, 56, 71, 72, 117; pictured, 119
Camp Butner, 139, 140, 145, 165, 195, 213
Camp Coëtquidan, 88
Camp Davis, 139, 140, 145, 190, 193, 194, 212, 213
Camp Greene, 47, 63, 71, 109, 117, 118
Camp Jackson, S.C., 63, 69, 70, 71, 73, 86, 94
Camp Lejeune, 80, 138, 139, 140, 141, 142, 143, 190, 193
Camp Mackall, 139, 141, 145, 167
Camp McClellan, Ala., 118
Camp Montford Point, 142
Camp Oglethorpe, Ga., 49
Camp Polk, 56, 72, 117, 118
Camp Sevier, S.C., 64, 69, 71, 73, 82, 111
Camp Sutton, 139, 141
Campaigns (political), 179, 180, 182
Camps: description of, 71; economic benefits of, 77; entertainment at, 88; location of, 138, 139; mentioned, 24, 41; types of, 47, 117, 122, 124, 145, 169. *See also by individual name*
Canadian army, 8
Canal Sector, Ypres, Belgium, 104
Canning (food), 47, 48, 50, 52, 56, 158, 159
Cannon, German: pictured, 94–95
Cannon Mills (Kannapolis, N.C.), 152
Canteen (Red Cross), 45, 46, 87
Canterbury, archbishop of, 36
Canton, N.C., 203

Cantonments, 71, 73
Cape Fear, 64
Cape Fear River, 118
Cape Gloucester, New Britain, 199
Cape Hatteras, 80, 124
Capitol Square (Raleigh), 85, 146
Caribbean, 187
Carnegie Foundation for the Advancement of Teaching, 120
Carolina Beach, N.C., 184, 187
Carolina Shipbuilding Corporation, 56
Caroline Islands, 207
Carrboro, N.C., 25
Carthage, N.C., 8, 11
Cartoons, 26, 207; pictured, 27, 29, 39
Cary, N.C., 34
Cassius Hudson (liberty ship), 152
Catawba County, 39
Cavalry, 7, 64, 86
Central America, 141
Chamberlain, Neville, 129
Champagne region (France), 86
Chapel Hill, N.C.: B-1 Band stationed in, 168, 169; infrastructure in, 174, 212; newspaper in, 138; residents of, 29, 56, 202; university in, 22, 49, 68, 120
Chaplin, Charlie, 60
Chapman, Victor: pictured, 10
Charleston, S.C., 56, 189
Charlotte, N.C.: camps located near, 63, 71, 72, 109, 117, 118; infrastructure in, 47, 64, 66, 140, 212; newspapers in, 201; nurses from, 193; polio cases in, 184; residents of, 3, 64, 123
Charlotte Daily Observer, 1–2, 5-6, 16
Charlotte News, 176
Charlotte Observer, 16, 17, 19, 26, 39, 40, 112, 123, 132
Charlotte-Mecklenburg School System, 203
Château-Thierry, 34, 103
Chatham County, 69
Châtillon (French town), 112
Cherry, R. Gregg: actions of, 97, 180, 213; addresses by, 211, 215; elected governor, 174, 180, 184; opinions about, 182; opinions of, 175, 212, 213; pictured, 181; quotations by, 159, 203–204

Faulkner, Yoder: quotation by, 143
Fayetteville, N.C., 47, 64, 71, 72, 73, 117, 141, 143, 165, 212
Fayetteville Observer, 3, 16, 17, 112
Fayetteville Street (Raleigh), 60, 113
Ferdinand, Archduke Francis, 1
Ferdinand, Sophie, 1
Ferebee, Thomas, 209; pictured, 210
Ferree, A. L., 180
Field artillery, 84, 93, 98, 112, 198. *See also* Artillery
Fifth Column, 149
"Fifth Columnists," 148
5th District (Congress), 174
5th Division, 119
15th Regiment, New York National Guard, 87
Filling stations. *See* Service stations
Finance School, 148
Financing (of war), 57, 162, 182, 213, 215
Finland, 132
"Fireside Chat," 129
1st Battalion, 107
First Battle of the Marne, 5, 90
1st District (Congress), 174
First Hundred Days, 123
1st Infantry Division, 2nd Brigade, 83
First U.S. Cavalry, 86
First World War. *See* World War I
540th Field Artillery Battalion, 198
541st Field Artillery Battalion, 198
Flag(s), 3, 19, 20, 40, 171, 203, 204
Flag Day, 40
Flanders, Belgium, 104, 111
Fletcher, Arthur Lloyd, 73, 88, 99, 109
Flora Macdonald College, 48
Florida, 63
Flu. *See* Spanish influenza
Flying Fortresses. *See* B-17s
Folger, John H., 173, 174
Food: canning, 159; demand for, 49, 104, 153; insufficient, 168, 177; prices, 160–161; for prisoners, 101; production of, 37, 50, 53, 154; quality of, 90, 102, 176; rationing of, 155; for soldiers, 142, 149, 167, 171, 187
Food Administration of North Carolina, 53
Football, 40, 49, 88, 155, 156–157

Foote, Percy W., 82
Ford (vehicles), 90, 91, 99
Foreign Affairs Committee, 173
Foreign Office, 36
Formidable (English ship), 168
Fort Bragg, N.C., 119, 138, 139, 145, 146, 167, 168, 170
Fort Des Moines, Iowa, 63, 86, 87
Fort McPherson, Ga., 99
Fort Monroe, Va., 138
42nd "Rainbow" Division, 63, 97, 109
Forum (publication), 34
Fosdick, Raymond B., 77, 78
Founders' Day, 22
Fountain, Richard T., 173
4-H, 166
"Four-minute speakers," 38
Fourragère of Belgium (award), 195
Fourteen Points, 115
4th District (Congress), 174
4th Division, 63, 71, 109, 195
4th Marine Brigade, 103
Fox, George L., 192
France: aid to and from, 2, 17, 22, 39, 129, 131; air raids in, 128, 214; Allied planes over, 59, 196; ambassador from, 11; ambulance corps in, 8; fighting in, 7, 11, 19, 34, 57, 73; and Germany, 5, 115, 126, 129; invasion of, 195, 205; Pershing arrived in, 79; prime minister of, 116; soldiers served in, 120; strengthened defenses, 130; training in, 84, 98; transporting soldiers to and from, 49, 71; views of, 127
Franco, Francisco, 127
French (language), 49, 98
French: army, 86, 90; coast, 81; fighting by, 5, 13, 79; flying corps, 11, 12; navy, 80; newspaper, 8; towns, 101, 104; troops, 73, 103, 195, 206
French Army Grand Headquarters, 7
French Consul in New Orleans, 9
French Croix de Guerre (award), 86
French foreign legion, 7
French Indo-China, 133, 206
French Legion of Honor, 86
French Morocco, 205
French-Belgian border, 104